Dennis Westermann

**Deriving Goal-oriented Performance Models
by Systematic Experimentation**

The Karlsruhe Series on Software Design and Quality
Volume 12

Chair Software Design and Quality
Faculty of Computer Science
Karlsruhe Institute of Technology

and

Software Engineering Division
Research Center for Information Technology (FZI), Karlsruhe

Editor: Prof. Dr. Ralf Reussner

Deriving Goal-oriented Performance Models by Systematic Experimentation

by
Dennis Westermann

Dissertation, Karlsruher Institut für Technologie (KIT)
Fakultät für Informatik
Tag der mündlichen Prüfung: 25. Oktober 2013
Referenten: Prof. Dr. Ralf Reussner, Prof. Dr. Hannes Hartenstein

Impressum

 Scientific
Publishing

Karlsruher Institut für Technologie (KIT)
KIT Scientific Publishing
Straße am Forum 2
D-76131 Karlsruhe

KIT Scientific Publishing is a registered trademark of Karlsruhe
Institute of Technology. Reprint using the book cover is not allowed.

www.ksp.kit.edu

Print on Demand 2014

ISSN 1867-0067
ISBN 978-3-7315-0165-7
DOI: 10.5445/KSP/1000037926

Abstract

The performance (i.e., resource usage, timing behaviour, and throughput) of a system influences the total cost of ownership (TCO) as well as the user satisfaction. Both are highly business critical metrics for software providers. In the field of software performance engineering, performance modelling approaches have been established that allow performance engineers to evaluate design decisions with respect to performance characteristics. However, when it comes to creating and maintaining performance models for software systems that are based on existing services and libraries, current performance modelling approaches can require substantial effort. Often, the size of the software systems, the heterogeneous technology stacks, and the fine-grained abstraction level of the approaches make the resulting models extremely complex and thus limit their acceptance among practitioners. Therefore, this thesis addresses the challenge of performance prediction in scenarios that involve existing software systems. It proposes a novel goal-oriented method for experimental, measurement-based performance modelling. The method guides performance engineers in finding a suitable abstraction level and supports the efficient derivation of performance models using automated statistical model inference. Moreover, it can be combined with other modelling approaches in order to limit the modelling effort of existing subsystems. We introduce (i) a language for the specification and execution of automatable experiment series and (ii) present and compare different strategies for the automated, adaptive generation of experimental designs for statistical model inference. We validated the approach in a number of case studies including standard industry benchmarks as well as a real development scenario at SAP. In general, our approach allows performance engineers to efficiently create and maintain accurate goal-oriented performance models of software systems that involve complex, existing components.

Kurzfassung

Die Performance-Eigenschaften eines Software-Systems (Ressourcennutzung, Antwortzeitverhalten oder Durchsatz) beeinflussen sowohl die Betriebskosten als auch die Zufriedenheit der Nutzer. Beides sind äußerst geschäftskritische Metriken für Software-Anbieter. Im Bereich Software Performance Engineering haben sich Modellierungsansätze etabliert, mit deren Hilfe Entwurfsentscheidungen bezüglich ihrer Performance-Eigenschaften analysiert und bewertet werden können. Zur Erstellung und Wartung von Performance-Modellen für bereits existierende Software-Systeme oder Software-Komponenten ist bei den existierenden Ansätzen ein erheblicher manueller Aufwand notwendig. Performance-Modelle für solche Systeme werden oft sehr komplex und daher in der Praxis selten erstellt. Gründe hierfür sind die Größe und Komplexität der Systeme, die heterogenen Technologie-Landschaften und die fein-granulare Abstraktionsebene bei der Modellierung. Die vorliegende Arbeit adressiert daher die Herausforderung Performance-Modellierung bestehender komplexer Software Systeme zu vereinfachen. Die Arbeit führt eine neue zielgerichtete Methodik zur experimentellen, messbasierten Performance-Modellierung ein. Performance-Experten erhalten durch die Methodik eine Hilfestellung bei der Suche nach einer geeigneten Abstraktionsebene bei der Modellierung. Des Weiteren unterstützt die Methodik das effiziente Ableiten von Performance-Modellen durch die automatisierte Kombination von Messpunktbestimmung und statistischer Modellbildung. Darüber hinaus kann die vorgestellte Methodik mit existierenden Ansätzen kombiniert werden, um deren Vorteile zu nutzen und dennoch den Modellierungsaufwand für bestehende Teilsysteme möglichst gering zu halten. In der Arbeit werden (i) eine Sprache und ein Framework zur Spezifikation und Ausführung von automatisierbaren Experiment Serien vorgestellt und (ii) verschiedene Strategien für die automatisierte Generierung von Versuchsplänen zur messbasierten, statistischen Modellbildung eingeführt und miteinander verglichen. Der Ansatz wurde in einer Reihe von Fallstudien validiert. Es konnte unter anderem in einer industriellen Fallsstudie bei der SAP AG gezeigt werden, dass Performance-Modelle für komplexe, bestehende Software-Systeme effizient und mit sehr guter Vorhersagegenauigkeit abgeleitet werden können.

Acknowledgements

Besides the computer science knowledge, writing a dissertation requires inspiration, confidence, will, motivation, and endurance. And while knowledge is something you can teach yourself, the other factors are influenced by the people that back you up along the way to the Dr.-Ing..

First of all, I'd like to thank my grandpa Rudolf that unfortunately could not go the whole way with me, but has been one of my major sources of will, confidence and motivation. I dedicate this thesis to him and my beloved grandma Helene.

If I had to name a person without whom this work would not have been possible, there would be only one answer: my long-time girlfriend, current fiancee and future wife Jenny. Jenny, it is impossible to put in words your support and my gratitude. Hence, I'll leave it to the plain and true - I love you.

Furthermore, I'd like to thank my parents, my whole family and all my friends. Each of you contributed in some way to this thesis, maybe without even knowing it.

Before I start to thank the numerous people which actively contributed to the content of this thesis, I'd like to mention my uncle Roland which has been the only IT guy in my circle of family and friends until I started to study computer science. He gave me my first PC and fixed it a dozen times after I managed to crash it. I haven't been a natural talent with respect to computers. So, thanks for your patience and for being an inspiring example.

Speaking of inspiration ultimately brings me to Ralf Reussner. I first encountered Ralf as a student sitting in his lecture. Ralf is a remarkable teacher and drummed up my enthusiasm for software engineering. I'd like to thank him for giving me the opportunity to write this thesis and for being a great supervisor and mentor. Furthermore, I'd like to thank Hannes Hartenstein for co-supervising my thesis and Walter Tichy and Sebastian Abeck for agreeing to be part of my examination committee.

When you start your work as a PhD, it is very important that there are people around you that steer you in a direction that is worth to be researched. In my case, Jens Happe did a perfect job in this matter. Jens not only gave me a direction but also provided guidance and support during my whole PhD time. Jens, I'm so thankful to have had you (and to still have you) as a companion on the way to achieving ambitious goals. Together with Jens, I worked in the magnificent LPE team at SAP Research. Thanks to Alexander Wert, Christoph Heger and Roozbeh Farahbod for all your input, the fruitful discussions, your reviews, bearing my reviews, and always being there with your support. And, of course, special thanks to Michael Hauck who served as my sparring partner in the final writing phase of the thesis. Moreover, I owe my sincere gratitude to all our students who contributed their piece to the puzzle of my thesis. Especially Christian Heupel, Christian Weiss, Marius Oehler, Michael Faber, Pascal Meier, Rouven Krebs, Tobias Pfeifer and Yusuf Dogan.

At SAP, I did my best to put research into practice and I'd like to give a special thanks to Wolfgang Theilmann and Martin Moser for their great support and mentoring in helping me to achieve this mission.

Unfortunately, I cannot write a direct word of thanks to each fellow of my PhD time. However, at least I can try to name all of the great colleagues at SAP, KIT and FZI. It has been a pleasure to work with you. Thanks to: Aleksandar Milenkoski, Andreas Friesen, Andreas Klein, Andreas Rentschler, Anne Koziolek, Axel Spriestersbach, Benjamin Klatt, Bernd Scheuermann, Bernhard Riedhofer, Christof Momm, Christoph Rathfelder, Daniel Scheibli, Elena Kienhöfer, Elmar Dorner, Erik Burger, Fabian Brosig, Fouad ben Nasr Omri, Frank Schulz, Franz Brosch, Heiko Koziolek, Henning Groenda, Hui Li, Johannes Stammel, Jörg Henß, Jörg Rech,

Klaus Krogmann, Lucia Happe, Markus Heller, Martin Küster, Matthias Huber, Max Kramer, Michael Altenhofen, Michael Kuperberg, Michael Langhammer, Mircea Trifu, Misha Strittmatter, Nikolas Herbst, Nikolaus Huber, Petr Zdrahal, Philipp Merkle, Piotr Rygielski, Qais Noorshams, Ralph Benzinger, Robert Heinrich, Ruediger Winter, Samuel Kounev, Simon Spinner, Steffen Becker, Steffen Kruse, Sylvia Scheu, Tatiana Rhode, Thomas Goldschmidt, Thorsten Sandfuchs, Vanessa Martin Rodríguez, Viktoria Firus, Wei Cheng, Wolfgang Schwach, Zoltan Nochta, Zoya Durdik.

Last but not least, I'd like to thank all those people that I forgot to mention in this acknowledgement and give a big thank you to No Budget Productions for shooting a wonderful movie about my time as a PhD.

Contents

1. Introduction

Quality aspects such as performance, security, and maintainability play an important role in software engineering. The performance (i.e., resource usage, timing behaviour, and throughput) of a system influences the total cost of ownership (TCO) as well as the user satisfaction which are highly business critical metrics [Bix10, Dix09, JN12, Cro12]. In [Liv08], the founders of companies like PayPal and Hotmail report on the large efforts they had to undertake in order to keep their first application versions responsive and make it scalable with the growing user base. To avoid these last-minute efforts, it is essential to integrate performance evaluation into the overall software engineering lifecycle and ensure early and continuous performance awareness [Jai91]. Williams and Smith [WS03] estimate the possible financial benefit of continuous performance consideration to be several million US-dollars in a business case for a medium sized project.

However, evaluating the performance of a system is a complex task as it requires detailed knowledge about the software itself, the platform on which the software runs, and the methods and tools to assess and interpret performance metrics. Usually, performance evaluations are conducted by performance analysts that team up with single members of the corresponding development units [SMF+07]. The methods that are applied to evaluate performance can be grouped in two categories: scenario-based load and regression testing and performance modelling [WFP07]. While load and regression testing are mostly used to define and monitor quality gates for software development, performance modelling is a suitable means to evaluate design decisions and get a detailed understanding of a system's performance characteristics early in the development process. A performance model is an abstraction of the actual software system that describes the performance behaviour depending on the system's usage [SW01]. For example, the results derived by a performance model can be used to answer what-if questions like "What happens to performance if I change the values of configuration parameter X and Y?" or "What happens to performance if I use design pattern A instead of B?".

Creating performance models for complex systems is a challenging task that is subject to ongoing research in the performance engineering field [Smi07, WFP07, Koz10]. Such complex systems are not developed from scratch but use existing services and libraries like middleware or legacy components, they comprise millions of lines of code designed and developed by multiple architects and hundreds of developers, and they are subject to continuous change. Performance analysts have to identify which of the many potential system components and parameters are performance-relevant. Moreover, they have to ensure that they have all major sources of disturbance under control in order to draw reliable conclusions. And ultimately, they have to quantify the relationship between the performance-relevant parameters and the performance metric of interest in order to provide this information to developers and architects. Classical model-driven approaches (such as surveyed in [BDIS04] and [Koz10]) require much human knowledge and effort to construct performance models of existing applications as they require a detailed description of the internal system behaviour. Re-engineering approaches [Kro10] can help to reduce efforts but get complex when applied to heterogeneous technology stacks. A common issue of all performance modelling approaches is the selection of the abstraction level. In most existing approaches, the abstraction level is too fine-grained which indeed provides a lot of information and flexibility but which makes the modelling process as well as the resulting models too complex [Smi07]. In the scenarios that we address in this thesis, software architects or developers are interested in the performance impact of very specific changes that do not require this flexibility [Jai91, WFP07]. In general, too much information and flexibility can sometimes lead to disinterest due to missing comprehensibility.

In this thesis, we introduce a novel method for experimental, measurement-based performance modelling which guides performance engineers in finding a suitable abstraction level and which addresses the challenge of dealing with existing and evolving software systems more efficiently. In order to support the implementation of the method, we introduce (i) a language for the specification and execution of automatable experiment series and (ii) present and compare different strategies for the automated, adaptive generation of experimental designs for statistical model inference. We validated the approach in a number of case studies including standard industry benchmarks as well as a real development scenario at SAP. In the industrial case study at SAP, we designed a performance model for enterprise web application front-ends. In general, our approach allows performance engineers to efficiently create and maintain accurate goal-oriented performance models of complex software systems.

1.1. Research Questions

In this thesis, we address three main areas:

- In the area of *Performance Modelling*, we aim at a better integration of performance models in industrial software development and therefore finding ways to deal with existing and evolving software systems more efficiently.

- In the area of *Experimental Performance Evaluation*, we aim at making the process of defining and running performance evaluation experiments more efficient.

- In the area of *Web Performance*, we aim at increasing the performance awareness of front-end developers in the design phase of enterprise web application screens.

In the following, we briefly introduce the research questions that we approach in the different areas. A detailed discussion of the scientific challenges is provided in each chapter.

Performance Modelling The most recent overviews on the achievements and outstanding problems in the area of software performance modelling are provided by Woodside et. al [WFP07], Smith [Smi07], and Koziolek [Koz10]. A common conclusion is that although the modelling methods and tools have evolved and it has been proven that the resulting models can provide accurate predictions for real-world software systems, there is a need to „[...] make Software Performance Engineering (SPE) more accessible to software developers rather than requiring modelling gurus, and to make SPE more likely to be adopted and used in development organisations.“ [Smi07]. Woodside et al. [WFP07] highlight the need for a convergence between measurement-based and model-based approaches towards more practicable and maintainable performance prediction models. A main challenge with respect to practical scenarios is to find proper mechanisms for determining the performance behaviour of systems or parts of a system (e.g. legacy systems or third-party components) that cannot be modelled formally (or only with large manual effort). Moreover, the abstraction level of performance models needs to be better aligned to the needs of software architects and developers [Jai91]. This can significantly reduce modelling efforts and increase the acceptance of performance models among practitioners. In this thesis, we address the aforementioned problems in the context of modelling existing software systems and thus aim at answering the following questions:

1. How to find a proper abstraction level for a performance model?

2. How to create and maintain performance models of existing software systems efficiently?

Experimental Performance Evaluation   In industrial practice, each performance evaluation scenario differs from another in, for example, the system under test, the tools used to monitor the system, or the tools used to generate load. In order to apply an experimental, measurement-based approach we need to be able to control these heterogeneous landscapes, i.e.,vary the values of input parameters and observe several performance metrics [Jai91]. Given a specific test environment, we can theoretically measure any point in the parameter space (i.e., any combination of input parameter values). Practically, this is impossible due to the huge amount of potential measurement points (i.e., experiments) even for simple systems. Furthermore, in order to derive a performance model based on experimentation, a large amount of different experiment series have to be conducted. And, in order to maintain the models experiment series have to be repeated on a regular basis. Thus, the efficient specification and automated execution of experiment series is an essential challenge that needs to be addressed. Generally, we need to approach the following research questions in the area of experimental performance evaluation:

1. How to find a trade-off between the number of experiments and prediction accuracy?

2. What is a suitable abstraction level to deal with heterogeneous scenarios?

3. How to specify automatable performance evaluation experiments?

Web Performance   In Chapter 5, we apply our approach in the web development domain. In this context, we address research questions in the area of Web Performance. Work in this field is based on the observation that a major fraction of the end-to-end response times of web applications is spent in the front-end [Sou07, Dix09]. Thus, improving front-end performance is a critical task for responsive applications. In his books [Sou07, Sou09], Steve Souders introduced a set of basic rules to optimize front-end performance. Inspired by these rules, tools like WebPageTest [Mee] and others allow developers to detect and automatically resolve the most common problems. For the development of web-based enterprise applications, companies often rely on JavaScript libraries that provide a uniform appearance, as well as a set of UI elements and utility functions commonly used in this kind of applications. Besides the classical challenges addressed by the guidelines and tools mentioned before, UI developers and designers need to evaluate the impact of the design of a screen on front-end performance. This involves questions like „How many columns and rows can I add to a table of type X in my web application without violating performance requirements?" or „What is the impact of back-end call Y on front-end performance?". Theoretically, these questions could also be answered with the existing performance measurement and analysis tools. However, practically the effort for applying measurement-based approaches to these kind of questions is too high, which hinders the flexible, performance-aware construction and evaluation of screen designs. Moreover, the development of a screen's design is usually conducted before the screen is actually implemented (e.g. using wireframe or mockup tools). As a consequence, early performance feedback (prior to implementation) is essential to drive the deployment of fast web applications [Fro13]. In order to provide this early feedback, we need to answer the following questions:

1. How to predict the performance of web applications?

2. What are performance-relevant influences in enterprise web application front-ends?

3. How to create a prediction model that captures all performance-relevant aspects and predicts front-end performance based on the planned UI design?

1.2. Existing Solutions

As discussed in the previous section, performance modelling needs closer integration in industrial software development processes and thus ways to deal with existing and evolving software systems more efficiently. In the following, we give a brief overview of approaches that deal with this challenge.

Several approaches build upon established architecture-based performance modelling methods (e.g. as surveyed in [BDIS04, Koz10]). Concerning the evaluation of already existing components, the main focus of these approaches lies on (i) the derivation or extraction of appropriate architecture models and (ii) the estimation of resource demands and other quantitative data needed to parametrize the performance models. Approaches focusing on the first issue analyse call traces [BKK09] or apply static code analyses [KKR10] to extract models of software systems. Approaches focusing on the second issue (e.g. [AW04, PSST06, SSN+08, TZV+08, KPSCD09, TDZN10, HKHR11]) use benchmarking and monitoring of systems to derive model parameters. The general drawback of these approaches is that they are bound to the assumptions of the underlying performance model [WFP07]. For example, if a network connection is modelled with FCFS scheduling, it won't capture the effect of collisions on the network. Another important issue is scalability. Creating architecture-based performance models for large systems requires considerable effort and can become too costly and error-prone as much work has to be done manually. For the same reason, many developers do not trust or understand performance models, even if such models are available. Concerning legacy systems and third party software, the required knowledge to model a systems architecture may even not be available at all, or the heterogeneous technology stack makes modelling infeasible.

Existing approaches that support an experimental, measurement-based performance evaluation process focus on (i) the efficient specification of experiments, and (ii) the (semi-) automated execution of experiments. However, none of the approaches supports the technology- and application-independent implementation of a holistic and systematic approach to the performance analysis of software systems such as, for example, defined by Jain [Jai91]. Existing experiment specification languages are often bound to the corresponding experiment management system which in turn are in most cases bound to a specific execution environment. Nimrod/G [AGK00] is for example a tool that allows performance analysts to conduct parametrised simulations in Grid environments. While the corresponding specification language supports the definition of input parameters and different types of value assignments, it also includes parts that are very specific to the execution of simulation models in Grid environments (such as task descriptions that are supposed to run on the selected node). ZEN [PF05] is a directive-based language which has the drawback that the experiment meta-information is defined in the application source code. This limits its scope to studies where the source code is available and easy to compile and deploy, as for every experiment a recompilation and redeployment is conducted by the corresponding experiment management system ZENTU-RION [PF04]. Approaches such as presented by Woodside et al. [WVCB01], Wu et al. [WW08] and Hauck et al. [HKHR11] apply experimental measurements to calibrate a prediction model that has been created in an upstream manual step. Thus, these approaches are tied to a certain type of performance models or a certain aspect of a software system. Another group of approaches [KM97, Wor05] perform experimental analysis on data measured at system runtime. Although these approaches use the notion of experimentation, they lack the capability to systematically control the execution of experiments based on experimental designs. Approaches from other domains, such as the ZOO experiment management system [ILGP96], lack the capability of specifying sophisticated experiment selection strategies for the automated control of large sets of experiments.

1.3. Contributions

In the scope of this thesis, we proposed a novel method for experimental, measurement-based performance modelling. In order to support the implementation of the method, we introduced (i) a language for the specification and execution of automatable experiment series and (ii) developed and compared different strategies for the automated, adaptive generation of experimental designs for statistical model inference. Moreover, we applied our method in an industrial case study at SAP, where we designed a performance model for enterprise web application front-ends. In the following, we discuss the contributions of this work in more detail.

A Method for Experimental, Measurement-based Performance Modelling   Our novel method for experimental, measurement-based performance modelling includes two main blocks: (i) a goal-oriented procedure for the specification of performance models, and (ii) a process definition for the experimental derivation of goal-oriented performance models. The explicit goal-oriented specification of a performance model based on our *Purpose, Consumption, Construction* methodology, supports performance engineers in finding an appropriate abstraction level and thus avoiding the construction of too detailed, general purpose performance models. The experimental, measurement-based process allows performance engineers to efficiently derive and maintain performance models of complex software systems. Based on a well-defined test environment and a set of initial assumptions on performance-relevant influences, performance engineers start an iterative specification and execution of experiment series, in which existing assumptions are validated and new assumptions are derived. Once all performance-relevant influences are understood and quantifiable, a second set experiment series is conducted that aim at deriving prediction functions for the performance model. Finally, the accuracy of the performance model is validated to ensure that the model is representative. In the scope of this thesis, we apply this method for the design of a performance model of SAP enterprise web application front-ends.

A Language for the Specification and Execution of Automatable Experiment Series   In order to support the method for experimental, measurement-based performance modelling, we developed a novel experiment specification language for automated performance evaluations. Unlike other experiment specification languages, it enables the definition of experiments independent of concrete domains, technologies or applications which allows performance analysts to focus on the problem that is investigated. Moreover, it allows performance analysts to reuse experiment definitions over multiple studies and share experiment meta-information and best practices in experimental design among each other. Another benefit of our language is the clear separation between experiment definition and automated experiment execution which facilitates the integration of the language in different experiment automation tools. In the scope of this work, we also developed a framework that uses the language to automate the execution of experiments and to iteratively combine experimental design and analysis. Moreover, the language and the framework allow researchers and engineers to apply and compare different experimental design and analysis strategies. The efficient specification and execution of performance evaluation experiments provides a basis for different performance engineering tasks. In this thesis, we applied the approach for deriving software performance models. In other case studies, it has already been applied for automated exhaustive performance regression testing [WWHM13] or to automatically detect performance anti-patterns [WHH13].

Automated, Adaptive Generation of Experimental Designs for Statistical Model Inference   We introduced an automated iterative process that combines experiment selection, function inference and function validation in order to derive experimental designs that optimize the trade-off between the number of executed experiments and the accuracy of multidimensional performance prediction functions. Performance analyst can flexibly introduce, combine, and evaluate different strategies for the three process steps. In our work, we systematically applied and evaluated (i) different strategies for automatically selecting new measurement points after each iteration, (ii) different validation strategies that allow us to automatically decide when to terminate the measurements, as well as (iii) different statistical model inference methodologies that make fewer assumptions about the underlying functional dependencies. We validated the approach by applying the different combinations in two case studies using industry standard benchmarks (SAP Sales & Distribution, SPECjbb2005). In general, the best results have been achieved by the combination Adaptive Equidistant Breakdown (AEB) measurement point selection, Dynamic Sector validation with Global prediction error (DSG), and Multivariate Adaptive Regression Splines (MARS) model inference. In the case studies our approach allows performance engineers to automatically derive performance prediction functions with a mean relative prediction error of less than 20% using only up to 10% of the potential measurement points.

Performance Model for Enterprise Web Application Front-ends
In the course of applying our method for experimental, measurement-based performance modelling in an end-to-end industrial case study at SAP. We evaluated the impact of different screen design alternatives on front-end performance for enterprise web applications developed with the JavaScript library SAP UI5 [SAP13b]. Based on the experiment results, we derived a set of heuristics to handle the large design space for web application screens. Moreover, we designed a performance model that allows estimating the impact of screen designs on performance for the three major browsers (Internet Explorer, Chrome, and Firefox). The derived performance model supports hundreds of UI designers and developers at SAP in building responsive screens. It allows them to assess the effect of different

UI design alternatives on front-end performance prior to implementation and with minimal overhead. We validated the accuracy of the performance model by comparing predictions to measurements for screens of two real-world enterprise web applications developed with the SAP UI5 library. The results show that we can predict the front-end performance for the screens of these applications with an average prediction error of 11% across all studied browsers. Due to the automatically executable experiments, our approach requires only limited manual effort for updating a performance model to system changes (e.g. new versions of the browser or the UI library).

1.4. Outline

- Chapter 2 describes the basic terms and concepts from the main areas relevant for this thesis. We give a short general introduction to software performance engineering and a more detailed view on performance measurements and web performance. We present the concept of experimental design and introduce a set of state of the art designs for the identification of performance-relevant parameters and parameter interactions. Furthermore, we introduce the statistical inference methods that have been applied in the context of this thesis.

- In Chapter 3, we introduce our method for deriving goal-oriented performance models. We describe a conceptual part that suggest a procedure on how to approach performance modelling in the context of a software development organisation, and an engineering part that introduces a detailed process on how to derive a performance model based on systematic, measurement-based experimentation. We applied the process in an industrial case study presented in Chapter 5.

- Chapter 4 describes our work that supports the implementation of the process introduced in Chapter 3. We present an overview on our approach for automatically executing and analysing experiments. We introduce a language for the definition of automatable performance evaluation experiments as well as a framework that allows to automatically run these experiments in different scenarios. Moreover, we provide a detailed description of the automated, iterative combination of experimental design and statistical analysis in order to derive multidimensional performance prediction functions. In multiple case studies, we validate that the approach can be applied to real applications and provides accurate results running only a relatively small set of measurements.

- In Chapter 5, we apply the method introduced in Chapter 3 using the strategies and tools introduced and validated in Chapter 4 in an end-to-end industrial case study that we conducted in cooperation with performance analysts and development groups at SAP. We provide a detailed description of how we derived and validated a performance model of the SAP UI5 JavaScript library for three major browsers (Internet Explorer, Chrome, and Firefox). We discuss the accuracy of the resulting performance models as well as the effort for creating and maintaining the models.

- In Chapter 6, we discuss state of the art approaches in the field of measurement-based performance evaluation that are related to our work presented in Chapter 4. Moreover, we discuss existing approaches in the field of performance modelling that apply measurements in order to deal with the complexity of modelling existing and frequently changing software systems, and compare these approaches to the method introduced in this thesis.

- Chapter 7 concludes this thesis. We summarise the most important scientific contributions of our work as well as the benefits to software performance engineering. Finally, we outline open questions and future research directions.

2. Foundations

In this chapter, we introduce the basic terms and concepts from the main areas relevant for this thesis: software performance engineering, experimental design, and statistical inference. In Section 2.1, we give a short general introduction to software performance engineering and a more detailed view on performance measurements and web performance. In Section 2.2, we present the concept of experimental design and introduce a set of state of the art designs for the identification of performance-relevant parameters and parameter interactions. Finally, Section 2.3 describes statistical inference methods that have been applied in the context of this thesis.

2.1. Software Performance Engineering

The term Software Performance Engineering (SPE) [Smi81, Smi82] has been established by Connie Smith in the early 80's and was originally focused on the use of performance prediction models to assess the performance behaviour of a software system in the early stages of the software development cycle. The idea was to support software architects in detecting and solving performance problems based on well-established performance modelling techniques like queueing network models [Laz84, BGdMT06], stochastic petri nets [Mar95, BK02], and stochastic process algebras [Hil96, ABC10]. Since then, the field has evolved towards modelling approaches that hide the analytical models behind the domain-specific languages of software architects and developers in order to simplify the modelling process [Smi86, UH97, Poo00, Smi01, DRSS01, BDIS04, Smi07, Koz10]. Furthermore, Woodside et. al [WFP07] established a broader definition of software performance engineering by including „[...] the entire collection of software engineering activities and related analyses used throughout the software development cycle, which are directed to meeting performance requirements." They group the field in measurement-based approaches like performance testing, diagnosis and tuning, model-based approaches as introduced by Smith, and approaches that combine measurements and modelling [WFP07]. The approach presented in this thesis supports software engineers in conducting measurement-based performance evaluations. In the remainder of this section, we present the basics of performance measurement which builds the foundation for our automated, experimental performance evaluation approach introduced in Chapter 4. Moreover, we present the state of the art regarding software performance engineering in web development which is the area where we conducted the industrial case study introduced in Chapter 3.

2.1.1. Performance Measurement

Performance measurement approaches can be grouped in active measurement and passive measurement [MA01]. Passive measurement approaches instrument and/or monitor a system in order to gather measurement data but do not add additional synthetic load on the system. This approach is also known as real user monitoring, runtime monitoring, or real-time application monitoring [AR10]. For example, passive measurement is used to track actual user behaviour and characterize workload or to monitor performance metrics and get alerted when a problem occurs. Active measurement approaches use measurement agents that simulate real user behaviour and observe the system's behaviour under the controlled workload [MA01]. As the approach presented in this thesis is an active measurement approach, we focus on this type in the remainder of this section. In the following, we describe the main components in an active measurement approach: Workload Generation, Data Collection, and Reporting.

Workload Basically, the term workload denotes either a real workload or a synthetic workload [Jai91]. A real workload is one observed in a productive system. Thus, real workloads are not repeatable and therefore generally not suitable for measurement-based performance predictions. Synthetic workloads are models of real workloads with similar characteristics. They can be applied repeatedly, are modifiable without affecting operation, may be portable to different systems, and may have built-in measurement capabilities [Jai91]. Furthermore, in literature workloads are grouped in coarse-grained benchmarks and fine-grained benchmarks while building benchmark hierarchies [KS00, MA01, Jai91]. Thereby, the granularity of the property that can be measured determines the granularity of the workload. A coarse-grained benchmark is for example a benchmark measuring the performance of an e-commerce system. In contrast, a benchmark measuring the CPU speed is considered as fine-grained.

Jain [Jai91] describes four major aspects that have to be considered when selecting workload:

- Services Exercised: One should clearly distinct between System Under Test (SUT) and Component Under Study (CUS) while taking into account the purpose of the study. SUT denotes the complete set of components of a system. CUS is a specific component of the SUT whose alternatives should be considered. Workload (as well as performance metrics) is determined primarily by the SUT. Moreover, the workload should exercise all services provided by the SUT.

- Level of Detail: After the SUT and the corresponding service interfaces have been identified; the next step is to choose the level of detail for the service request that should be generated. Jain lists the possibilities as follows: Most frequent requests (e.g. the addition instruction to compare ALUs), frequency of request types (e.g. instruction mixes), time-stamped sequence

17

of requests (e.g. trace of requests on a real system), average resource demand (based on resource demand per request), and distribution of resource demands (e.g. if there is a large variance in the resource demands).

- Representativeness: The test workload should match the real application. That means the arrival rate, the total resource demands, and the resource usage profile should be the same or proportional to that of the application.

- Timeliness: User behaviour often changes over time, so synthetic workloads could become obsolete over time. Thus, it is important to monitor the user's behaviour on an ongoing basis.

To convert the logical description of the workload into actual load drivers that run the tests, one needs to decide how to generate the load. Podelko [Pod05] categorizes the approaches as follows:

- Record and Playback (Virtual Users): Record communication between two tiers of a system and playback the automatically created script. The users simulated in such kind of tools are referred as virtual users. The real client systems are not necessary to replay the scripts. That allows simulating a high number of users. Instead, the most important factor is the protocol used between the considered tiers.

- Record and Playback (GUI Users): The second record and playback approach comprises tools that record all actions of a real user (e.g. mouse moving and clicking). Thus, the communication between user and client GUI is recorded and replayed. While this approach delivers real end-to-end times, the problem is that one needs a machine for each user that has to be simulated. This makes the approach infeasible for measurements where a large amount of users have to be simulated.

- Manual: In some cases the manual generation of workload might be a pragmatic option. For example, when you need to simulate just one (or a few) user and you do not want to install a tool or develop scripts. However, problems with manual testing are that tests are not exactly reproducible, they cause high effort, and thus are not feasible over longer periods or for multiple users.

- Programming: The programming approach means that a special program is developed to generate multi-user workload. Therefore, the API or the source code of the system under test is used. In simple cases, this might be a time- and cost-effective solution, if the programmer is familiar with the API of the system under test. However, features like complex user scenarios or centralized test management and result analysis can drastically increase the effort to develop and maintain such programs.

- Custom Load Generation: This is a mixed approach as it combines some of the above mentioned approaches. One could develop lightweight custom software clients to create the workload but use powerful tools to manage them and analyse the results [PSG01]. Or one could develop programs that control workload generation tools in order to automate measurements [WHHH10].

Data Collection   There are several ways to gather the values of the performance metrics required for an analysis. Lilja [Lil05] groups them in four categories: Event-driven, Tracing, Sampling and Indirect.

- Event-driven: Event-driven data collection techniques gather information whenever a certain event is triggered (e.g. a method is entered or a specific error occurs).

- Tracing: Tracing extends the event-driven techniques by adding additional information on the system state when the event occurs (e.g. storing which method called the method that is observed).

- Sampling: In contrast to the event-driven techniques, sampling methods gather information at fixed time intervals. When analysing sampled data, performance analysts need to consider that events which only occur occasionally might not be captured by this technique. However, data gathered via the sampling method provides a good statistical summary of the system's overall behaviour.

- Indirect: If a performance metric can not be measured directly, performance analysts need to gather data based on which the target metric can be derived or estimated. For example, when using cloud-based runtime environments, direct system access to measure CPU consumption might not be available. In such a case, performance analysts need to collect data that is available from the outside (e.g. service response times [KPSCD09]).

Usually, the data is recorded using either standard performance measurement tools or instrumentation. Instrumentation is a methodology where code is inserted into the system under test which gathers customized data. The benefits of instrumentation are convenience (one can record exactly the data that is required), data granularity (compared to standard tools one can measure at any detail level), and control (one can turn selected measurement points on and off) [SW01].

Reporting   The data that has been collected during the execution of performance measurements needs to be analysed and visualized in an appropriate way. Therefore, performance analyst can use, for example, spreadsheet or charting software, advanced statistical analysis tools such as R [R F13], or self-coded reporting software. In the course of this thesis, we mainly use box-and-whisker plots (short: box plots) to summarize and display measurement data. Box plots have been introduced by Tukey [Tuk77] and are a powerful means to illustrate the distribution of measurement data and to compare different data sets. Figure 2.1 shows a box plot as well as the basic terms for its interpretation [Nat12, Tuk77]. The horizontal axis represents

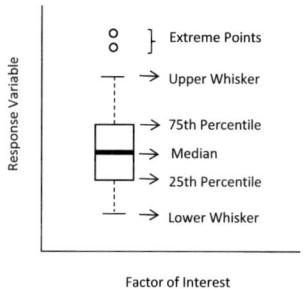

Figure 2.1.: Box plot

the factor of interest while the vertical axis represents the response variable (i.e., the performance metric). The horizontal line within the box depicts the median of a data set. The box itself represents the middle 50% of the data points in the data set. The top and the bottom of the box represent the 75th and the 25th percentile which indicate that 75% or 25%, respectively, of the data points are below this response variable value. The distance between these two values is called the interquartile range (IQR). The upper whisker represents the largest measured data point that lies between the 75th percentile and 1.5 * IQR and the lower whisker represents the smallest measured data point that lies between the 25th percentile and 1.5 * IQR.

The values above or below the whiskers are depicted as extreme points and are usually outliers.

2.1.2. Web Performance Optimisation

In our industrial case study (see Chapter 5), we apply our approach in the context of web applications. In recent years, several studies [Bix10, Dix09], books [Sou07, Sou09, Ste12], and tools [Mee, Yah] have been published under the umbrella of web performance optimisation. Work in this field is based on the observation that a major fraction of the end-to-end response times of web applications is spent in the front-end [Dix09, Sou07]. In fact, an investigation of the top 10 U.S. web sites has shown that all of these sites spend less than 20% of the total response time for retrieving the HTML document [Sou07]. Hence, improvements in front-end performance are more likely to significantly improve the end-user experience. In our case study presented in Chapter 5, the front-end performance metric that we aim to improve is the CPU time consumed by the browser process between the loading of a page is initiated (by typing a URL or clicking a link) until the requested page is fully loaded. In the following, we describe the basic tasks that have to be performed by a browser when a user requests a page. Figure 2.2 shows a reference architecture that adheres to most modern browsers [GG05]. The main components of a browser are:

- User Interface: Includes all visible parts of the browser except the window that shows the screens (e.g. address bar, tool bars, search field).

- Browser Engine: Provides a high-level interface to the rendering engine. Moreover, it is responsible for loading URIs and simple browsing actions (e.g. reload, forward, back).

- Rendering Engine: Creates the visual representation for a given URI. This involves parsing HTML and XML documents, dis-

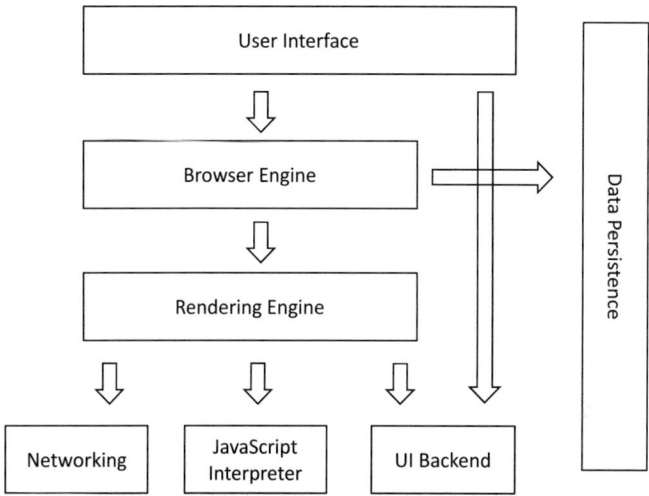

Figure 2.2.: Reference architecture for web browsers [GG05]

playing embedded content (e.g. images), formatting contents according to the definition in Cascading Style Sheets (CSS), as well as calculating the exact page layout.

- Networking: Implements the file transfer protocols (e.g. HTTP and FTP) and caches for recently retrieved resources.

- JavaScript Interpreter: Executes the JavaScript code that is embedded in a web page.

- XML Parser: Responsible for parsing XML documents into a Document Object Model (DOM) tree.

- Display Back-end: Is coupled to operating system interfaces and provides drawing and windowing primitives as well as a basic set of UI widgets and fonts.

- Data Persistence: Stores data on disk. The data can be either user-related settings and bookmarks, or web page specific information such as cookies, caches or certificates.

With respect to front-end performance, the networking component, the rendering engine, and the JavaScript interpreter are the most important components. The workflow of the networking component is described in [Ost11] and starts as soon as the user requests a page. In the first step, the browser looks up the IP address for the given domain in a recursive search through several caches (e.g. browser, operating system) up to the name server of the domain. Then, the browser sends a HTTP request to the web server and waits until the server responds with a permanent redirect which needs to be followed or with an immediate HTML response. Next, the rendering engine starts rendering the HTML document. In the course of that, the browser sends additional requests to the web server in order to fetch the files that are embedded in the HTML document (e.g. images, CSS style sheets or JavaScript files) and are not available in the cache. For each of these files, the browser goes through the same steps as described for the HTML file. When using, for example, the AJAX technology [Hol08], the browser continues the communication with the server even after the page is fully rendered. In that way information can be added dynamically without re-rendering the whole screen. Examples for such asynchronous requests are online status updates on chat or social networking websites.

The handling of these JavaScript request is done by the JavaScript engine (see for example Google's V8 engine [Goo13] or the SpiderMonkey engine of Firefox [Moz13b]). The Java Script engine is also responsible for parsing and executing the JavaScript code in the course of the rendering process. Whether JavaScript code is executed immediately during the rendering process depends on its position in the HTML document [W3C12a].

The rendering engine is the central component of the browser. The browsers that we use in our industrial case study are built upon the following rendering engines: Firefox uses Gecko [Moz13a], Chrome uses

Webkit [App13] and Internet Explorer's rendering engine is called Trident [Mic13]. Figure 2.3 illustrates the basic workflow of a rendering engine as described in [Gar11]. Once the contents of the requested page are

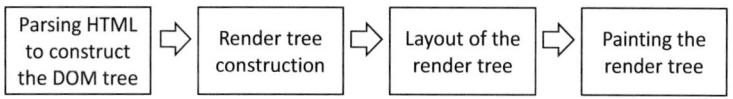

Figure 2.3.: Basic workflow of a rendering engine [Gar11]

loaded from the networking component, the HTML parser in the rendering engine parses the HTML document and creates the DOM tree. Moreover, the CSS parser extracts the style information specified within the HTML document and in external CSS files in order to create a set of style rules.

Based on the DOM tree and the style rules, the rendering engine constructs the render tree which contains the visual elements of a screen in the order in which they will be displayed. Moreover, the render tree holds the visual attributes of the elements such as color and dimensions. Non-visual elements of the DOM tree will not be inserted in the render tree (e.g. the head element or elements whose display attribute is set to none).

In the next step, the render tree is traversed to calculate and add layout information (i.e., exact position and size). Each element in the render tree contains a *layout* method which is invoked by its parent node. The layout process can either be triggered for the entire tree (e.g. when a screen is initially loaded or resized) or only for those elements that are to be updated (e.g. when additional dynamic content is loaded).

Finally, the render tree is traversed again and the *paint* method of each element in the tree is called. This method uses the browser's display backend component (see Figure 2.2) to display the content on the screen. Like the layout process, the painting can be global or incremental.

In order to help performance analysts in understanding what happens in the browser between the time a user initiates the loading of a page (by typing a URL or clicking a link) until the requested page is fully loaded, the W3C Web Performance Working Group [W3C13] recently released a set of standards [Ste12]. These standards define APIs that, when implemented by the browsers, provide detailed information on how long each phase of the page-loading process takes. For a detailed description of the timings, we refer to the specification document [W3C13].

2.2. Experimental Design

Jain [Jai91] states that „What maximum information means depends on the purpose of the design and the analysis method which is used applied on the data.' In Chapter 4, we introduce advanced experimental designs for deriving performance prediction functions. In this section, we describe the basic terms and concepts used in experimental design). Moreover, we introduce three classical experimental designs that we use in the course of this thesis for identifying performance-relevant influences and interaction effects.

2.2.1. Basic Terms

In this section, we introduce some terms and concepts of experimental design (a.k.a. Design of Experiments (DOE)). Figure 2.4 shows the basic experimentation environment that we use in this thesis for our measurement-based approach.

The input parameters i_1 to i_n (a.k.a. factors) and its potential values (a.k.a. levels) can be controlled and can be subject to variation in an experimental design. The observation parameters o_1 to o_n (a.k.a. response variable) are the parameters or metrics that are observed when an experiment is executed. The experimental design consists of specifying the number of experiments, the number of repetitions for each experiment, as well as the parameter value combinations for each experiment [Jai91]. Usually, the experiment results are evaluated based on a linear model. According

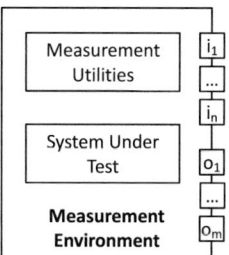

Figure 2.4.: Experiment environment

to [Nat12], for the input parameters i_1 and i_2 such a linear model can be defined as follows:

$$o_1 = \beta_0 + \beta_1 i_1 + \beta_2 i_2 + \beta_{12} i_1 i_2 + \varepsilon \tag{2.1}$$

Thereby, o_1 denotes the observation parameter whose values are measure for a given experiment which specifies the values of the input parameters i_1 and i_2. The constant value β_0 describes the offset value that is independent of the input parameters. The terms $\beta_1 i_1$ and $\beta_2 i_2$ describe the change in the value of o_1 for which each of these input parameters is accountable. These effects are also called main effects. Furthermore, changes in the value of o_1 that are caused by the interaction of the input parameters i_1 and i_2 are denoted by the term $\beta_{12} i_1 i_2$. In general, effects that are caused by the interaction of multiple input parameters are called interaction effects. Finally, ε describes the experimental error, and thus the deviation between the model and the measured values which cannot be described by the other terms.

2.2.2. Identifying Significant Main and Interaction Effects

In the following, we present three classical experimental designs that are most frequently used for identifying the important parameters and interaction effects between parameters [Nat12, Jai91]. We also discuss the applicability of the designs in the context of this thesis.

2.2.2.1. Experimental Designs

Full Factorial Designs   Full factorial designs utilize every possible combination of values and parameters. Hence, the number of experiments n in a performance study with k input parameters can be calculated as

$$n = \prod_{j=1}^{k} n_j$$

where n_j is the number of possible values for the jth parameter [Jai91]. Usually, for each parameter the highest (+1) and lowest (-1) values are used in the design. This special kind of a full factorial design is called 2^k design. Table 2.1 shows an example 2^k full factorial design for three parameters (i.e., $k = 3$).

For our experiments, we try to use only the high and low values in order to keep the number of experiments small. However, especially for non-numeric values it is sometimes not possible to determine the high and low values upfront. The advantage of a full factorial design is that it examines all possible combinations and thus allows us to find all parameter interactions. However, especially when the number of parameters is large, the number of experiments that are to be executed can result in an overall measurement time that is not feasible in real performance evaluation scenarios.

Fractional Factorial Designs   If the number of experiments required by a full factorial design is too large, a fractional factorial design might be an appropriate alternative [Jai91]. Fractional factorial designs are similar to full factorial designs. They are also usually applied with high and low values and are represented in the form of a design matrix. However, in

Experiment	i_1	i_2	i_3
1	-1	-1	-1
2	+1	-1	-1
3	-1	+1	-1
4	+1	+1	-1
5	-1	-1	+ 1
6	+1	-1	+1
7	-1	+1	+1
8	+1	+1	+1

Table 2.1.: 2^k full factorial design for three parameters

fractional factorial designs there is not for every combination of parameter values an experiment executed. Instead, a subset of the full factorial design is chosen depending on the degree of interaction effects that should be detected [Nat12]. The design generators create a full-factorial design for a subset of the input parameters (e.g. for 2 out of 3). The values of the remaining input parameter are derived by the design generator based on the values of the selected parameters for the full factorial design. Table 2.2 shows such an example design where the values for the third parameter are set to $i_1 * i_2$.

Using this example design, one can derive all main effects using only half of the experiments compared to a full factorial design. However, as the third column is used for calculating the main effect of input parameter i_3, we cannot derive an estimate for the interaction $i_1 * i_2$ that is separate from an estimate of the main effect for i_3. This overlapping of effects is called confounding or aliasing [Nat12].The degree to which estimated main effects are confounded with interaction effects is described by the resolution

Experiment	i_1	i_2	i_3
1	-1	-1	+1
2	+1	-1	-1
3	-1	+1	-1
4	+1	+1	+1

Table 2.2.: 2^{3-1} fractional factorial design

of a design. The higher the resolution of a design, the less confounded is the design, but the more experiments are required. The most important resolution levels are [Nat12]:

- Resolution III designs where main effects are confounded with two-parameter interactions and thus only main effects can be estimated reliably.

- Resolution IV designs where no main effects are confounded with two-parameter interactions, but two-parameter interactions are confounded with each other. Thus main effects and some two-parameter interactions can be estimated reliably.

- Resolution V designs where no main effect or two-parameter interaction is confounded with any other main effect or two-parameter interaction, but two-parameter interactions are confounded with three-factor interactions. Thus all main effects and all two-parameter interaction effects can be reliably estimated.

While such designs can significantly reduce the number of experiments, they require the assumption that interaction effects of a certain degree are negligible.

Plackett-Burman Designs   If one can make the assumption that interaction effects are completely negligible, Plackett-Burman designs can be very efficient designs to identify main effects [Nat12]. Compared to full factorial and fractional factorial designs, the Plackett-Burman designs require fewer experiments. However, this efficiency comes with the cost that interaction effects cannot be detected.

Table 2.3 gives an overview on the characteristics of the three experimental designs introduced in this section. The four columns include the name of the experimental design, the number of experiments required for the experimental design, the effects that can be detected by a design, and a classification for the number of parameters n for which the design is usually applied.

Design	Experiments	Detectable Effects	# Parameters
Full Factorial	2^n	*Main,* *Interaction*	small
Fractional Factorial	2^{n-k}	*Main,* partially *Interaction*	medium/large
Plackett-Burman	$n+1$	only *Main*	large/very large

Table 2.3.: Overview of experimental designs with n parameters and two values for each parameter

The classification for the number of parameters is kept on an abstract level as the concrete number depends on the time it takes to execute a single experiment. This time differs strongly between performance evaluation scenarios but has to be considered when selecting an experimental design. Hence, when selecting an experimental design, the performance analyst has to consider the interaction effects that should be detected as well as the number of experiments that is executable in a reasonable amount of time. The three designs are integrated in the SoPeCo framework (see Chapter 4), so that a performance analyst can simply select and configure a proper design which is then executed automatically by the framework.

2.2.2.2. Analysis

In the course of this thesis, we use three techniques to analyse the measurement data derived by the three experimental designs presented in Section 2.2.2.1: Box plots, two-way interaction plots, and analysis of variance (ANOVA).

Box plots can be useful to test the distribution of the observed values (see also Section 2.1). Moreover, they can be used as a visual test to see if changing the value of an input parameter has a significant effect on the values of a observation parameter.

Two-way interaction plots visualize all main effects and two way interactions for designs with more than one parameter [HH04]. The rows and columns are defined by the Cartesian product of the parameters. The diagonal panels show box plots to illustrate the main effect of a parameter. The off-diagonal panels show standard interaction plots. Each point in a plot is the mean of the observation parameter conditional on the values of the two parameters that are investigated. Each line in a plot connects the means for a constant value of a trace parameter. If the lines for the two parameters run parallel, there is no interaction effect between these parameters.

ANOVA is a method for comparing different samples against each other. The basic idea behind ANOVA is to determine and compare the variation caused by random errors within one sample and the variation between the samples. In our experiments, we mainly apply Factorial ANOVA (i.e., we compare multiple input parameters where each parameter has at least two values). In the following, we introduce Factorial ANOVA based on an example with two input parameters A and B that is described in [Nat12]. For a detailed description of ANOVA we refer to [Jai91] and [Nat12]. Assuming we have K measurements at each combination of I values of parameter A and J values of parameter B, we define the following model:

$$y_{ijk} = m + a_i + b_j + (ab)_{ij} + e_{ijk} \qquad (2.2)$$

The equation says that the kth measured value for the ith value of parameter A and the jth value of parameter B is the sum of the following components: the common value (grand mean m), the effect of the value for parameter A (a_i), the effect of the value for parameter B (b_j), the interaction effect between A and B ($(ab)_{ij}$), as well as the residual (e_{ijk}). Table 2.4 summarizes the calculation of variations and forms the basis for determining if the values of a parameter are significant.

The ratio of the mean square for the parameter or parameter interactions, respectively, and the residual mean square follows an F distribution with degrees of freedom as shown in Table 2.4. Hence, if the F_0 value is significant at a given confidence level, there is a significant effect present in the data that is caused by the parameter or the parameter interaction, respectively.

2.3. Statistical Inference

Statistical inference is the process of drawing conclusions by applying statistics to observations or hypotheses based on quantitative data [HTF09]. The goal is to determine the relationship between input and output parameters observed at some system (sometimes also called independent and dependent variables). Statistical inference of performance metrics does not require specific knowledge on the internal structure of the system under study.

Source	Sum of Squares	DoF	Mean Square	F_0
A	$SSA = IK \sum (\bar{y}_{i..} - \bar{y}_{...})^2$	$I-1$	$MSA = SSA/(I-1)$	MSA/MSE
B	$SSB = JK \sum (\bar{y}_{.j.} - \bar{y}_{...})^2$	$J-1$	$MSB = SSB/(J-1)$	MSB/MSE
Interaction	$SSI = K \sum \sum (\bar{y}_{ij.} - \bar{y}_{i..} - \bar{y}_{.j.} - \bar{y}_{...})^2$	$(I-1)(J-1)$	$MSI = SSI/((I-1)(J-1))$	MSI/MSE
Residuals	$SSE = \sum \sum \sum (\bar{y}_{ijk} - \bar{y}_{ij.})^2$	$IJ(K-1)$	$MSE = SSE/(IJ(K-1))$	

$$\bar{y}_{i..} = \frac{1}{JK} \Sigma_{j=1}^{J} \Sigma_{k=1}^{K} y_{ijk}$$

$$\bar{y}_{.j.} = \frac{1}{IK} \Sigma_{i=1}^{I} \Sigma_{k=1}^{K} y_{ijk}$$

$$\bar{y}_{ij.} = \frac{1}{K} \Sigma_{k=1}^{K} y_{ijk}$$

$$\bar{y}_{...} = \frac{1}{IJK} \Sigma_{i=1}^{I} \Sigma_{j=1}^{J} \Sigma_{k=1}^{K} y_{ijk}$$

Table 2.4.: Factorial ANOVA table for two input parameters [Nat12]

However, statistical inference can require assumptions on the kind of functional dependency of input and output variables. The inference approaches mainly differ in their degree of model assumptions. For example, linear regression makes rather strong assumptions on the model underlying the observations (it being linear) while the nearest neighbour estimator makes no assumptions at all. Most other statistical estimators lie between both extremes. Methods with stronger assumptions, in general, need less data to provide reliable estimates, if the assumptions are correct. Methods with less assumptions are more flexible, but require more data. For our black-box inference approach presented in Chapter 4, we focus on flexible methods with less assumptions about the underlying functional dependencies. In the following, we introduce four methods that fulfill this characteristic and that have been applied in the course of this thesis.

2.3.1. Multivariate Adaptive Regression Splines (MARS)

Multivariate Adaptive Regression Splines (MARS) [Fri91] is a non-para-metric regression technique which requires no prior assumption as to the form of the data. The method fits functions creating rectangular patches where each patch is a product of linear functions (one in each dimension). MARS builds models of the form $f(x) = \sum_{i=1}^{k} c_i B_i(x)$, the model is a weighted sum of basis functions $B_i(x)$, where each c_i is a constant coefficient [Fri91]. MARS uses expansions in piecewise linear basis functions of the form $[x - t]_+$ and $[t - x]_+$. The + means positive part, so that

$$[x-t]_+ = \begin{cases} x-t & \text{, if } x > t \\ 0 & \text{, otherwise} \end{cases}$$

and

$$[t-x]_+ = \begin{cases} t-x & \text{, if } x < t \\ 0 & \text{, otherwise} \end{cases}$$

The model-building strategy is similar to stepwise linear regression, except that the basis functions are used instead of the original inputs. An independent variable translates into a series of linear segments joint together at points called knots [CW00]. Each segment uses a piecewise linear basis function which is constructed around a knot at the value t. The strength of MARS is that it selects the knot locations dynamically in order to optimize the goodness of fit. The coefficients c_i are estimated by minimizing the residual sum-of-squares using standard linear regression. The residual sum of squares is given by $RSS = \sum_{i=1}^{N}(\hat{y}_i - \bar{y})^2$, where $\bar{y} = \frac{1}{N} \sum \hat{y}_i$, N is the number of cases in the data set and $\hat{y}_i$ is the predicted value.

2.3.2. Classification and Regression Trees (CART)

CART is a simple and popular method for tree-based regression and classification. Tree-based methods partition the feature space into a set of rectangles, and then fit a simple model in each one [HTF09]. Figure 2.5 illustrates an example with output Y and input parameters $X1$ and $X2$. CART

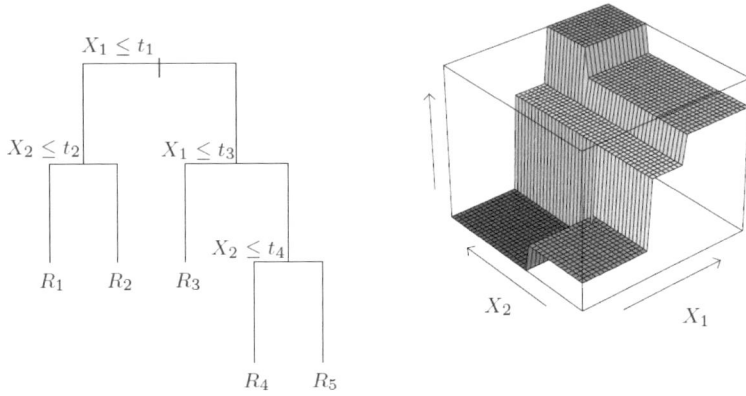

Figure 2.5.: Regression tree model [HTF09]

first splits the space into two regions, and models the output parameter by the mean of Y in each region. Then one or both of these regions are split into two more regions, and this process is continued, until a stopping rule is applied. For example, in the left panel of Figure 2.5, there is a split at $X1 = t1$. After that, the region $X1 \le t1$ is split at $X2 = t2$ and the region $X1 > t1$ is split at $X1 = t3$. Finally, the region $X1 > t3$ is split at $X2 = t4$. The result of this process is a partitioning into the five regions $R1, R2, ..., R5$ shown in the figure. The corresponding regression model

$$\widehat{f}(X) = \sum_{m=1}^{5} c_m I\{(X_1, X_2) \in R_m\}$$

predicts Y with a constant c_m in region R_m [HTF09]. The right panel of Figure 2.5 depicts a perspective plot of the prediction surface from the model above. The decision when and where to split is based on the criterion minimisation of the sum of squares $\sum(y_i - f(x_i))^2$ where the best $\widehat{c_m}$ is the average of y_i in region R_m: $\widehat{c_m} = ave(y_i|x_i \in R_m)$. Finding the best pair of splitting variable and split point in terms of minimum sum of squares is done via a greedy algorithm (see [HTF09] for details). The implementation that we use in our case studies is part of the rpart package [TAR11] of the statistic tool R.

2.3.3. Genetic Programming (GP)

Genetic Programming (GP) aims at deriving computer programs or mathematical equations and is thus well-suited for symbolic regression [Koz93]. GP does not require any assumptions about the input/output parameter dependency and optimizes the structure of the equation simultaneously with the coefficients. It uses an iterative approach to approximate an optimal solution [Koz93]. During each iteration (*generation*), the *population*, consisting of a certain number of *individuals*, evolves. This evolution is performed by *reproducing*, *mutating* and *crossing-over* individuals of the previous generation. Each individual represents a candidate solution and has a *fitness* value expressing the quality of the solution. The aim is to maximize the fitness over many generations. The individuals in GP are usually represented as tree structures and recombinations are tree operations such as randomly exchanging subtrees between two trees. The GP algorithm applied in this thesis is specially optimized for the inference of performance prediction functions [FH12]. To improve the generalisation of the result models, the GP algorithm further applies techniques to prevent overfitting. Figure 2.6 depicts the idea of GP applied to software performance engineering [FH12]. In the first step, GP is initialized with randomized data. After the initialisation, the genetic algorithm begins to evolve the individuals. The evolution starts with an evaluation of individuals by using the measurement data (Step 2). Then, the algorithm selects and reproduces fit individuals (Step 3 and 4) and repeats steps 2-4 for a given number of iterations (generations). Finally, the algorithm terminates (Step 5) when

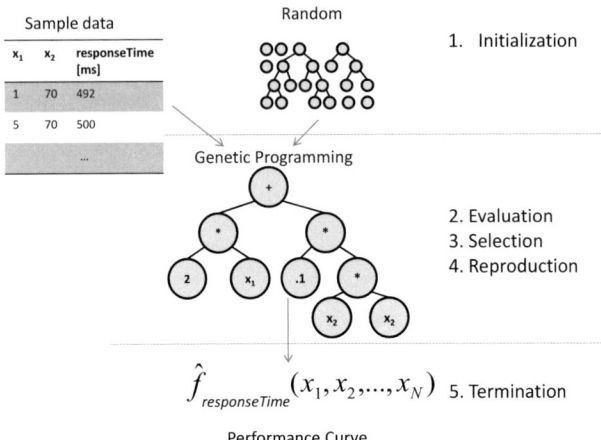

Figure 2.6.: Genetic programming

a given termination criteria, such as the desired accuracy level or runtime constraints, are fulfilled. The result of the algorithm is a performance prediction function expressed through a mathematical equation.

For example, the goal of the GP algorithm might be to find the function $\hat{f}(x_1, x_2)$, which predicts the dependent variable *responseTime* using provided measurement data. Two input parameters x_1 and x_2 influence the *responseTime*. The algorithm receives independent response time measurements with different input configurations (values for x_1, x_2). To evaluate the fitness of each individual, the algorithm calculates the averaged relative error based on the provided training data. New individuals are created by recombining the genes (represented as trees) of two individuals. The trees comprise *operators* (e.g. +, -, *, /) serving as inner nodes and *constants* and *variables* (here x_1, x_2) serving as leaves. When the evolution of individuals finishes, the algorithm returns the fittest individual representing the prediction function identified by the algorithm. The exemplary individual in the centre of Figure 2.6 depicts one possible representation for the curve $(\hat{f}(x_1, x_2) = 2 * x_1 + 0.1 * x_2^2)$ in the internally-used tree representation.

2.3.4. Kriging

Kriging is a generic name for a family of spatial interpolation techniques using generalized least-squares regression algorithms [LH08]. It is named after Daniel Krige who applied the method to a mineral ore body [Kri51]. Examples of Kriging algorithms are Simple, Ordinary, Block, Indicator, or Universal Kriging. In [LH08], the authors provide a comprehensive re-view of multiple Kriging algorithms as well as other spatial interpolation techniques. Generally, the goal of spatial interpolations is to infer a spatial field at unobserved sites using observations at few selected sites. According to [LH08], nearly all spatial interpolation methods share the same general estimation formula:

$$\hat{Z}(x_0) = \sum_{i=1}^{n} \lambda_i Z(x_i)$$

where the estimated value of an attribute at the point of interest x_0 is rep-resented by $\hat{Z}$, the observed value at the sampled point x_i is Z, the weight assigned to the sampled point is λ_i, and the number of sampled points used for the estimation is represented by n. Furthermore, the semivariance (γ) of Z between two data points is an important concept in geostatistics. It is defined as:

$$\gamma(x_i, x_0) = \gamma(h) = \frac{1}{2} var[Z(x_i) - Z(x_0)]$$

where h is the distance between point x_i and x_0 and $\gamma(h)$ is the semivari-ogram (commonly referred to as variogram)[LH08].

Figure 2.7 shows an example variogram with an exponential variogram model. The *nugget* (or nugget effect) is a contribution to variability without spatial continuity [Swi06]. The *range* is the distance where the model first flattens out and the *sill* is the value at which the variogram model reaches the range.

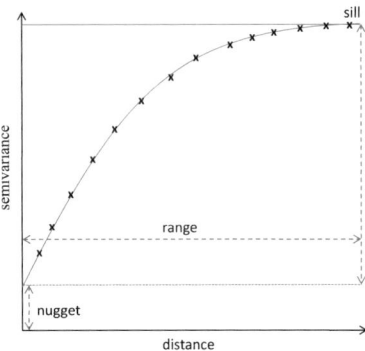

Figure 2.7.: Sample variogram

The Kriging implementation [Peb04] that we applied in our experiments uses the Ordinary Kriging algorithm to estimate unknown points. As described above the estimated values are computed as simple linear weighted average of neighboring measured data points. The weights are determined from the fitted variogram with the condition that they must add up to 1 which is equivalent to the process of reestimating the mean value at each new location [DGL].

As in geostatistics the problems typically have two input parameters (the geo-coordinates), we could not find an implementation of Kriging that allows more than two input parameters. Hence, we decided to combine Kriging with Classical Multidimensional Scaling (CMDS) [CC00] in order to use the method for problems with more than two input variables. Using CMDS we reduce the dimensionality of the input parameter space from n to 2. The implementation [R D11] takes a set of dissimilarities and returns a set of points such that the distances between the points are approximately equal to the dissimilarities. We selected CMDS as although it reduces the dimensions it keeps the distances between the different points which is an essential characteristic for combining it with Kriging.

3. Deriving Goal-oriented Performance Models by Systematic Experimentation

While existing performance modelling approaches have demonstrated the value of early performance feedback, the effort to create and maintain the models is still large. Especially in practical scenarios where models have to integrate existing components such as middleware, platforms, or third-party services, software vendors struggle to value the return on investment (ROI) of performance modelling. The modelling approaches often require information and flexibility which complicates the model construction. Such a flexibility is not required in most cases. Stakeholders in the software development process are usually interested in answering what-if questions that are important for their design decisions.

Moreover, the success of performance engineering in practical scenarios depends on the performance awareness of an organisation and how good performance engineering is integrated in the software development process [SMF+07]. For example, Shopzilla.com did a complete re-development of their software and made performance a design decision that has been considered during the whole software development cycle [Dix09]. As a consequence, page views increased by 25%, conversion rate increased from 7% to 12% and infrastructure costs have been halved.

In this chapter, we introduce our approach for goal-oriented performance modelling. The approach consists of two parts:

- a conceptual part that suggest a procedure on how to approach performance modelling in the context of a software development organisation, and

- an engineering part that introduces a detailed process on how to derive a performance model based on systematic, measurement-based experimentation.

For the first part, the approach adopts the *Why? How? What?* model that has been introduced by Sinek [Sin09] in the field of inspirational leadership. This approach can help to explicitly derive the goal of the performance model before the modelling process actually starts. The core idea is to state the purpose of the performance model first. *Why* do you need a performance model? If that purpose is clearly stated and project leads belief in the *Why*, one can start looking into *How* a performance model can help to fulfil the purpose. In this step, we suggest to adopt approaches like Design Thinking [Bro09] or The Lean Startup [Rie11] from the field of innovation building. Such approaches can help to figure out what developers and architects actually need to develop faster software. If there is a clear understanding about *How* a performance model can fulfill a purpose, one can start to define *What* needs to be done in order derive this performance model.

As a result of the first part, we get a specification of a goal-oriented performance model. We define a goal-oriented performance model as an abstraction of a software system which is specifically tailored to the needs of the stakeholders in a certain scenario. To actually derive the models, we propose a measurement-based, experimental process that neglects internal details of a system. Measurements are an established performance evaluation methodology in practice. Hence, expertise and professional tools are already available. Our experimental process leverages these tools and expertise and provides guidance towards the derivation of a performance model. Moreover, each experiment provides already valuable insights, independent of the resulting performance model.

This chapter is structured as follows. Section 3.1 introduces the scientific challenges in the field of performance modelling that we address with our approach. Section 3.2 describes the idea of goal-oriented performance models and provides a template for specifying goal-oriented performance models. Moreover, two example scenarios are provided for further illustration. In Section 3.3, we introduce our measurement-based, experimental process for deriving goal-oriented performance models. The limitations and assumptions of the approach are discussed in Section 3.4. Finally, Section 3.5 summarises the chapter and highlights the scientific contributions.

3.1. Scientific Challenges

The scientific challenges in the field of performance modelling that we address in this chapter are as follows:

- **How to find a proper abstraction level for a performance model?** Performance engineering in general and especially creating and maintaining performance models always requires effort and expertise. Hence, software vendors need to invest in creating and maintaining performance models. As this investment has to be made upfront (i.e., before the product is actually developed or shipped to customers), its value is often unclear and not directly visible. This is also a reason why the acceptance of performance modelling in practical communities is still low [SMF+07]. Besides the size and complexity of the software system that is subject to modelling, the selection of the abstraction level for creating a performance model is an important factor for the effort and thus the investment required to create and maintain a performance model. Hence, it is subject to research to identify methodologies that support software vendors in finding the balance between modelling effort and a clear return on investment [Smi07].

- **How to create and maintain performance models of existing software systems efficiently?** Today's software systems

43

are usually built on existing software (middleware, legacy applications, or third party components) and rarely developed from scratch. Reflecting the influence of such existing and often very complex components on the performance of the software that is under development is a large challenge in the field of performance modelling [WFP07]. While there are many established approaches for modelling a software system that is built from scratch, those approaches face problems when it comes to complex existing components. The approaches do not scale with respect to size and complexity of software systems and thus they require considerable effort and can become too costly and error-prone as much work has to be done manually. Concerning legacy systems and third party software, the required knowledge to model the systems may even not be available at all. Furthermore, companies continuously adapt their applications to changing market requirements and technological innovations which requires an efficient way of maintaining the performance models during the software lifecycle [SMF$^+$07, WFP07, Smi07].

3.2. Specifying Goal-oriented Performance Models

The acceptance of software performance engineering in industry is not only a matter of having proper modelling and analysis approaches. A significant factor for a successful implementation is also the commitment of software vendors to integrate performance engineering in the software development process and to explicitly provide resources for such tasks [SMF$^+$07]. In order to get that commitment, we propose to specify a clear goal using the procedure presented in this chapter. A clear and systematic specification of the goal of a performance model, allows performance engineers to decide on a proper abstraction level for model derivation which can limit the effort for creating and maintaining performance models.

The proposed procedure arose from combining best practices described in literature of the performance engineering domain [SW01, Jai91, BCR94] and other domains [Sin09, Bro09, Rie11], industrial experience reports [SMF⁺07, Dix09, JN12], and our own experience gathered in the course of conducting different performance projects at SAP (see for example Chapter 5). In the following sections, we provide a description of how to apply the *Why? How? What?* approach [Sin09] in the context of performance modelling, as well as two example specifications from the SAP context in which we applied our overall approach.

3.2.1. Purpose, Consumption, Construction

The *Why? How? What?* model has been introduced by Sinek [Sin09] in the field of inspirational leadership. The actual target group of the model are companies and people that are in a leadership position. The basic idea of the approach is that if, for example, one wants to start a successful company, create a successful product, or convince other people of something, one should start with the *Why*. The *Why* defines the higher purpose, e.g. what is the main driver of a company. The *How* says how this purpose is fulfilled by the company. And finally, the *What* describes the product or service that the company sells. In the following, we adopt this approach and map it to the performance modelling domain, i.e., we define which information performance engineers should gather in order to describe the why, how, and what of a performance model. This approach can help to explicitly derive the goal of the performance model before the modelling process actually starts and to identify the required abstraction level for the actual performance modelling process.

Purpose (Why?)

The core idea is to state the purpose of the performance model first. Why do you need a performance model? As the derivation and maintenance of a performance model requires effort and commitment from several experts, it is very important to identify and clearly state the benefits of having a performance model. It should become clear that, for example, the performance model can help to reduce efforts of target stakeholders, or to significantly increase product quality.

Consumption (How?)

If the purpose is clearly stated and project leads belief in the why, one can start looking into how a performance model can help to fulfil the purpose. In this step, we suggest to adopt approaches like Design Thinking or The Lean Startup from the field of innovation building. Such approaches can help to figure out what developers and architects actually need to develop faster software. Defining the concrete needs of those stakeholders that are supposed to consume the results provided by the performance model helps to identify the required resources and limits the scope of the performance model. The definition should include the concrete target stakeholders, the task that is supported by the predictions, the (sub-)system that should be modelled, the usage profiles that are used as input to the model, and the level of desired prediction accuracy. In order to further cut the modelling efforts to what is really needed for supporting the target stakeholders in their tasks, it is important to specify in advance how the model should be consumed by the stakeholders. This includes for example how the inputs for the performance model are provided and how the results are presented to the stakeholder. The simpler the model consumption, the less effort is put on the stakeholders and thus it becomes more likely that the predictions are actually considered and lead to better product quality.

Construction (What?)

If there is a clear understanding about how a performance model can fulfil a purpose, one can start to define what needs to be done in order derive this performance model. This includes the selection of the actual method for the derivation process. In order to evaluate early lifecycle architectural design decisions, tools like the Palladio Component Model or the approaches surveyed in [Koz10] might be appropriate. In scenarios where large parts of the system that is to be modelled already exist, approaches like the one presented in this thesis might be the best choice. Details on the model derivation process proposed in this thesis are presented in Section 3.3.

3.2.2. Examples

In the following, we provide two example scenarios for how to specify goal-oriented performance models using our *Purpose, Consumption, Construction* approach. The first example deals with the effect of screen design on front-end performance and has been implemented in an industrial case study at SAP which is introduced in detail in Chapter 5. The second example illustrates the application of goal-oriented performance models in the context of the development of data models using the Java Persistence API.

3.2.2.1. Effect of Screen Design on Front-end Performance

Purpose

In today's web applications front-end performance contributes significantly to the overall user experience [Sou07] and thus affects business-critical metrics like conversion rate. Often, performance problems are caused by flawed screen designs [Fro13]. Changing the design of a screen in late development cycles implies large efforts and high costs. Hence, the effect of the screen design should be considered as early as possible. At SAP there are hundreds of developers using the SAP UI5 JavaScript library to build web application front-ends. Having a performance model that allows developers to easily evaluate the performance of their screen design, would significantly reduce the need for setting up and running performance tests by each individual developer. Moreover, it would significantly reduce the number of performance problems that are casued by flawed screen designs. Hence, the efforts to construct and maintain the performance model by an expert team are relatively small compared to the efforts that are necessary to achieve the same test coverage without the performance model (i.e., each developer needs to setup and run performance tests for each screen).

Consumption

The performance model should support developers in designing responsive web application screens by warning them when the design contains potential performance problems. Therefore, the model should predict the influence of different UI elements, their configuration and their interference on performance. The focus of the model is on screens developed with the SAP UI5 library, influences of custom coding or other libraries can be neglected. Furthermore, the model should be derived for a reference client machine and current versions of the most common browsers (Internet Explorer, Firefox, and Chrome). Thereby, it is important that the model reflects performance influences accurately for the reference setup. The transferability to other machine sizes or browser versions is neglectable. For the given scenario, we identified two potential consumption channels: a web-based prediction tool and an integration in a screen design editor. The web-based tool allows designers to quickly evaluate different screen designs by varying the screen configuration based on check boxes, sliders and input fields. It is a valuable tool for making rough estimations about front-end performance before actually starting the screen design. It hclps answering questions like „How many columns and rows can I add to a table of type X in my web application without violating performance requirements?" or „What is the impact of back-end call data size on front-end performance?". Moreover, the web-based prediction tool can be used in developer trainings to clarify the impact of bad screen designs on front-end performance. The second consumption channel is the integration of the prediction model in a screen design editor used by developers to create SAP UI5 based web applications. Having the prediction integrated in the editor allows us to give immediate feedback on the expected performance while the screen is under development. Developers can get a warning when the screen design does not meet SAP's performance requirements and detailed views.

Construction

To derive the prediction model an experimental, measurement-based process is applied. The experiments are conducted using a screen generator software that allows to generate screens with different SAP UI5 library elements and configurations. The performance of the generated screens is measured on the latest versions of the main browsers on a test client machine.

3.2.2.2. Effect of Data Model Design on Application Throughput

Purpose

In data-centric applications, the data model can significantly limit performance and scalability of the overall application. When developing the data model it is often unclear to developers, how different design decisions or usage profiles affect the application's performance. Setting up and running performance tests that are tailored towards data model performance require special expertise and cause significant overhead for developers. Standard benchmarks such as provided by SPEC [SPE12] and TPC [TPC13] do not test broad enough in order to enable a detailed understanding of performance characteristics of a particular data model. SAP offers a Java-based cloud plattform on which Independent Software Vendors (ISVs) can develop and run their applications. A major component of this plattform is the persistence service that can be accessed using the Java Persistence API (JPA). Supporting ISVs in developing scalable JPA-based data model designs is an additional feature of the platform that helps SAP's customers to run their software faster and more efficient. Deriving a performance model that maps the service usage (i.e., the design of the JPA data model and its expected usage profile) to the expected performance and providing that information to the ISVs can have positive effects on customer satisfaction and platform sales.

Consumption

The performance model should support developers in designing scalable JPA-based data models by providing them information about the expected performance of the data model under development. The performance characteristics of the data model should be estimated for different reference workload types which represent common usage patterns in business applications. Moreover, the performance model should only be derived on the reference test platform. Instead of providing exact prediction numbers, it is sufficient to provide relative estimates on the performance characteristics of different data model variants under different reference usage profiles. Developers can use the feedback provided by the model to continuously track the performance impact of changes applied to the data model, and to evaluate design alternatives with respect to data model entities (e.g. distribution of attributes across entity classes) and entity usage (e.g. number of parallel reads). We aim at two scenarios of developer support: (i) continuous tracking of the performance impact of changes applied to the data model, and (ii) evaluating design alternatives with respect to data model entities. For the first usage type, the performance feedback relates to the currently focused data model entity and the performance values are updated when changes are applied to the software artefact. Figure 3.1 sketches how this could look like in the IDE of the developer.

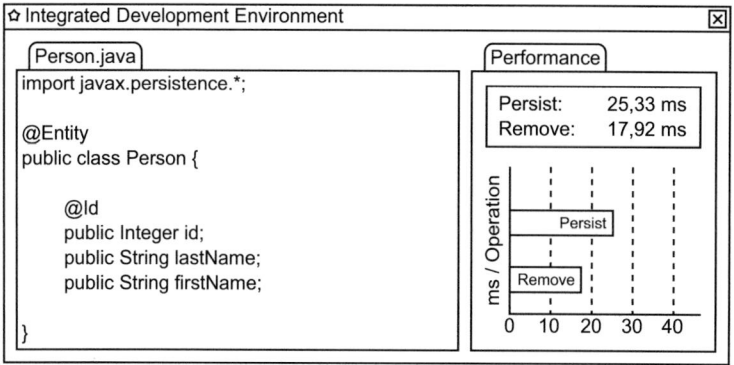

Figure 3.1.: Immediate feedback in the IDE

While the developer is developing the entity *Person* and adding additional attributes, the performance feedback view on the right side of the figure shows how the changes affect the average response time for persist and remove operations on this entity for a predefined test workload.

In the second scenario, developers directly compare different implementation alternatives against each other in order to understand the performance characteristics of each alternative. Figure 3.3 shows an example for this kind of feedback.

Figure 3.2 sketches the two implementation alternatives. The functional requirement for the developer is to store 32 numbers in a *Container* entity. *Alternative 1* implements this requirement by adding 32 fields of type *Long* to the entity. *Alternative 2* uses a list field that can hold values of type Long. Figure 3.3 illustrates the performance feedback view for that example. It shows the throughput that can be achieved for the insert, update, remove, and persist operations using the respective alternative. In the example, the throughput that can be achieved with *Alternative 1* is 4 times higher than with *Alternative 2*.

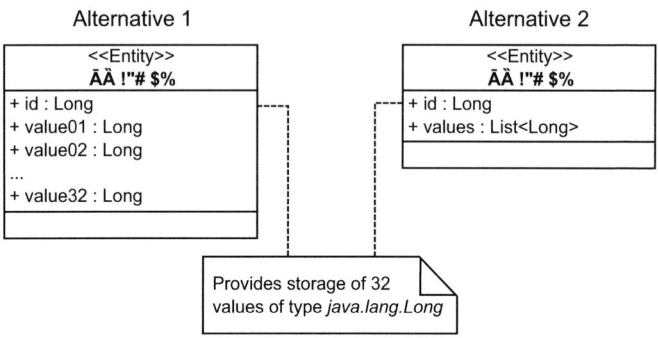

Figure 3.2.: Two design alternatives

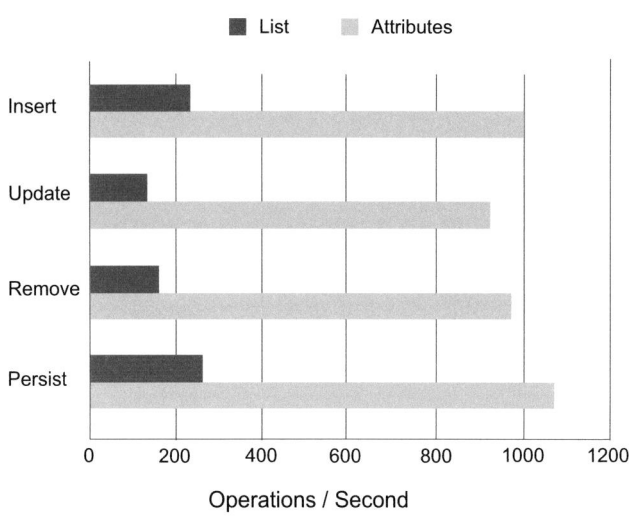

Figure 3.3.: Evaluation of design alternatives

Construction

To derive the prediction model an experimental, measurement-based process is applied. The experiments are conducted using a JPA benchmarking framework [WWHM13] that allows us to automatically create, run and analyse tailored benchmark applications. The Benchmark Framework is parametrisable via information specified in a JPA Benchmark Model (e.g. the characteristics of the data model that is to be tested). In the construction step the modelled information is used to trigger the generation of code and configuration files, and package the benchmark application to a deployable unit. In the execution phase the benchmark application is deployed to the test platform for which the performance model is to be derived. Having this framework in place allows us to efficiently experiment with different data model characteristics and derive a performance model.

3.3. Systematic, Measurement-based Experimentation

To derive goal-oriented performance models, we propose a measurement-based, experimental approach. The approach consists of the four basic steps depicted in Figure 3.4

1. *Define Context:* Includes all tasks that are necessary to set up the test environment and to prepare experimentation (e.g. finding and documenting known issues and finding a proper reference system and performance metric).

2. *Understand Performance Behaviour:* An iterative process where assumptions about performance-relevant influences are identified and tested. Moreover, proper heuristics and analysis methods for performance model derivation are identified.

3. *Derive Performance Model:* Based on the knowledge gained in the previous process step, a set of experiments is defined and executed in order to derive the performance prediction functions of the performance model.

4. *Validate Performance Model*: Includes a comparison of the predictions made by the performance model with measurements from a real systems in order to further validate if the assumptions and heuristics are valid and all relevant performance influences have been captured.

The process illustrated in Figure 3.4 is based on a method for experiment-based performance model derivation introduced by Happe [Hap08]. As with the performance evaluation process described by Jain [Jai91], Happe highlights that the design of a performance model should be driven by a specific goal that directs and limits the design effort to the factors that are important for the specific scenario. To define the performance goal properly, we propose to apply the template introduced in Section 3.2. Another important characteristic of the process is its highly iterative nature around the core activities. In the following, we provide a detailed description of the four process activities that should be implemented by an experts team consisting of performance analysts and domain experts.

3.3.1. Define Context

In the first step, the experts team needs to define the context of the experiments. This includes the interpretation and the refinement of the information provided in the performance evaluation template (see Section 3.2). All information and known issues in the context of the performance evaluation scenario need to be gathered and properly documented. Another major task in this process step is setting up the test environment that is to be used for running the experiments. The experts team has to prepare the hardware and software used for the system under test as well as for supporting tasks like load generation and monitoring. Furthermore, in some cases an artefact generation component needs to be developed (see Section 3.2). Based on the goal of the performance model, the performance metrics that should be used for prediction have to be defined. Usually, these are response time, throughput, or resource utilisation metrics [Jai91]. Ultimately, the test environment has to expose an interface that allows the experts team to vary the values of a set of input parameters and observe the values of a set of output parameters (i.e.,the performance metrics of interest). In summary, the results of this process step are as follows.

- A sound documentation of the performance evaluation goal and the known facts and issues in the context of the evaluation scenario.

- A ready-to-use test environment that provides an interface for varying input parameter values and observing performance metrics.

3.3.2. Understand Performance Behaviour

The goals of this activity are

a) to get a sound understanding of the basic performance characteristics of the system under test, and

b) to minimize the parameter space for model derivation.

The first goal involves, for example, questions like:

- What are the performance-critical system components and parameters in the scenario?

- Does the selected metric provide a sufficient description of the performance characteristics of the system?

- What are potential measurement biases and how to avoid or control them?

Once a proper measurement environment is in place and a basic understanding of the performance-critical parameters has been established, the experts team needs to identify how to minimize the parameter space for model derivation. Usually, the amount of performance-critical parameters is too large to derive a single prediction function (see also "curse of dimensionality"). Instead, proper abstractions and heuristics have to be identified that limit the parameter space. Here, the following example questions are to be answered:

- Which parameters can be neglected?

- What are reasonable boundaries for parameter values?

- Are their groups of parameters that can be measured in isolation?

- What are appropriate analysis methods to derive functional relationships between parameters?

To answer the questions introduced above, we propose the process illustrated in Figure 3.5.

Identify Assumptions   In the first step of the process, performance analysts identify a set of assumptions with respect to the relevant performance influences. This can be done based on experience in the scenario context or documentation. In our industrial case study presented in Chapter 5, we build upon a rich base of screens that have already been available to identify potential contributors to front-end performance. Based on this knowledge, we came up with a set of assumptions. For example, one assumption that we test in Chapter 5 states: „The larger the number of UI elements on a screen, the lower the front-end performance."

Define Experiments to Test Assumptions   Once an initial set of assumptions has been identified, the experts team defines a set of experiments that explicitly test the assumptions and quantify the influences. For example, in our industrial case study we defined experiments to capture the effect of different configurations of an UI element on performance. To guide the experiment design and help performance analysts in resolving the issues that come with this task, we propose to apply the SoPeCo approach introduced in Chapter 4 of this thesis. Especially if multiple parameters are to be varied, the number of required experiments may grow exponentially. This behaviour is known as curse of dimensionality [HTF09]. In this case, good experimental designs (such as those proposed in Chapter 4.4) can help to keep the number of experiments manageable.

Run Experiments and Analyse Results   Once the experimental designs have been defined, performance experts can run the experiments and analyse the results. We use the SoPeCo approach (see Chapter 4) to automate the experiment execution and to collect the relevant data. To analyse the results, different techniques can be appropriate depending on the experiments executed and the questions to be answered. If, for example, performance analysts want to check if a certain parameter affects performance, fractional factorial experimental designs (see Chapter 2.2) can be a proper choice. The experiment results and the analyses may point out missing assumptions and influences that need to be tested in further experiments.

In summary, the results of the activities introduced in this section, which are part of the overall process depicted in Figure 3.4, are as follows.

- A set of validated assumptions with respect to relevant performance influences in the scenario.

- A set of heuristics and analysis methods that enable an efficient derivation of a performance model.

3.3.3. Derive Performance Model

Based on the assumptions and heuristics that have been identified in the previous process step, a set of experiments is defined that aims at deriving performance prediction functions. The defined set of experiments is automatically executable and thus the construction of the prediction function can be easily repeated if the system is updated or a new parameter has to be added. The main question that is to be answered in this process step is „How to combine the different experiment results into a single performance model?" Therefore, we propose to implement the process illustrated in Figure 3.6.

Define Experiments for Model Derivation   In the first step, the learnings from the previous experiments are used to define the complete set of experiments that is necessary to derive the required prediction functions. For example, in our industrial case study we define an experiment for each performance-critical UI element which derives the functional relationship between the number of this UI elements on a screen and the performance of the screen.

Run Experiments and Analyse Results   In this step, the experiments are automatically executed on the test environment. Moreover, the analysis results are checked for any issues (e.g. failed measurements, too many outliers, performance behaviour differs from assumption).

Construct Prediction Functions   In order to construct the prediction functions of the performance model, the experts team has to combine the functions derived by model fitting, regression techniques, or machine learning (e.g. as introduced in Chapter 4.4.2) with the assumptions and heuristics derived in the previous process step. In our industrial case study (see Chapter 5), we come to the assumption that different UI elements do not interfere with each other and thus their performance influence on the front-end performance is additive. This assumptions heavily reduces the number of required experiments and allows us to construct the performance model by adding up the prediction functions for each UI element.

In summary, the result of the process step introduced in this section is a set of prediction functions that support stakeholders in the software development process in conducting the tasks stated in the performance evaluation goal.

3.3.4. Validate Performance Model

The prediction functions derived in the previous process step form a performance model that captures the known assumptions and influences tested by the experiments. However, the model needs to be validated before it can be used in practice. The validation aims at answering the following questions.

- Are the assumptions and heuristics good enough to derive an accurate performance model?

- Are there any influences in the validation objects that have not been captured by the performance model?

This validation is the final step in the process illustrated in Figure 3.4. The predictions provided by the performance model have to be compared to measurements of a real system as there is a good chance that some major influences are still missing. If this is the case, further experiments have to be added and the prediction model has to be refined.

Finally, the process results in a validated performance model that can be applied by the target groups. In our case study (see Chapter 5), UI designers and developers can use the predictions provided by the performance model to asses front-end performance of web applications for different browsers before the screens are actually implemented.

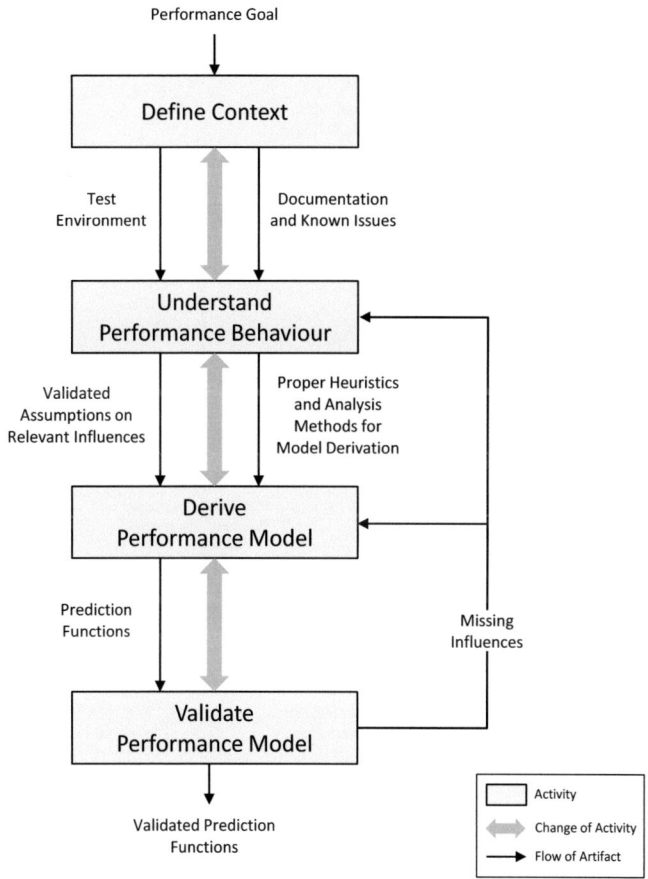

Figure 3.4.: Process for deriving goal-oriented performance models

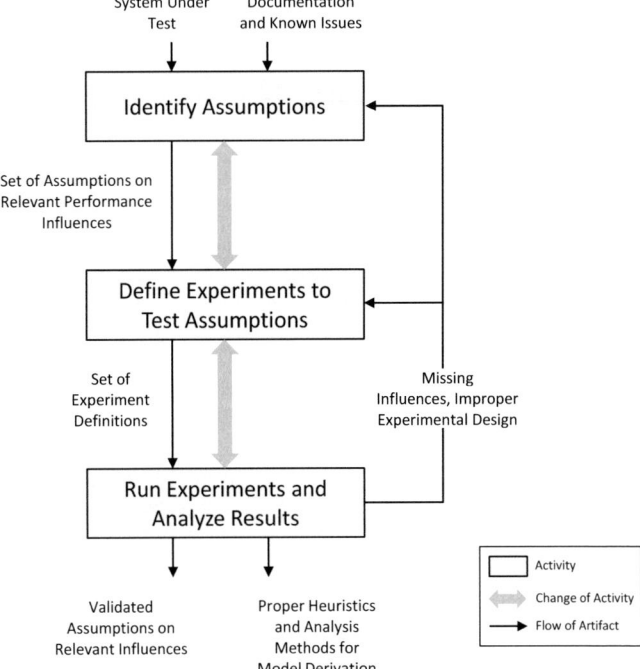

Figure 3.5.: Process for understanding performance behaviour

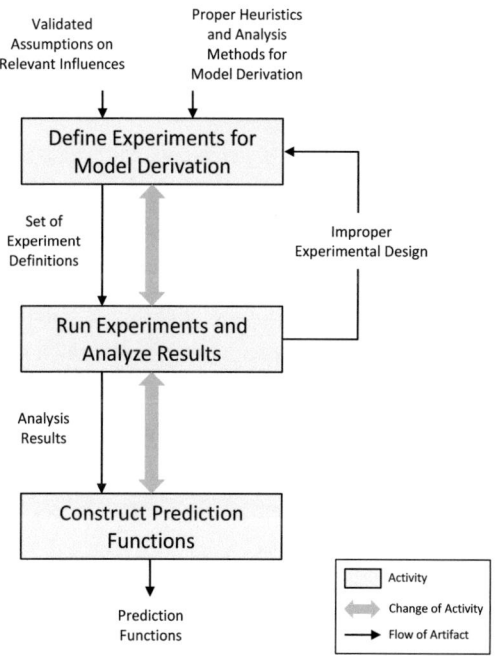

Figure 3.6.: Process for deriving performance model

3.4. Discussion of Assumptions and Limitations

In the following, the limitations and assumptions of the general performance model construction approach that is presented in this chapter will be discussed. As the performance model construction builds upon the SoPeCo approach introduced in Chapter 4, it inherits all the assumption and limitations described in Chapter 4.6. Additionally, we see the following restrictions.

Number of Experiments   In order to deal with the complexity of real-world software systems, we use experiments to derive assumptions and heuristics that enable us limit the number of experiments that are to be executed. For example, in the case study presented in Chapter 5, we could reduce the number of experiments due to the assumption that different UI elements do not interfere with each other and thus are additive. If it is not possible to limit the number of experiments, the approach might not be applicable due to the curse of dimensionality [HTF09] that occurs when too many parameters have to be varied in combination.

Transferability of Models   The performance models that are derived using the approach presented in this chapter are focused on a very specific goal. On the one hand, this allows performance analysts to deal with the complexity of the systems and limits the complexity of the resulting performance model. On the other hand, it reduces the transferability of the performance model to other scenarios and goals. However, in similar scenarios the measurement environment as well as some of the experiment definitions can be reused to create a performance model.

Also the fact that the performance model is only valid for the test system on which it has been derived limits its transferability. However, as described in Section 5.4, the capability to rerun experiments on different systems with minimal manual effort compensates the restricted generality.

Availability of Model Inputs   When conducting the experiments potential usage and configuration parameter values are varied and used to
derive a performance model. While at the time of experimentation these
values are set by the corresponding tools in the measurement environment,
they have to be accessible at the time when the performance model is used
for prediction. For example, in order to assess the performance of the design of a web application screen, the developer has to provide the corresponding design characteristics as an input to the model. These inputs can
be provided manually (e.g. via the web application introduced in Section
5.4) or automatically by a supporting tool (e.g. the „what you see is what
you get" editor also described in Section 5.4). In the course of the case
study, we also tried to derive the inputs from a regular source code editor
by parsing the JavaScript code. However, this failed due to the vast amount
of potential representations of the same JavaScript code and the complexity
of the parser.

3.5. Summary and Contributions

In this chapter, we introduced a novel approach for software performance
modelling that aims at being tightly integrated in the software development process. We presented a procedure for specifying goal-oriented performance models using the *Purpose, Consumption, Construction* methodology, as well as an experimental, measurement-based process for deriving
performance models. Our measurement-based approach is close to the industrial practice and thus more likely to be applied by practitioners than
other approaches.

The contributions of this chapter are

- A goal-oriented procedure for the specification of performance models.

- A process definition for the experimental derivation of goal-oriented performance models.

In summary, the approach allows performance analysts to efficiently derive and maintain goal-oriented performance models of complex software systems. Based on these models developers, software architects or administrators can asses the performance impact of their design decisions with only minimal overhead. The goal-oriented specification of the models increases the probability of creating a performance model that is actually adopted in development organisations. The iterative and measurement-based nature of the experimental derivation of performance models helps to deal with complex software systems as many tasks can be supported or automated by an appropriate experimentation infrastructure (see Chapter 4).

4. Automated Performance Evaluation Experiments

The overall goal of this thesis is to provide a practical means to performance analysts that helps them in constructing performance models of software systems. In Chapter 3, we introduced our overall approach for deriving goal-oriented performance models based on systematic experimentation. In this chapter, we introduce an approach to support performance analysts in deriving such goal-oriented performance models efficiently. Figure 4.1 illustrates the basic idea of the approach that has been introduced in Chapter

.

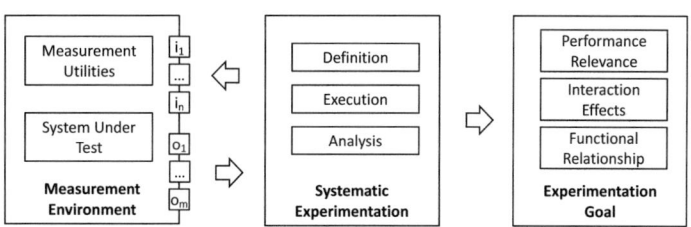

Figure 4.1.: Experimental performance evaluation

We assume that a measurement environment is in place that allows us to vary the values of a set of input parameters and observe the values of a set of output parameters. The parameters can either belong to the system under test or to a measurement utility such as a benchmark application, a monitoring tool or a load driver. In the following, we refer to a concrete measurement environment that has a defined set of input and observation parameters as performance evaluation scenario or just scenario. Our systematic experimentation approach enables performance analysts to define a set of experiments based on the input and observation parameters. An experiment is defined as a concrete valuation of input parameters for which the values of one or many observation parameter are gathered. Moreover, we define an experiment series as a set of experiments derived by an experimental design [Nat12]. If, for example, the measurement environment allows us to set the number of users simulated by a load driver and observe the average response time for this users, the performance analyst could define an experiment series that investigates the effect of a growing number of users on the average response time of the system under test. Experiment series are executed and analysed automatically. Depending on the goal of the experiment series, the performance analyst gets information about the performance-relevance of input parameters, interaction effects between input parameters or a description of the functional relationship between a set of input parameters and an observation parameter of interest (such as the functional relationship between the number of users and the average response time).

This chapter introduces our approach to automatically execute and analyse experiments that target a specific goal. The approach is called SoPeCo, named after the Software Performance Cockpit framework that we developed to implement and derive the contributions of this thesis. SoPeCo eases the definition of performance evaluation experiments and combines experimental design and analysis in an automated, iterative way which allows deriving goals efficiently. Another benefit of the approach is that once the experiments are defined and the measurement environment is in place, one can simply rerun the experiments whenever necessary (e.g. due to a new version of a component in the measurement environment). The SoPeCo framework allows performance analysts to apply the approach in different scenarios including different technologies and tools. Based on the capabilities of the SoPeCo approach presented in this chapter, we can automatically run systematic series of experiments to derive performance models for complex software systems (see Chapter 3).

The chapter is structured as follows. In Section 4.1, we illustrate the scientific challenges when implementing an automated performance engineering approach. Section 4.2 provides an overview on the SoPeCo approach. In Section 4.3, we introduce a language for the definition of performance evaluation experiments as well as an architecture that allows to automatically run these experiments in different scenarios. A detailed description of the automated, iterative combination of experimental design and statistical analysis follows in Section 4.4. In multiple case studies, we validate that the approach can be applied to real applications and provides accurate results running only a small set of measurements (Section 4.5). Finally, Section 4.6 lists limitations of the approach and Section 4.7 summarises the chapter.

4.1. Scientific Challenges

As described above, our approach is based on the assumption that we have an existing test environment on which we can vary the values on input parameters and observe several performance metrics. Theoretically, we can measure any point in the measurement environment (i.e., any combination of input parameter values) . Practically, this is impossible due to the huge amount of potential measurement points (i.e., experiments) even for simple systems. Moreover, performance measurements are indeterministic, which requires the repeated execution of a single experiment in order to get statistically stable results. Hence, each experiment that is required for a performance evaluation is costly and endangers the practicability of the approach. The scientific challenges in the field of measurement-based performance evaluations that arise from these circumstances are as follows:

- **How to derive accurate prediction functions efficiently?** Finding the trade-off between accuracy and efficiency is the main

69

research challenge when trying to quantify the relationship between one or many factors and the response variable. The number of potential measurement points is a function of the number of factors and their levels which results in a space that is impossible to measure completely. Moreover, real software systems usually do not show a simple (e.g. linear) behaviour for this relationship. Hence, performance engineering research needs to investigate what kind of models can be used to quantify this relationship. Furthermore, smart experimental designs are required that provide enough and proper measurement data to fit these models accurately and with the least number of measurement points possible.

- **What is a suitable abstraction level to deal with heterogeneous scenarios?** In industrial practice, each performance evaluation scenario differs from another in, for example, the system under test, the tools used to monitor the system, or the tools used to generate load. How to cope with this variety of technologies, tools and potential performance behaviours in a unified approach is subject to research.

- **How to specify automatable performance evaluation experiments?** Performance evaluation projects are often conducted over a certain period of time until a problem has been fixed or a new release is tested. In most cases, the environment setup and the experiments that have been conducted are not clearly documented [SMF⁺07]. However, especially these tasks require a lot of effort and knowledge. Providing a means to document this knowledge and transfer it between the stakeholders of different performance evaluation projects would significantly improve productivity. The challenge is to define a language that allows to

reuse assets across a wide range of different performance evaluation projects. Moreover, the language has to encapsulate all
information necessary to automatically execute and analyse experiments.

4.2. Overview

Based on the research challenges identified above, the main goals of the
SoPeCo approach are

- simplifying and unifying the definition of performance evaluation experiments,

- automating the execution of experiments based on a definition,
  as well as

- providing methods and heuristics that optimize the trade-off between result accuracy and the number of required measurements

in different, heterogeneous real-world performance evaluation projects.

Figure 4.2 outlines the main activities in an experiment-based performance evaluation and indicates how these activities are supported by the
SoPeCo approach. Following this process, performance analysts can evaluate the performance properties of complex systems by applying systematic
experimentation in a goal-oriented way. Our process for deriving goal-
oriented performance models presented in Chapter 3, includes the activities
presented in this chapter in several steps. The SoPeCo framework (see
Section 4.3) allows performance analysts to capture important information
and automate common tasks within this process. Based on the manual definition of a scenario (*Scenario Definition*) and one or more experiments
for that scenario (*Experiment Definition*), the SoPeCo framework automatically executes the experiments (Experiment Execution). The loop between

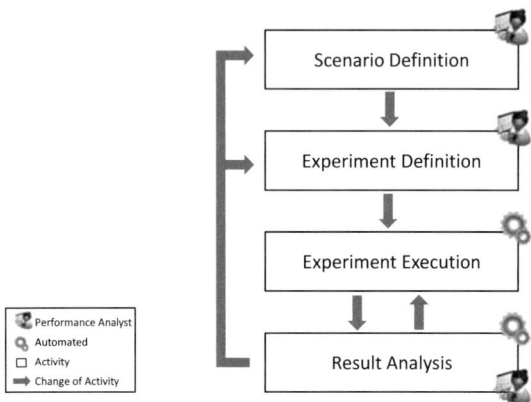

Figure 4.2.: Overview on the SoPeCo approach

the *Experiment Execution* and the *Result Analysis* activity (see Figure 4.2), reflects the iterative combination between these activities targeting the automated derivation of experimental designs that optimize the trade-off between result accuracy and the number of required experiments (see Section 4.4). After the results have been analysed, the performance analysts might need to adjust the scenario or the experiment definitions and re-run the evaluation in order to improve the evaluation results or get more insights.

Jain [Jai91] lists a set of common mistakes done by performance analysts within these activities. To avoid these mistakes, he introduces a systematic approach consisting of ten steps that guide analysts through a performance evaluation process (similar process guidelines are defined in [MA01] and [SW01]). In the remainder of this section, we describe how the ten steps defined by Jain are integrated in and supported by our approach. For a detailed description of the ten steps we refer to [Jai91] .

Scenario Definition The *Scenario Definition* activity comprises all steps that need to be done by a performance analyst before the actual experimentation begins. This includes:

1. State goals and define the system: One main mistake in many performance evaluation projects is that the goal is not set properly. Analysts often start with gathering vast quantities of measurement data or building models that are supposed to answer any design question. However, the proper way is to consider carefully what the goals of the study are. Based on these goals the performance analyst can define which components to include in the system under test (SUT), which performance metrics to measure or which workloads to choose. Once these decisions are made, the performance analyst can set up the test environment which comprises the SUT, monitoring tools and load generation tools. This is a manual task that has to be done by the performance analyst together with the other stakeholders of the study (e.g. development groups or system administrators). In our approach, we assume that the goals are clearly defined and the test environment is ready-to-use.

2. List services and outcomes: Listing the services the SUT provides and the potential outcomes of these services is a preparatory step for the next step which is selecting the criteria based on which performance should be compared.

3. Select metrics: In performance evaluations metrics are usually related to timing behaviour, throughput and resource consumption [Jai91]. It is important to select those metrics that help understanding the questions that need to be answered in order to achieve a certain goal. Moreover, performance analysts have to check whether these metrics can be monitored in the test environment. There might be cases where a metric cannot be monitored because the overhead would be too high or the instrumentation of a system component is too complex. Once the met-

rics are defined by the performance analyst, they can be documented using the experiment specification language included in the SoPeCo framework [WHF13] (see Section 4.3). In general, the language-based definition of a performance evaluation scenario, as proposed in this thesis, has the advantages that (i) the information is captured in a structured way and thus it is less likely that the analyst forgets to add important information, (ii) the information can be reused in the definition of different experiments possibly conducted by different performance analysts, and (iii) the information can be processed automatically by a corresponding tooling. In the experimental design terminology the metrics are called response variables (see Chapter 2.2.1).

4. Select workload: Depending on the goal of the performance evaluation different workloads can be selected by the performance analyst. For the success of the study it is important that the workload is representative for the scenario that is subject to evaluation. However, deriving and characterizing workloads is out of the scope of this thesis. In the SoPeCo approach, we assume that the performance analyst has identified a set of appropriate workloads and thus also workload parameters that can be varied in the experiment series.

5. List parameters: As with the metrics, the performance analyst has to define which parameters potentially affect performance and thus should be included in the experiments. These parameters are either system parameters, such as component configurations and feature selections, or workload parameters like user request characteristics and instruction mixes. Like the metrics, the parameters are documented using the experiment specification language of the SoPeCo framework [WHF13] (see Section

4.3). The list of parameters and metrics might need to be adjusted after some experiments have been conducted and analysed (see Figure 4.2).

Experiment Definition   Once the scenario for the performance evaluation project is properly defined, the performance analyst can start designing experiments. Mapped to Jain's systematic approach to performance evaluations [Jai91], the *Experiment Definition* activity comprises the following steps:

6. Select factors to study: For each experiment, the performance analyst has to specify which input parameters should be varied and how. The performance analyst specifies this information using the experiment specification language included in the SoPeCo framework [WHF13] (see Section 4.3). The framework provides several ways to express the possible values of a parameter (e.g. a list of values or a range of values). Moreover, the language as well as the framework are designed to enable the flexible introduction of new parameter variation strategies.

7. Select evaluation technique: In this step, Jain lists three main techniques for performance evaluation: analytical modelling, simulation, and measuring. The performance analyst has to chose the one he wants to use for the study. Although the SoPeCo approach could also be used for the efficient execution of experiments based on simulation models, the focus of this thesis is on measurement-based performance evaluations.

8. Design experiments: Depending on the complexity of the scenario, the design of experiments (or experimental design) can be one of the most complex and error-prone steps in a perfor-

mance evaluation (see for example the list of common mistakes in experimental designs listed by Jain [Jai91]). In this step, it has to be decided which experiments (i.e., one concrete valuation of input parameters) should be executed. The challenge for the performance analyst is to select the values in a way that the experiments provide maximum information and can be executed within a limited period of time. With our SoPeCo approach, we support the performance analyst in this task by providing a set of sophisticated methods that dynamically create experimental designs for common performance evaluation questions (see Section 4.4):

a) What are the most performance-relevant factors?

b) Which factors interact with each other?

c) What is the functional relationship between the levels of a list of factors and a response variable?

Using our approach, the performance analyst does not have to create the experimental design. He only has to select one of the methods that we provide for the respective question. These methods dynamically create the experimental design based on the iterative application of measurements, statistical methods and result validation (see Section 4.4). In the following paragraphs, we describe how this interaction between *Experiment Execution* and *Result Analysis* is applied in the SoPeCo approach in order to answer the three questions stated above.

Experiment Execution   Usually the execution of an experiment is only triggering the start of a measurement. Hence, Jain does not list this step in his systematic approach to performance evaluation [Jai91]. However, in the SoPeCo approach the *Experiment Execution* is the connector between the automated derivation of experimental designs based on a strategy defined in the *Experiment Definition* and the *Result Analysis* activity. That is, we shift tasks that are usually conducted manually by the performance analyst to the automated *Experiment Execution* activity which makes this activity an important part of the approach. In Section 4.3, we describe in detail how we automate this step in the SoPeCo framework [WHHH10] and combine it with analysing the measured data and deriving smart, goal-driven experimental designs for different real-world performance evaluation projects.

Result Analysis The *Result Analysis* activity includes the two final steps of Jain's systematic approach [Jai91].

9. Analyse and interpret data: This step requires the most experience and knowledge as the performance analyst has to decide, for example, which methods to choose to analyse data, when the results are good enough to draw conclusions, or if there has been a mistake in the experiment definition. In our approach, we automate many analysis and interpretation tasks based on a set of heuristics. Hence, we support the performance analyst in making these decisions. In addition, the SoPeCo approach analyses the data with respect to the question which further experiments are likely to provide the maximum information gain and thus dynamically creates the experimental design [WKH11]. Moreover, our analyses are usually black-box analyses, i.e.,without making strong assumptions about the underlying functional dependencies. this increases the range of scenarios in which our automated approach can be applied.

For the three main performance evaluation questions outlined in step 8, we analyse and interpret the data as follows. For questions a) and b), we combine existing experimental designs that are executed automatically. The problem behind question c) is subject of research in this thesis. The space of potential experiments spanned by the input parameters and their possible values is growing exponentially with the number of parameters. Thus, it is even more important to accurately quantify the functional relationship with the least possible amount of measurements. If the performance analyst has to do this with existing approaches, he has to execute a set of experiments using a manually predefined experimental design. Furthermore, he has to determine the underlying model, i.e.,the type of the relationship (e.g. a linear relationship), in order to fit the model using the measured data as training data (see Chapter 2.3). In a next step, the analyst has to conduct additional measurements to validate whether the model is accurate enough. If not, further experiments are required to extend the training data for the model fitting process.

Executing these steps manually is not efficient (usually too many experiments are executed that do not provide significant information gain), error-prone (there might not be enough and suitable validation measurements so that a bad model fit in a certain area might not be detected), complex (in real software systems the underlying models are usually not trivial and do not follow a certain rule), and finally causes a lot of effort (determining the model, running the measurements, analysing the data). In Section 4.4.2, we introduce an approach that combines experimental design, statistical model inference and model validation in order to derive the functional relationship between a list of input parameters and a performance metric of interest. The approach iterates automatically over the three tasks until a prediction function with a sufficient accuracy has been derived. We developed and compared different algorithms that derive experimental designs which efficiently fit a model (i.e.,using as few experiments as possible). Moreover, we evaluated a set of statistical regression and interpolation methods that make less assumptions about the underlying functional dependencies and thus are able to represent a large set of functions. This allows us to fit accurate prediction functions for real applications without knowing any details about the internal behaviour of the application. The automated, black-box inference of prediction functions [WHKF12] makes our approach applicable to a large set of scenarios and frees the performance analyst from the manual tasks described above.

10. Present Results: This final step deals with the communication of the evaluation results to the corresponding target groups. Although Jain [Jai91] already mentions that it is important to present the results in an understandable way, he basically means that one should avoid statistical jargon and plot correct graphs. In our approach, we aim at going one step further and integrate the evaluation results in the daily life of the stakeholders in the software development process [Wes12]. In Chapter 3, we present an industrial case study where we provide direct performance feedback to UI developers by integrating the evaluation results in the design process of web application front-ends.

In the following sections, we provide a detailed introduction of our contributions that support performance analysts in implementing the presented process.

4.3. Experiment Definition and Execution

Each performance evaluation project is different. Projects differ for example in their goals, the system under test, the workload type, and the monitoring tools. However, as described in the previous section, there are tasks that are common to all performance evaluation projects (e.g. defining the parameters and metrics to study, triggering measurements, gathering measurement data, analysing measured data). Hence, in order to enhance reusability and automate common tasks, it is important to distinct between those parts of a project that are scenario-specific and those that are to be conducted for every experiment-based performance evaluation. Moreover, the commonalities between projects have to be expressed in a well-defined way in order to allow for knowledge exchange between projects and provide a basis for automating tasks.

In this section, we present an approach for handling different projects in a unified way. Section 4.3.1 introduces the abstract syntax of a language for the definition of scenarios and experiments [WHF13]. The language can be used to describe experiments for any performance evaluation project. When applied by a concrete syntax (e.g. a graphical editor) it directs the performance analyst through the experiment definition process and reduces the risk of making common mistakes (such as those described by Jain [Jai91]). Moreover, it increases maintainability and reusability of experiment definitions due to the specified semantics that allows other performance analysts to comprehend existing definitions. Another benefit of such a language is that it captures the information in a machine-readable form and thus provides the basis for the automated execution of experiments described in Section 4.3.2. The capability to automatically execute experiments independent of the actual performance evaluation project [WHHH10, WH11] is a basic prerequisite for the work presented in Chapter 3. Without automation it would not be feasible to derive performance models for real-world software systems based on experimentation (such as demonstrated in Chapter 5). The large amount of experiments that need to be conducted would make a manual execution too time-consuming for the performance analyst.

4.3.1. Experiment Specification Language

This work introduces a novel experiment specification language [WHF13] that forms a basis to capture information required to implement a systematic performance evaluation process (such as described by Jain [Jai91] or Smith [SW01]). Unlike other languages, it enables the definition of experiments independent of concrete domains, technologies or applications which allows performance analysts to focus on the problem that is investigated. Moreover, it allows performance analysts to reuse experiment definitions over multiple studies and share experiment meta-information and best practices in experimental design among each other. Another benefit of our language is the clear separation between experiment definition and automated experiment execution which facilitates the integration of the language in different experiment automation tools.

Section 4.3.1.1 outlines the requirements for the design of the language. Section 4.3.1.2 introduces the abstract syntax of the language in form of a UML diagram and explains its design rationale. Section 4.3.1.3 provides an example SoPeCo experiment definition.

4.3.1.1. Requirements

In this section, we outline the requirements that drive the design of the experiment specification language.

Targeting Automated Experiment Execution The goal of the approach presented in this thesis is to run goal-oriented performance evaluation experiments automatically. Hence, we require a language that has the capabilities to express experimental designs in way so that they can be automatically executed and analysed. For example, we need to describe what parameters to vary in which way or how to analyse the measured data to achieve a certain goal.

Supporting a Broad Range of Scenarios As we do not want to focus on evaluating the performance only for a certain software domain, the language should not include any domain-specific elements nor should it predefine a fixed set of goals, experimental designs, or analysis strategies. Furthermore, it should be independent of the programming language and the experiment automation tool used to implement the automated experiment execution.

Flexible Extensibility The third requirement arises from the first two requirements. As the language should be independent of a concrete automation tool implementation and support the automated execution and analysis of experiments without explicitly defining concrete strategies, we need to allow automation tool implementations to flexibly adapt to concrete goals, domains, or scenarios. That means it is up to experiment automation tool implementations to provide a set of parameter variation strategies, experimental design methods, or result analysis techniques. Hence, our language has to provide an abstract syntax that sets the frame for an automated performance evaluation but is flexibly extensible by a concrete syntax implemented in an experiment automation tool. As a result of this thesis, we provide a hosted version of the SoPeCo framework [WHW+13] that includes implementations of commonly used methods as well as a concrete web-based syntax for the experiment specification language.

4.3.1.2. Abstract Syntax and Informal Semantics

Due to the requirements describe above, we decouple the generic abstract syntax, presented in this section, from a concrete implementation that would (i) provide the concrete syntax and additional semantics (e.g. concrete analysis strategies), and (ii) automate the experiment selection and execution (as realized by the SoPeCo framework (see Section 4.3.2) in our approach). Thus, we also shift tasks like type safety and misuse checks to the experiment automation tool in order to keep the language independent and flexibly extensible. We implemented the abstract syntax in XML format. However, for the purpose of illustration we present it in the form of UML class diagrams.

In the following, we refer to a concrete performance evaluation project as a scenario. According to the systematic performance evaluation process introduced in Section 4.2, a clear definition of the scenario should be the first step of any performance evaluation. Figure 4.3 shows the Scenario-Definition as the root element of the abstract syntax.

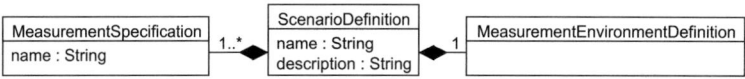

Figure 4.3.: Scenario Definition

A ScenarioDefinition is identified by its name and should have a description. In the description attribute the performance analyst can provide information concerning the scenario set up and evaluation goals. Furthermore, a ScenarioDefinition contains exactly one MeasurementEnvironmentDefinition and one or many MeasurementSpecifications.

MeasurementEnvironment: The measurement environment denotes the complete set of systems and tools involved in the performance evaluation. This includes the system under test as well as load generation tools or monitoring applications. In the MeasurementEnvironmentDefinition the performance analyst defines the parameters and metrics that can be controlled or measured by the measurement environment.

We introduce the notion of namespaces in order to group parameters and allow for duplicate parameter names in different contexts (e.g. a parameter *CPUUtilisation* for different machines in the measurement environment) if needed (see Figure 4.4). Each ParameterDefinition is contained in a ParameterNamespace which is structured hierarchically. Besides the name, a ParameterDefinition has a description, a type and a role. The ParameterRole indicates whether the parameter value can be controlled

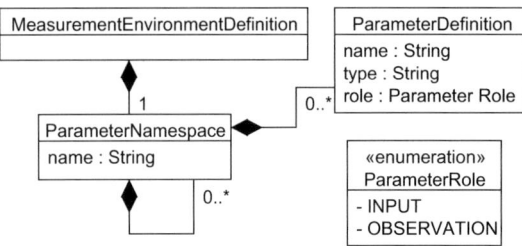

Figure 4.4.: Measurement Environment Definition

(i.e., it is an input to the measurement environment) or measured (i.e., it is observed by the measurement environment). The type can be specified by a textual representation. For the purpose of general applicability, we do not introduce detailed typing in the model as types are often technology-, domain- or application-specific (see also Section 4.3.1.1). Hence, the concrete types have to be interpreted by corresponding tooling that uses the language. The description field allows performance analysts to specify additional semantics with respect to the parameter such as to which component it belongs or what possible values are.

MeasurementSpecification: The MeasurementSpecification deals with the specification of experiments based on the scenario and the parameters defined in the MeasurementEnvironmentDefinition. Figure 4.5 illustrates the measurement specification part of the abstract syntax. A MeasurementSpecification contains one or many ExperimentSeries-Definitions. We define an experiment series as a set of experiments that are designed to answer a specific question. An experiment is defined as one concrete valuation of all input parameters (a.k.a. factor level combinations in experimental design terminology [Jai91]). An ExperimentSeriesDefinition contains all information necessary to automatically derive experiments that fulfil the purpose of the experiment series. Possible purposes of an experiment series are, for example, the identification of performance-relevant parameters, the identification of parameter interdependencies, or the quantification of functional dependencies between input parameters and an observed performance metric.

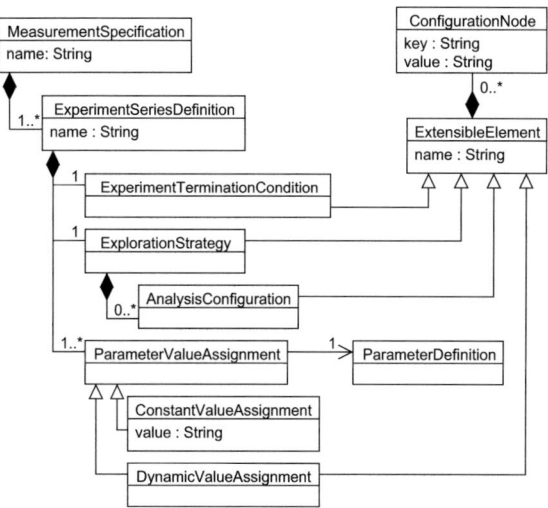

Figure 4.5.: Measurement Specification

Each `ExperimentSeriesDefinition` contains exactly one `Experi-`
`mentTerminationCondition`, exactly one `ExplorationStrategy`, and one or many `ParameterValueAssignments`. For the purpose of universality and extensibility, we do not include concrete implementations of these elements in the abstract syntax (see also Section 4.3.1.1). If we would for example integrate the concrete `ExplorationStrategy` elements in the abstract syntax, we would have to adjust the language for each new `Explo-rationStrategy`. Instead, we introduce a generic element that serves as an extension point and provides the information required by these concrete implementations. This `ExtensibleElement` is identified by its name and can contain a list of key value pairs for its `Configuration` (see Section

4.3.1.3). Please note that in a concrete syntax (i.e., the view for the performance analyst), these extensions look like regular language elements. Hence, the performance analyst does not have to specify the names of the extensions or the configuration keys but selects existing extensions and specifies only the values for the configuration.

- `ParameterValueAssignment`: Specifies the parameters that are to be controlled in the experiment series and defines the possible values for each parameter. The possible values can either be defined via a `ConstantValueAssignment` or a `DynamicValueAssignment`. The `ConstantValueAssignment` simply defines a fixed value which does not change throughout the experiment series. The `DynamicValueAssignment` allows the performance analyst to define different types of value assignment such as a linear variation rule with a minimum value, a maximum value and a step size, or a simple comma separated list of values. We use the `ExtensibleElement` to flexibly define concrete value assignment strategies. For example, a dynamic value assignment with name "Linear Value Assignment" will at runtime be resolved to the implementation of Linear Value Assignment provided by its corresponding plugin. Based on the list of `ParameterValueAssignments` in an `ExperimentSeriesDefinition` one can calculate the size of the measurement space (i.e., the number of potential experiments). The actual selection of an experiment is part of the experimental design which is derived by an `ExplorationStrategy`.

- `ExperimentTerminationCondition`: Due to the stochastic nature of performance measurements, all samples that we take for an experiment have different values. This requires repeated sampling for an experiment in order to minimize the effect of errors and outliers and derive statistically significant results [Jai91]. The ExperimentTerminationCondition specifies when enough repetitions for an experiment have been conducted. Examples are a fixed number of repetitions, a certain time frame in which the experiment is repeated, a certain confidence interval that has to be achieved, or a combination of the aforementioned conditions. Similar to parameter value assignments, termination conditions are also defined by ExtensibleElements. For example, a *NumberOfRepetitions* termination condition will be resolved at runtime to a concrete implementation that is provided by an extension with the same name.

- ExplorationStrategy: Specifies the strategy for exploring the input parameter space (i.e., the input parameter value combinations are selected). This strategy can, for example, implement a simple one-at-a-time experimental design [Nat12] or more sophisticated strategies such as those presented in Section 4.4. In the latter case, the strategies use different analysis methods in order to derive goal-oriented, efficient experimental designs. Hence, an ExplorationStrategy can contain multiple AnalysisConfigurations. Both, the exploration strategies as well as the analysis methods are modelled as an ExtensibleElement that allows performance analysts to flexibly bind them to available implementations.

Based on the information described above, large parts of a performance evaluation can be automated (see Section 4.3.2). However, it is subject to research to come up with appropriate methods for automated experiment selection, experiment termination, and experiment analysis methods that support performance analysts in evaluating complex software systems. This work aims at facilitating these research activities by providing a common language that allows scientists and engineers to combine and compare different methodologies in a unified and structured way (such as demonstrated in this thesis).

4.3.1.3. Example

To demonstrate the usage and complete the description of the language, Figures 4.6 to 4.8 show an example of a scenario definition in form of a diagram. It contains at least one representative instance for each abstract syntax element of the language (enclosed in angle brackets, <<Element-Class>>). We use a representation that is close to the abstract syntax in order to highlight the links to the previously introduced language elements. For the SoPeCo framework, we developed a concrete syntax in form of a web-based editor in order to improve the user experience for the performance analysts [WHW+13].

The example illustrates an experiment definition for a customisation project of an SAP ERP 2005 application. In this project, a performance analyst addresses the problem of customizing an SAP ERP application installation to an expected customer workload. The workload of an enterprise application can be coarsely divided into batch workload (background jobs like monthly business reports) and dialogue workload (user interactions like displaying customer orders). This workload is dispatched by the application server to separate operating system processes, called work processes, which serve the requests [Sch06]. Among other tasks, such as sizing the underlying hardware, the IT administrator of an SAP system has to allocate the available number of work processes (depending on the size of the machine) to batch and dialogue jobs, respectively. To support the IT administrator, the performance analyst has to find the optimal amount of work processes required to handle the dialogue workload of a sales and distribution scenario with the constraint that the average response time of dialogue steps should be less than one second. In order to derive this information, the performance analyst documents this scenario using our experiment specification language (see Figures 4.6 to 4.8) and runs an automated performance analysis based on this specification. Please note that for illustration purposes we do not include the complete set of experiment series and parameters required for a successful enterprise application customisation in the example.

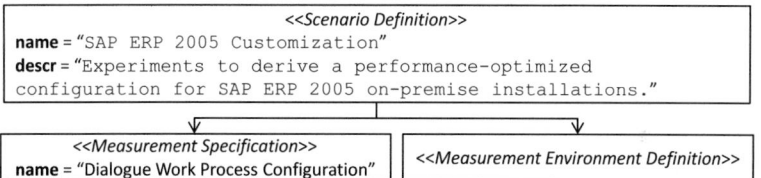

Figure 4.6.: Example for Scenario Definition

The measurement environment definition (Figure 4.7) contains two parameter namespaces, one for the input parameters and one for the observation parameters. In this example setup, the input parameters are (i) the number of active users in the sales and distribution (SD) scenario (*numSDUsers*) and (ii) the number of work processes (WPs) for dialogue workload (*numDialogueWPs*). The observed parameter is the average response time for the dialogue steps (*avgDialogueResponseTime*).

The measurement specification (Figure 4.8) defines the experiment series that should be conducted on the measurement environment in order to meet the scenario goal. In the example, the performance analyst wants to infer a function that describes the relationship between the two input parameters and the observation parameter (i.e., $f(numSDUsers, numDialogueWPs) = avgDialogueResponseTime$). Therefore, the experiment series definition contains two dynamic value assignments that describe the possible values for each input parameters. In the example, the values are specified via a *"Linear Variation"* assignment which means that the parameter can take any value between *min* and *max* in the defined *step* width (i.e., 3, 4, 5, and 6

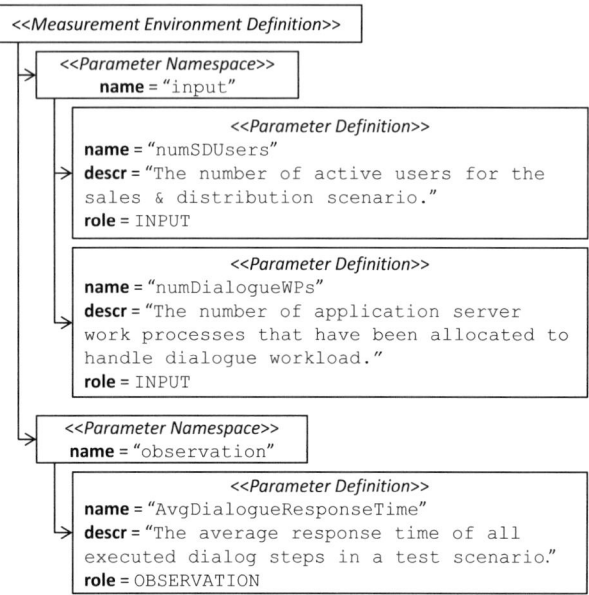

Figure 4.7.: Example for Measurement Environment Definition

for the number of dialogue work processes). The number of potential experiments in the experiment series is $4*30 = 120$. Using an experiment termination condition, the performance analyst determines that every experiment should be repeated 30 times. Moreover, the performance analyst defines the *"Random Breakdown"* method as an exploration strategy. This method runs iteratively, and randomly selects a fixed number of experiments in each iteration (see Section 4.4.2.1). Moreover, it derives a prediction function based on the data measured by the already executed experiments. Therefore, the Multivariate Adaptive Regression Splines (MARS) [Fri91] method is defined using the analysis configuration. As a last step in each iteration, the method validates whether the prediction function is accurate enough. In the example, the performance analyst specifies that the function is accurate enough if the mean relative prediction error on the validation data is less

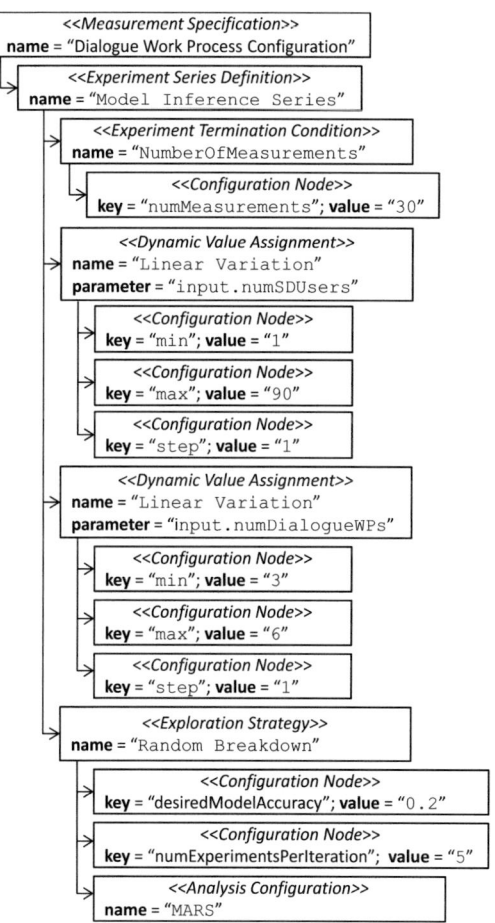

Figure 4.8.: Example for Measurement Specification

than 20%. If this is the case, the exploration strategy terminates and the execution of the experiment series is finished.

Based on the information provided in this example, the performance analyst can automatically run the experiments for customizing an SAP ERP application installation to an expected customer workload. Moreover, he or his colleagues can reuse the specification for customizing the installations of other customers.

4.3.2. Automated Experiment Execution

Based on the information specified in the experiment definition, the SoPeCo framework automatically executes and analyses a series of experiments. A description of the automated process as well as the basic architecture of the SoPeCo framework and its design rationale [WHHH10, WH11] can be found in Appendix A.

4.3.3. Summary

We introduced a novel approach for automating software performance evaluations in a wide range of scenarios. Our approach consists of an experiment specification language [WHF13] and a framework for the automated execution of experiments [WHHH10, WH11]. The experiment specification language is flexibly extensible and provides all necessary information to execute the defined experiments automatically. Moreover, the language supports performance analysts in defining proper experiments and enables reuse among different stakeholders and performance evaluation scenarios. In the following sections, we introduce and evaluate a set of strategies for the automated combination of experimental design and statistical analyses that target at finding a good trade-off between the number of experiments that are to be executed and the accuracy of the analysis result.

4.4. Automated Combination of Experimental Design and Statistical Methods

In the previous section, we introduced the basic experiment automation process of the SoPeCo approach. In the following, we describe how we leverage this process to implement advanced methodologies that support the performance analyst in efficiently evaluating the performance of complex software systems [WKH11, WHKF12]. We combine experimental designs with statistical analysis methods in order to provide an integrated solution to answer three main performance evaluation questions:

1. What are the performance-relevant parameters?

2. Which parameters interfere with each other?

3. What is the functional relationship between a set of parameters and a performance metric of interest?

To support answering the first two questions, we integrated several state-of-the art experimental design methods into the SoPeCo framework. Full factorial, fractional factorial and Plackett-Burman designs are examples that are well-understood and often applied for performance analyses [Jai91, JE06]. In Chapter 2.2, we present these designs and provide an overview that supports performance analysts in selecting a proper design for a specific application scenario.

In Section 4.4.2, we introduce an approach to support performance analysts in answering the third question. Following the goals of this thesis, the approach is designed to meet the requirements listed in Section 4.4.1.

4.4.1. Requirements

Automating as much as Possible   In order to support performance analysts in evaluating the performance of software systems efficiently we need

93

to automate as many tasks as possible. Furthermore, the automated execution of experimental designs is a key prerequisite to keep the experiment-based approach presented in this thesis feasible for real-world scenarios.

Limited Assumptions about System Under Test Statistical analysis methods can require assumptions on the kind of functional dependency between input and output variables. The methods mainly differ in their degree of model assumptions. For example, linear regression makes rather strong assumptions on the model underlying the observations, while the nearest neighbour estimator makes no assumptions at all. Most other statistical estimators lie between both extremes. In general, methods with stronger assumptions need less data to provide reliable estimates, if the assumptions are correct. Methods with less assumptions are more flexible, but require more data (see also 2.3). As we aim at a flexible approach that is applicable to a wide range of scenarios, we focus on flexible methods with less assumptions about the underlying functional dependencies.

Using a Minimum Set of Experiments Running a single experiment on a software system in order to get performance measures takes time. Often it requires warm-up runs, multiple repetitions to get stable numbers and clean-up procedures. Moreover, when varying the values of multiple parameters in an experiment series, the „curse of dimensionality" [HTF09] leads very quickly to a parameter space that is not measurable in a reasonable amount of time. Hence, approaches are required that gain maximum information with as few experiments as possible [Jai91].

4.4.2. Automated Inference of Performance Prediction Functions

Inferring functional relationships from quantitative data is required in many disciplines. Various regression and interpolation techniques exist that can

94

be used to estimate the value of an unknown point in a partially measured space [HTF09]. In the following, we refer to the data based on which the relationship between parameters is inferred as training set. Moreover, we refer to the data that is used to determine the quality of the estimates as validation set. We assume that theoretically we can measure any point in the parameter space. However, as this is in most cases not feasible, we have to provide a means to decide which points we should add to the training and validation set in order to derive an accurate prediction function. In general, the quality of the estimation depends on four main factors:

Number of Known Points   Usually, a larger number of known points increases the probability to derive a good estimation.

Structure of Known Points   At least as important as the number of known points is the structure of the known points, i.e., if the space is covered properly. Having many points from a certain area in the space, but none from other areas will most likely not result in a good overall estimation. In order to achieve best results, the structure of the points should be aligned to the combination of underlying functional relationship and applied inference method.

Appropriateness of Inference Method   The proper selection of an inference method that is able to fit the underlying dependency is another crucial step when inferring functional relationships from measurement data.

Deviation in Measured Values   Due to the stochastic nature of performance measurements, all samples that we take for a certain point in the parameter space have different values [Jai91]. Hence, the value that we derive for a single point is always different from the real value for this point. This deviation can influence the quality of estimations.

The challenge addressed by the approach presented in this section is to find a trade-off between automatically deriving an accurate prediction function and executing only a minimal set of experiments. Moreover, the approach should be applicable to a large set of scenarios and thus should not make too many assumptions about the functional dependencies that are to be inferred. In particular, we answer the following questions:

1. What are appropriate statistical inference methods to derive performance prediction functions without knowing the underlying dependencies?

2. What are appropriate strategies for automatically selecting measurement points in a parameter space?

3. Which measurement point selection strategies and statistical inference methods are good or bad matches with respect to the trade-off between number of measurement points and prediction accuracy?

4. How to derive prediction functions with sufficient accuracy using a minimal set of measurements?

In the context of this thesis the value of a single measurement point is derived by an experiment (see Section 4.3.1). The basic procedure of our approach for finding a good trade-off between number of experiments and prediction accuracy is depicted in Figure 4.9.

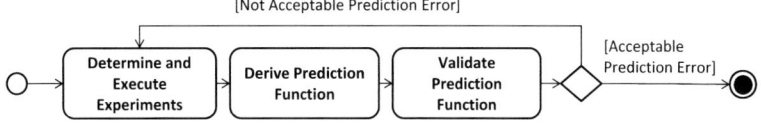

Figure 4.9.: Overview on automated, iterative function inference

We use an automated iterative approach that executes new experiments until a prediction function with sufficient accuracy has been inferred. Within one iteration the following steps are executed. The first step is determining and executing a set of experiments. We developed different strategies that decide which and how many experiments are selected in each iteration (see Section 4.4.2.1). In the next step, a statistical analysis is conducted to derive a prediction function based on the data measured so far. In Section 4.4.2.3, we introduce multiple inference methods that meet the requirements of the approach. Once the prediction function has been derived, it is automatically validated against the data in the validation set using one of the strategies described in Section 4.4.2.2. The validation provides a prediction error metric for the inferred prediction function. If this error is below a predefined threshold, the process terminates. If the error is above the threshold, a new iteration is started.

Figure 4.10 illustrates the process by a simplified example with a single controlled parameter. The underlying functional relationship between the controlled parameter and the performance metric of interest follows an exponential model (as indicated by the solid exponential curves in the graphs on Figure 4.10).

In the first step, the algorithm runs two experiments and adds the values t_1 and t_2 to the training set (see Figure 4.10(a)). Then, a linear function is derived from the data in the training set (dashed line in Figure 4.10(b)). In the next step, the prediction function is validated. For this purpose, two more experiments are executed and the values v_1 and v_2 are added to the validation set. Now, the measured values in the validation set are compared to the predicted values for those points and the difference between the measured and the predicted values is calculated (indicated by Δp and the vertical dotted line in Figure 4.10(c)). As Δp is larger than the predefined threshold, a second iteration is started running an additional experiment and adding the value t_3 to the training set (see Figure 4.10(d)). Based on the new training set, a stepwise linear function is derived (dashed lines in Figure 4.10(e)). Finally, the new predictions are compared to the measured values $v1$ and $v2$ in the validation set and the prediction error Δp is

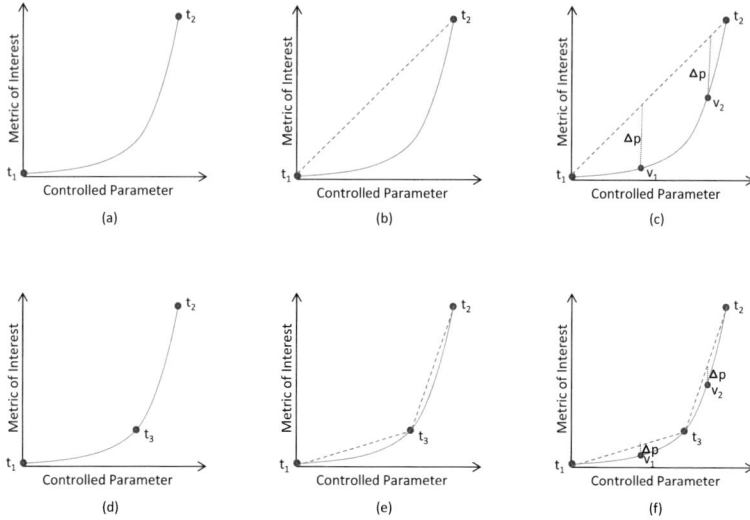

Figure 4.10.: Example for iterative function inference

calculated again (see Figure 4.10(f)). Now, the prediction error is smaller than the predefined threshold and the algorithm terminates.

In the remainder of this chapter, we introduce different methodologies and strategies to implement and combine the three steps of the process. Moreover, we validate the efficiency and prediction accuracy of the approach in different case studies (see Section 4.5).

4.4.2.1. Experiment Selection Strategies

In the following, we describe three concrete experiment selection strategies that implement the iterative process described above. The *Random Breakdown* algorithm selects a number of random experiments in the whole parameter space. In contrary, the adaptive strategies continuously split the parameter space in different sectors and select new experiments in those sectors that have the worst prediction accuracy. Thereby, the *Adaptive Ran-*

dom Breakdown algorithm randomly selects experiments within a sector, while the *Adaptive Equidistant Breakdown* algorithm follows an equidistant pattern when selecting new experiments in a sector.

Random Breakdown   The Random Breakdown algorithm randomly selects a number of experiments in each iteration of the process outlined in Figure 4.9. The selected experiments are always distributed across the whole parameter space. The algorithm is formalized in Algorithm 4.1 and illustrated in Figure 4.11 using an example with two controlled parameters.

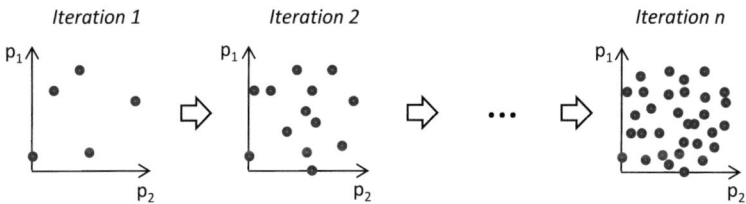

Figure 4.11.: Example for Random Breakdown

At the beginning of the algorithm the training set T is empty. V is a predefined validation set that contains n randomly selected validation experiments. The set of experiments E from which the strategy can select candidates is defined by the number of all possible experiments in the parameter space $e_1, \ldots, e_m$ minus the experiments that have been selected for the validation set V. The algorithm can be configured via two parameters. $\varepsilon_{maxPredErr}$ is a threshold that defines at which prediction error the algorithm can terminate. This threshold allows performance analysts to adjust the trade-off between prediction accuracy and number of executed experiments according to their needs. $\varepsilon_{expPerIter}$ denotes the number of experiments that are to be executed in each iteration. Hence, it allows performance analysts to control the length of a single iteration. In some cases it might be more efficient to execute more experiments before conducting an analysis while in other cases one wants to build the prediction models more frequently. This

---

Algorithm 4.1 Random Breakdown

1: $err := \infty$
2: $T := \{\}$
3: $V := \{v_1, \ldots, v_n\}$
4: $E := \{e_1, \ldots, e_m\} \setminus V$
5: Initialise configuration values $\varepsilon_{maxPredErr}$, $\varepsilon_{expPerIter}$

6: **while** $err > \varepsilon_{maxPredErr} \wedge E \neq \{\}$ **do**
7:     $E_{iter} := \varepsilon_{expPerIter}$ random experiments from E
8:     Execute all experiments in E_{iter}
9:     $T := T \cup E_{iter}$
10:     $E := E \setminus E_{iter}$
11:     Build prediction function using T
12:     Predict points in V and calculate err
13: **end while**

---

mainly depends on the size of the parameter space, the time it takes to get one measurement point and the time it takes to conduct an analysis. In the body of the algorithm, a loop is executed until the prediction error is less than $\varepsilon_{maxPredErr}$ or all possible experiments have been executed. In each iteration of the loop $\varepsilon_{expPerIter}$ random experiments are selected, executed and added to the training set T. Then, the prediction function is derived based on the training set and the predictions are compared against the data in the validation set V.

The benefit of the random breakdown strategy is its simplicity. Moreover, it is not prone to local over-optimisations. However, it also does not optimize the structure of the selected experiments with respect to the analysis. Hence, it is possible that a lot of experiments are executed that do not provide much information gain. See Section 4.5, for a detailed discussion.

Adaptive Equidistant Breakdown In contrast to the algorithm described above, the Adaptive Equidistant Breakdown algorithm as well as

the Adaptive Random Breakdown algorithm (described in the next paragraph) take the locality and the size of single sector prediction errors into
account when determining experiments for the next iteration. Both adaptive
algorithms split the parameter space in sectors depending on the locality of
the points with the largest prediction errors. We assume that a new experiment in the area with the highest prediction error raises the accuracy
of the overall prediction function at most. Thus, only those sectors that
have a prediction error larger than the predefined threshold will be split
into equidistant sub sectors and only in these sub sectors new experiments
will be selected.

In the following, we describe the algorithm in detail. First, we introduce
some basic data types, variables and functions followed by a listing of the
algorithm (see Algorithm 4.2) and a figure illustrating the basic idea by an
example (see Figure 4.12).

We define $E = \{\vec{e}|\vec{e} \in F^i\}$ as a set of all possible experiments in a mul-
tidimensional parameter space with normalized values $F = [0..1]$. Ele-
ments of E are declared as $\vec{e}$. Let the elements $\vec{e}_1 \neq \vec{e}_2$ be two positions
describing the multidimensional space. Function $f_{center} : E \times E \rightarrow E$ returns the center of the two given experiments which is calculated by the
element-wise arithmetic middle of the two vectors. This center is again
an experiment named $\vec{e}_{center}$. Furthermore, function $f_{corners} : E \times E \rightarrow E^*$
returns a set of all corner points of the embraced space given by $\vec{e}_1$ and
$\vec{e}_2$ (i.e., $E^* \subset E$). A corner point is an experiment $\vec{e}_{corner}$ that contains
only the minimal or maximal possible value of an input parameter in a
multidimensional space. In addition, let $err_{sector} \in \mathbb{R}^+$ describe the error
of the prediction function in a multidimensional space called *sector* that
is defined by two corner points $\vec{e}_{corner1}$ and $\vec{e}_{corner2}$. Furthermore, $S =$
$\{\vec{e}_{corner1} \times \vec{e}_{corner2} \times err_{sector}|\vec{e}_{corner1} \in E \wedge \vec{e}_{corner2} \in E \wedge err_{sector} \in \mathbb{R}^+\}$
is defined as the set of sectors in a multidimensional space. $Q \subset S$ is a
priority-controlled queue which contains sectors where the error of the prediction function runs out of the acceptable threshold. The order of priority

is based on err_{sector}. The training set T holds the measurement results of the experiments used to create a prediction function. V is the validation set used to calculate the prediction error. With respect to the contained experiments Q, T, and V are mutually disjoint. The function $f_{predict} : E \rightarrow \mathbb{R}$ creates a prediction results for a specific experiment $\vec{e}$ based on the data in the training set T. The parameter $\varepsilon_{maxPredErr} \in \mathbb{R}^+$ is predefined by the performance analyst and gives an option to control the expected accuracy and thus the runtime of the iteration process. To derive the validation set which is used to calculate the prediction error, the performance analyst can choose between three strategies $VS = \{vs | vs \in \{DSL, DSG, RVS\}\}$, where DSL is the *Dynamic Sector with Local scope*, DSG is *Dynamic Sector with Global scope*, and RVS is the *Random Validation Set* strategy (see Section 4.4.2.2 for a detailed description of the validation strategies). For the sake of simplicity, we illustrate only the DSL validation strategy in Algorithm 4.2 and Algorithm 4.3. In general, all methods are based on the assumption that the prediction error of the derived function for $f_{center}(e_1, e_2)$ is representative for the error in the spatial field embraced by $\vec{e}_1$ and $\vec{e}_2$.

After setting the preconditions, the actual experiment selection starts with a loop over Q in line 7 of Algorithm 4.2. Within this loop, those sectors with the highest error are selected for further processing and stored in the set I (lines 8 to 15). Starting at line 16, the algorithm iterates over the selected sectors and executes the experiments that define the corners of the sector as well as the experiments that lies in the center of the sector (lines 17 to 20). Furthermore, it calculates the prediction error err_{sector} for these sectors (lines 21 and 22). If err_{sector} is greater than the defined $\varepsilon_{maxPredErr}$, new sub sectors are created to be measured in further iterations (lines 24-28). If the err_{sector} is less than $\varepsilon_{maxPredErr}$ and the validation strategy is one of the *Dynamic Sector* strategies (see also Section 4.4.2.2), the current sector is used for validation (line 30). To provide faster convergence against the underlying performance functions it brings significant advantages to execute this breadth-first approach over all sectors with the same prediction

---

Algorithm 4.2 Adaptive Equidistant Breakdown

1: $\vec{e}_1 := (1, 1, \ldots, 1)$
2: $\vec{e}_2 := (0, 0, \ldots, 0)$
3: $err_{sector} := \infty$
4: $T := \{\}$
5: $V := \{\}$
6: $Q := \{< \vec{e}_1, \vec{e}_2, err_{sector} >\}$

7: **while** $Q \neq \{\}$ **do**
8:    $I := \{\}$
9:    Sort Q descending by err_{sector}
10:    **repeat**
11:       $s_{tmp1} :=$ first sector in Q
12:       $Q := Q \setminus \{s_{tmp1}\}$
13:       $I := I \cup \{s_{tmp}\}$
14:       $s_{tmp2} :=$ first sector in Q
15:    **until** $s_{tmp1}.err_{sector} > s_{tmp2}.err_{sector}$

16:    **for all** s in I **do**
17:       $E := f_{corners}(s.\vec{e}_1, s.\vec{e}_2)$
18:       Execute all experiments in E and add results to T
19:       $\vec{e}_{center} := f_{center}(s.\vec{e}_1, s.\vec{e}_2)$
20:       $r_{measured} :=$ measured value for $\vec{e}_{center}$
21:       $r_{predicted} := f_{predict}(\vec{e}_{center})$
22:       $err_{sector} := \frac{|r_{measured} - r_{predicted}|}{r_{measured}}$
23:       **if** $err_{sector} > \varepsilon_{maxPredErr}$ **then**
24:          **for all** $\vec{e}$ in E **do**
25:             $s_{tmp} :=< \vec{e}, \vec{e}_{center}, err_{sector} >$
26:             $Q := Q \cup \{s_{tmp}\}$
27:             $T := T \cup \{< r_{measured}, \vec{e}_{center} >\}$
28:          **end for**
29:       **else**

30:     $V := V \cup \{s\}$
31:     **end if**
32:   **end for**
33:   **for all** s in V **do**
34:     $r_{measured} :=$ measured value for $s.\vec{e}_{center}$.
35:     $r_{predicted} := f_{predict}(\vec{e}_{center})$
36:     $s.err_{sector} := \frac{|r_{measured} - r_{predicted}|}{r_{measured}}$
37:     **if** $s.err_{sector} > \varepsilon_{maxPredErr}$ **then**
38:       $V := V \setminus \{s\}$
39:       $Q := Q \cup \{s\}$
40:     **end if**
41:   **end for**
42: **end while**

43: **for all** s in V **do**
44:   $r_{measured} :=$ measured value for $s.\vec{e}_{center}$.
45:   $T := T \cup \{< r_{measured}, \vec{e}_{center} >\}$
46: **end for**

error err_{sector}. It ensures that the algorithm goes deeper in those areas with the highest prediction faults. Since nearly all interpolation or regression techniques cannot absolutely avoid the influence of new elements in T onto preliminary well predicted sectors, the validation repository V is checked for negative effects in sectors that have been well predicted before the last modifications (lines 33 to 41). If for any sector s in V the prediction is not accurate enough, the sector is returned to Q and thus measured in more detail in later iterations. We expect that the heuristic converges more efficiently if a new measurement has only local effects on the interpolation function. Finally, all elements from V are copied to T as the experiments have been executed before and thus the data is available but not yet added to the training data (lines 43-46). Figure 4.12 illustrates the experiment selection process of the Adaptive Equidistant Breakdown strategy based on two controlled parameters p_1 and p_2. The red points mark the experiments that have been used in the training set. For the sake of readability, we do not show the experiments used for validation.

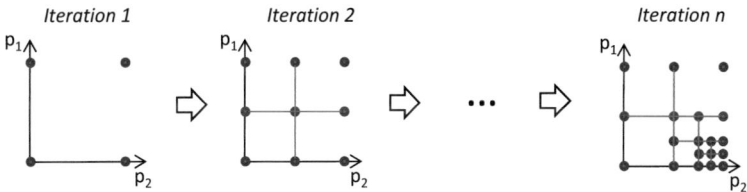

Figure 4.12.: Example for Adaptive Equidistant Breakdown

The benefit of the strategy is the smart coupling between experiment selection, prediction function derivation and validation. The fact that new experiments are selected in those areas where the highest prediction error has been observed can result in a faster convergence against the desired overall prediction accuracy defined by the performance analyst. Moreover, the strategy is very economical with respect to the number of executed experiments. However, a drawback of the strategy is that the decision if the points in a sector are represented accurately enough is based on a single center point experiment which might lead to wrong conclusions. The Adaptive Random Breakdown Strategy presented in the following paragraph aims at compensating this drawback by selecting multiple random experiments for each sector.

Adaptive Random Breakdown   The Adaptive Random Breakdown algorithm is very similar to the Adaptive Equidistant Breakdown algorithm. It also takes the locality and the size of single sector prediction errors into account when determining experiments for further iterations. The only difference to the Adaptive Equidistant Breakdown algorithm is that instead of selecting only the center point of the sector, the Adaptive Random Breakdown algorithm selects a given number of random experiments within the sectors. Figure 4.13 illustrates the selection process based on two controlled parameters.

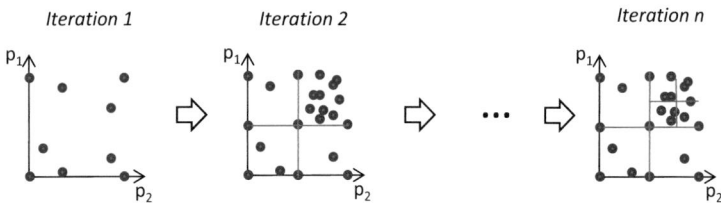

Figure 4.13.: Example for Adaptive Random Breakdown

The frame of the algorithm as well as the basic data types and variables correspond to Algorithm 4.2. The main difference in Algorithm 4.3 is that the function $f_{random} : E \times E \rightarrow E^R$ which returns n random experiments ($E^R \subset E$) located in a sector s replaces function f_{center}. Thus, the training set T and the validation set V contain the set of randomly selected experiments E^R and the corresponding measured results $R^M = \{r_m | r_m \in \mathbb{R}^+\}$. The predicted results are stored in an array $R^P = \{r_p | r_p \in \mathbb{R}^+\}$. The number of experiments that are selected in each iteration can be configured by the performance analyst.

Compared to the Adaptive Equidistant Breakdown Strategy, more experiments are selected within an iteration which can lead to a faster termination in critical sectors (due to less necessary sector splits). However, that depends on the size of the parameter space, the configured number of experiments per iteration, the applied inference method and the complexity of the underlying function. In Section 4.5, we discuss the interaction between the different combinations of problems, experiment selection strategies, validation strategies and inference methods in detail.

4.4.2.2. Validation Strategies

The decision on how to derive the data for the validation of the prediction function can be a crucial one for the automated experiment selection approach presented in this thesis. As with the experiment selection for the training set, the number of experiments and the structure of selected experiments determine the quality of the validation set. However, while a larger validation set leads to better results, it also requires more time to execute these experiments. As the number of executed experiments is the metric we want to minimize in our approach, it is important to find and add those points to the validation set that provide maximum information gain (i.e., which are most likely to improve the prediction accuracy). In the algorithms introduced in Section 4.4.2.1, we have already implicitly shown two strategies for adding experiments to the validation set. In the remainder of this section, we introduce and discuss the validation strategies applied in this thesis in more detail.

Random Validation Set In this strategy, a set of random experiments out of the whole parameter space is used to determine the accuracy of the prediction model during the automated iterative process depicted in Figure 4.9 . The size of the validation set can be defined by a performance

---

Algorithm 4.3 Adaptive Random Breakdown

1: $\vec{e}_1 := (1, 1, \ldots, 1)$
2: $\vec{e}_2 := (0, 0, \ldots, 0)$
3: $err_{sector} := \infty$
4: $T := \{\}$
5: $V := \{\}$
6: $Q := \{< \vec{e}_1, \vec{e}_2, err_{sector} >\}$

7: **while** $Q \neq \{\}$ **do**
8:   $I := \{\}$
9:   Sort Q descending by err_{sector}
10:   **repeat**
11:     $s_{tmp1} :=$ first sector in Q
12:     $Q := Q \setminus \{s_{tmp1}\}$
13:     $I := I \cup \{s_{tmp}\}$
14:     $s_{tmp2} :=$ first sector in Q
15:   **until** $s_{tmp1}.err_{sector} > s_{tmp2}.err_{sector}$

16:   **for all** s in I **do**
17:     $E := f_{corners}(s.\vec{e}_1, s.\vec{e}_2)$
18:     Execute all experiments in E and add results to T
19:     $E^R := f_{random}(s.\vec{e}_1, s.\vec{e}_2)$
20:     $R^M :=$ measured values for E^R
21:     $R^P := f_{predict}(E^R)$
22:     $err_{sector} := \dfrac{\sum_{i=1}^{E^R.size} \frac{|R^M[i] - R^P[i]|}{R^M[i]}}{E^R.size}$
23:     **if** $err_{sector} > \varepsilon_{maxPredErr}$ **then**
24:       **for all** e in E **do**
25:         $s_{tmp} :=< \vec{e}, E^R, err_{sector} >$
26:         $Q := Q \cup \{s_{tmp}\}$
27:         $T := T \cup \{< R^M, E^R >\}$
28:       **end for**
29:     **else**

30:            $V := V \cup \{s\}$
31:       **end if**
32:    **end for**
33:    **for all** s **in** V **do**
34:       $R^M :=$ measured values for $s.E^R$.
35:       $R^P := f_{predict}(E^R)$
36:       $s.err_{sector} := \dfrac{\Sigma_{i=1}^{E^R.size} \frac{|R^M[i]-R^P[i]|}{R^M[i]}}{E^R.size}$
37:       **if** $err_{sector} > \varepsilon_{maxPredErr}$ **then**
38:          $V := V \setminus \{s\}$
39:          $Q := Q \cup \{s\}$
40:       **end if**
41:    **end for**
42: **end while**

43: **for all** s **in** V **do**
44:    $R^M :=$ measured values for $s.E^R$.
45:    $T := T \cup \{< R^M, E^R >\}$
46: **end for**

analyst. In each validation run, all experiment results in the validation set are compared to the predicted values of the prediction model, and the average relative prediction error is calculated.

The advantages of this strategy are that the validation experiments are distributed across the whole parameter space and that the performance analyst can control the size of the validation set and thus its significance. However, the disadvantages are that a large validation set requires the execution of many experiments that cannot be used for function building, it can cause long processing times of the validation step, and due to the random selection of the experiments we might not get enough validation experiments in those areas that are the most critical.

Dynamic Sector The Dynamic Sector validation is a strategy developed to further improve the efficiency of the adaptive breakdown algorithms (see Section 4.4.2.1). Thus, it is closely connected to the adaptive algorithms and can only be applied in combination with one of these. The goal of the strategy is to minimize the measurement overhead for the validation step but providing enough validation points in order to confidently calculate the prediction error of the derived function. The strategy uses only experiments that have been measured anyway during the breakdown of the parameter space by the respective algorithms. After a new experiment has been executed, the strategy decides based on the prediction error in the corresponding sector whether the new experiment result will be part of the validation set or training set. If the prediction error of a sector is below a predefined threshold, the adaptive algorithms do not further split the sector (as formalized in Algorithm 4.2 and 4.3). The experiments measured in the course of this last split will not be added to the training set but to the validation set. After each iteration of the adaptive algorithms, the strategy checks the prediction errors of the sectors in the validation set. If a change in the model during an iteration causes the prediction error in a sector to go above the predefined threshold, the experiment results for this sector will be removed from the validation set and added to the training set. Moreover, the sector is split in multiple sub sectors in order to execute more experiments in the critical sector. Hence, the experiments that are part of the validation set change dynamically based on the sector prediction errors at a certain point in time. The validation terminates the overall measurement process if (i) all sectors have a prediction error that is less than the predefined threshold (in the following referred to as Dynamic Sector validation with Local prediction error scope (DSL)), or (ii) the average prediction error of all sectors is less than the predefined threshold (in the following referred to as Dynamic Sector validation with Global prediction error scope (DSG)).

The advantages of this strategy are that it requires no additional measurements in order to build a validation set and that the size of the validation set grows with the number of splits executed by the adaptive algorithms. As the number of splits is an indicator for the complexity of the function that has to be predicted, we get more validation points if we have to infer a more complex function. However, the fact that only those experiments measured by the breakdown algorithm are used for the validation set implies that the confidence of the calculated prediction error relies on the quality of the breakdown algorithms.

4.4.2.3. Statistical Inference Methods

In this section, we introduce four analysis methods that can be applied in the presented approach. It is not a goal of this thesis to develop a novel function inference method or to compare all existing approaches and find the best one. Instead, we aim at demonstrating that our approach provides good results by integrating state of the art analysis methods. Furthermore, we want to demonstrate that the flexibility of the approach allows to combine different experiment selection algorithms with different analysis methods. This flexible combination of methods allows scientists and engineers to benchmark new experimental design and analysis strategies against state of the art approaches. In the course of this thesis, we focus on flexible analysis methods that make less assumptions about underlying functional dependencies and thus are generally applicable to a large set of scenarios. In the remainder of this section, we briefly introduce and discuss the four analysis methods applied in the course of this thesis. A detailed description of the methods is provided in Chapter 2.3. In Section 4.5, we apply the different combinations of analysis methods and experiment selection strategies to several problems and discuss which combinations are good and which are bad matches.

Multivariate Adaptive Regression Splines (MARS) Multivariate Adaptive Regression Splines (MARS) [Fri91] is an analysis method which has already been successfully employed in software performance engineering [CW00, HWSK10]. MARS is a non-parametric regression technique which requires no prior assumption as to the form of the data. The method fits functions creating rectangular patches where each patch is a product of linear functions (one in each dimension) [Fri91]. We selected this method due to its general applicability and the good results that have been reported in existing performance engineering literature.

Classification and Regression Trees (CART) CART is a simple and popular method for tree-based regression and classification. Tree-based methods partition the feature space into a set of rectangles, and then fit a simple model in each one [HTF09]. CART has also been successfully applied in recent performance evaluation case studies [WAA+04, TDZN10]. Moreover, it is a very simple predictor that can analyse a large data sets very quickly.

Kriging Kriging is a generic name for a family of spatial interpolation techniques using generalized least-squares regression algorithms [LH08]. It is named after Daniel Krige who applied the method to a mineral ore body [Kri51]. Generally, the goal of spatial interpolations is to infer a spatial field at unobserved sites using observations at few selected sites. The underlying assumption that values that are closer to each other are more likely to have a similar effect on the metric of interest is also true for most performance evaluation studies which is why we decided to include Kriging in the list of methods studied in the course of this thesis. Moreover, it demonstrates one of the main benefits provided by the presented approach, which is the relatively simple application and evaluation of analysis methods from other research fields into software performance engineering.

As in geostatistics the problems typically have two input parameters (the geo-coordinates), we could not find an implementation of Kriging that allows more than two input parameters. Hence, we decided to combine Kriging with Classical Multidimensional Scaling (CMDS) [CC00] in order to use the method for problems with more than two input variables. We selected CMDS as although it reduces the dimensions it keeps the distances between the different points which is an essential characteristic for combining it with Kriging.

Genetic Programming (GP)   Genetic Programming (GP) aims at deriving computer programs or mathematical equations and is thus well-suited for symbolic regression [Koz93]. GP does not require any assumptions about the underlying dependency and optimizes the structure of the equation simultaneously with the coefficients. The GP algorithm that we apply in the course of this thesis has been published by Faber and Happe [FH12] and is specially optimized for the inference of performance prediction functions. This example demonstrates another benefit of the approach which is that it allows to benchmark novel analysis methods against existing state of the art.

4.4.3. Summary

We introduced an automated iterative process that combines experiment selection, function inference and function validation in order to derive experimental designs that optimize the trade-off between the number of executed experiments and result accuracy [WKH11]. Our approach, which is integrated in the SoPeCo framework presented in Section 4.3, allows performance analyst to flexibly introduce, combine, and evaluate different strategies for the three process steps. The set of strategies that we presented aim at fitting the functional dependency between a set of input parameters and a performance metric of interest without making strong assumptions about the underlying model. As a result, we get 32 possible combinations of strategies that we applied to three case studies. The results of this evaluation are presented in the following section.

4.5. Validation

In this section, we evaluate and discuss the applicability, efficiency and accuracy of the approach introduced in this chapter. The Software Performance Cockpit (SoPeCo) introduced in Section 4.3 allows Performance Analysts to define and automatically execute performance evaluation experiments in different scenarios. Moreover, as presented in Section 4.4, our approach enables the flexible combination of experiment selection and data analysis strategies for the automated and efficient inference of performance prediction functions (see Section 4.4.2).

We applied the approach in two real-world scenarios and a set of simulated functions in order to answer the following questions.

Q1 Can we automatically derive accurate prediction functions in different scenarios using only a small subset of all possible experiments and without making assumptions on the underlying dependencies?

Q2 What are appropriate statistical inference methods to derive performance prediction functions without knowing the underlying dependencies?

Q3 What are appropriate strategies for automatically selecting experiments in a parameter space?

Q4 Which experiment selection strategies and statistical inference methods are good or bad matches?

In general, we consider a method as good or appropriate if it yields a good trade-off between the number of executed experiments and the accuracy of the prediction functions. Hence, the metrics that we use in the case studies to compare the different combinations against each other are the following.

Metric 1: The *number of selected experiment (NE)* compared to the possible number of experiments spanned by the parameter space. We aim at generating an accurate prediction model with only a minimal set of experiments.

Metric 2: The *time it takes to execute NE experiments (ET)* in hours (h) or days (d). This metric is calculated as the product of the number of executed experiments (NE) and the average execution time for a single experiment. The time for analysing the measured data is not included in this metric. Moreover, we discuss the ET metric only in the context of the real-world use cases.

Metric 3: The *mean relative error (MRE)* of the predictions (in %). To derive this metric, we measured the complete set of possible experiments within the parameter space and used the measured data as the validation set. This validation set is independent of the training and validation sets used during the derivation of the prediction models. The validation sets used for this MRE metric aim at the general validation of the approach, which is why measured all points in the parameter space.

Metric 4: The mean relative error alone can sometimes cause misleading conclusions. For example, in cases where a large (simple) part of a function is fitted very well, the mean relative error can be under a certain threshold although there might be an important area where the predictions are bad. That is why we also use the metrics LT15, LT30, and *Highest Error (HE)* as an indicator for the reliability of the predictions. The first two metrics define *the percentage of predictions that have a prediction error that is less than 15% (LT15) or 30% (LT30)*, respectively. HE is the highest single point prediction error (in %) observed in the validation.

Based on these metrics, we discuss the results of our case studies. The following subsections are structured as follows. In Section 4.5.1, Section 4.5.2, and Section 4.5.3 we describe a case study using simulated functions and two real-world case studies. After an introduction to each case study, we list the five best and worst performing *combinations of experiment selection algorithm, validation strategy and model inference technique (Comb)*. Moreover, we briefly comment the results. A detailed evaluation and discussion of the overall results is then provided in Section 4.5.4. Table 4.1 gives an overview on the abbreviations used in the result tables for the different methodologies.

The selection of the best five and the worst five entries in the tables is based on a combined consideration of the aforementioned metrics. The goal of the evaluation is to identify those combinations that provide a good trade-off between the number of experiments and the prediction accuracy. Figure 4.14 illustrates the process that we applied to select the best combinations. The threshold ε_{MRE} determines the mean relative prediction error

Abbreviation	Methodology
RB	Random Breakdown
AEB	Adaptive Equidistant Breakdown
ARB	Adaptive Random Breakdown
RVS	Random Validation Set
DSL	Dynamic Sector Validation \w Local Scope
DSG	Dynamic Sector Validation \w Global Scope
MARS	Multivariate Adaptive Regression Splines
CART	Classification and Regression Trees
Kriging	Kriging
GP	Genetic Programming

Table 4.1.: Abbreviations in result tables

that is considered as acceptable by the performance analyst in the respective scenario. For the scenarios presented in this section, we set $\varepsilon_{MRE} = 30\%$ following standard performance literature [MA01]. From all the combinations that yield a MRE that is less than ε_{MRE}, we select the five that required the least number of experiments. For the five worst combinations we selected those that could not find a trade-off (i.e.,very large number of experiments and/or very large prediction error). Please note, that although we list only the top five and the worst five combinations (for the sake of readability), we considered all results when deriving our conclusions. The complete list of results can be found in Appendix B. Moreover, we also consider the second threshold (ε_{NE}) depicted in Figure 4.14 in our discussion. The number of required experiments determines the time it takes to derive a prediction function. If NE gets too large, the required measurement time might render the approach inappropriate for a certain scenario,

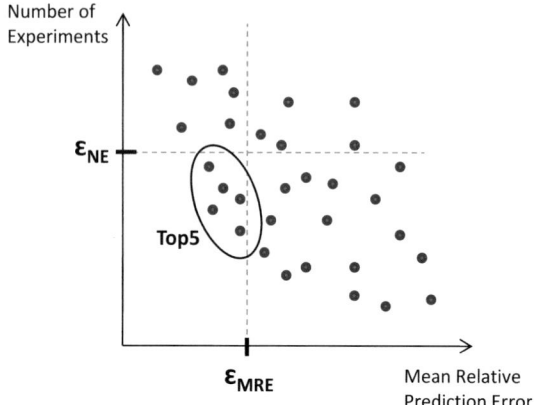

Figure 4.14.: Selecting the best combinations

4.5.1. Simulated Functions

In this case study, we test the approach against two functions that simulate typical performance behaviour of software systems. The reason for this case study with simulated functions is to test the approach in a clean environment where we know the function that we try to fit and where we do not have to deal with fluctuating or misleading measurement results. The goal is to later on identify those combinations that work in clean environments but have problems when dealing with real world measurement data.

Context   Table 4.2 shows the two functions that we selected for this case study.

For function f_1, we configured the domain for each of the three input parameters (x_0, x_1, x_2) from 1 to 20 in steps of 1. Thus, the total number of possible experiments is 8000. For function f_2, we configured the domain for each of the five input parameters $(x_0, x_1, x_2, x_3, x_4)$ from 1 to 10 in steps of 1 which calculates to 10000 possible experiments.

Nr.	Function
1	$f_1(\vec{x}) = 0.025 \cdot \exp(0.35 \cdot x_0) + 0.81 \cdot x_1 + 0.08 \cdot x_2^2 + 100$
2	$f_2(\vec{x}) = 0.005 \cdot \exp(0.999 \cdot x_0) + 105.5 \cdot \left(\frac{x_1}{(5.1+x_1)}\right)$ $+7.8 \cdot x_2 + \frac{1}{0.66^{x_3}} + 0.58 \cdot x_4^2 + 100$

Table 4.2.: Simulation functions for function inference validation

Results   Table 4.3 and Table 4.4 outline the five best and worst performing combinations of experiment selection algorithm, validation strategy, and statistical model inference method for the two simulated functions of this case study.

Table 4.3 shows that for function f_1 in Table 4.2 the combination of Adaptive Equidistant Breakdown (AEB) and Dynamic Sector validation with global error calculation (DSG) performed very good with all statistical model inference techniques and outperformed all other combinations of measurement point selection and validation strategy. For function f_2 in Table 4.2 the results are not that clear (see Table 4.4), although AEB is still the dominating measurement point selection strategy. Especially in combination with CART and MARS models, the Dynamic Sector validation with local error calculation (DSL) performed as good as DSG when fitting function f_2. When looking at the five worst combinations for the two equations, the combination of Adaptive Random Breakdown (ARB) measurement point selection and Random Validation Set (RVS) validation strategy does not seem to be efficient.

4.5.2. Enterprise Application Customisation

This case study has already been introduced in Section 4.3.1.3. It describes a customisation project of an SAP ERP 2005 application. In this

Top 5					
Comb	NE	MRE	HE	LT15	LT30
AEB DSG MARS	22	2.4	9.9	100.0	100.0
AEB DSG GP	22	5.3	14.9	100.0	100.0
AEB DSG CART	22	8.8	22.1	85.3	100.0
AEB DSG Kriging	36	4.4	24.1	97.2	100.0
ARB DSG MARS	41	0.6	2.0	100.0	100.0
Worst 5					
Comb	NE	MRE	HE	LT15	LT30
AEB DSL Kriging	288	8.5	26.8	85.7	100.0
ARB RVS Kriging	304	5.0	19.1	94.5	100.0
RB RVS GP	314	2.6	12.3	100.0	100.0
ARB DSL GP	909	1.7	7.9	100.0	100.0
ARB RVS GP	974	1.6	5.4	100.0	100.0

Table 4.3.: Results for function f_1 (Table 4.2)

project, a performance analyst addresses the problem of customizing an SAP ERP application configuration to an expected customer workload (see also [Sch06]). The workload of an enterprise application can be coarsely divided into batch workload (background jobs like monthly business reports) and dialogue workload (user interactions like displaying customer orders). This workload is dispatched by the application server to separate operating system processes, called work processes, which serve the requests [Sch06]. At deployment time of an SAP system the IT administrator has to allocate the available number of work processes (depending on the size of the machine) to batch and dialogue jobs, respectively. With the performance prediction function derived in this case study, we enable IT administrators to find the optimal amount of work processes required to handle the dialogue

Top 5					
Comb	NE	MRE	HE	LT15	LT30
ARB DSL CART	103	10.9	48.8	73.1	96.8
AEB DSG MARS	114	5.5	30.7	80.4	99.8
AEB DSL MARS	114	5.5	30.7	80.4	99.8
ARB DSG MARS	134	1.4	8.1	100.0	100.0
ARB DSL MARS	134	1.4	8.1	100.0	100.0
Worst 5					
Comb	NE	MRE	HE	LT15	LT30
ARB RVS CART	603	9.9	43.2	77.4	98.3
ARB RVS GP	640	7.1	26.9	90.6	100.0
ARB RVS MARS	1002	1.0	5.4	100.0	100.0
ARB RVS Kriging	1002	12.6	43.2	64.4	94.6
ARB DSG CART	3215	11.2	46.7	71.0	98.0

Table 4.4.: Results for function f_2 (Table 4.2)

workload with the constraint that the average response time of dialogue steps should be less than one second.

Context The system under test consists of the enterprise resource planning application SAP ERP2005 SR1, an SAP Netweaver application server and a MaxDB database (version 7.6.04-07). The underlying operating system is Linux 2.6.24-27-xen. The system is deployed on a single-core virtual machine (2,6 GHz, 1024KB cache). To generate load on the system we used the SAP Sales and Distribution (SD) Benchmark [SAP12]. This standard benchmark covers a sell-from-stock scenario, which includes the creation of a customer order with five line items and the corresponding delivery with subsequent goods movement and invoicing. Each benchmark user has its own master data, such as material, vendor, or customer master data to avoid data-locking situations [SAP12]. The performance metric of interest is the average response time of dialogue steps (*AvgResponseTime*). The input parameters in this setup are (i)

- the number of active users (*NumSDUsers*) where the domain ranges from 60 to 150 and

- the number of work processes for dialogue workload (*NumDialogueWPs*) varied from 3 to 6.

Thus, we are looking for the function

$$f(NumSDUsers, NumDialogueWPs) = AvgResponseTime. \qquad (4.1)$$

The full parameter space consists of 360 experiments. The range of values measured for the *AvgResponseTime* is between 125 ms and 3500 ms. The execution of a single experiment (including repetitions to control measurement noise) takes approximately one hour, which means that in the worst case the IT administrator has to measure 15 days in order to determine the optimal configuration. We do not aim at modelling the complete ERP system and varying all potential configuration, workload and tuning parameters of a system at once. Instead, the goal is to provide a practical automated evaluation that helps the administrator to determine the optimal allocation of work process for a given workload type and a given system configuration. In the process of enterprise application customisation this is only one question among many others which is why it is important to provide a flexible, automated approach that does not make assumptions about underlying functional dependencies.

Results Table 4.5 shows the five best and worst performing combinations of our prediction approach. Even the worst combination can derive a prediction model with an acceptable prediction error while requiring only one fourth of the measurement points. For the combinations that performed best, the result is even better. For the combination of Adaptive Equidistant Breakdown (AEB), Dynamic Sector Global (DSG) and Genetic Programming (GP) we were able to build a prediction model with an average relative prediction error of 8.7% using only 21 measurement points. The Kriging method in combination with AEB and DSG also performed very good with a relative prediction error of only 6% and 38 required measurement points. Thus, applying our approach can reduce the time necessary to derive an optimal configuration from 15 to one or two days of measurement. Here, one can see that although we varied only two independent parameters it is essential to provide efficient evaluation methods in order to derive results in a reasonable time frame.

Top 5						
Comb	NE	ET	MRE	HE	LT15	LT30
AEB DSG GP	21	21h	8.7	36.0	81.8	98.7
AEB DSG Kriging	38	38h	6.0	43.3	88.3	96.1
ARB DSG MARS	38	38h	7.3	31.8	89.6	98.7
AEB DSG MARS	53	43h	7.4	31.7	87.0	98.7
AEB DSL Kriging	54	54h	2.8	38.8	94.8	98.7
Worst 5						
Comb	NE	ET	MRE	HE	LT15	LT30
AEB RVS CART	69	69h	31.7	92.9	26.0	51.3
ARB RVS CART	77	77h	28.7	92.0	35.1	57.9
ARB DSG CART	77	77h	28.7	92.0	35.1	57.9
ARB DSL CART	77	77h	28.7	92.0	35.1	57.9
RB RVS CART	77	77h	28.7	92.0	35.1	57.9

Table 4.5.: Results for enterprise application customisation case study

4.5.3. Java Virtual Machine Tuning

The Java Virtual Machine (JVM) is one of the most important components when it comes to performance tuning of a Java-based applications [Jam, Shi03]. However, getting the best performance out of the JVM often requires detailed hand tuning of command line options with respect to heap sizes or garbage collection. In this case study, we address the problem of tuning the parameters of a JVM to the special characteristics of an application. The application that we use in our experiments is the SPECjbb2005 Java Server Benchmark [SPE05]. The benchmark emulates a three-tier client/server system (with emphasis on the middle tier) and exercises the implementations of the JVM, JIT (Just-In-Time) compiler, garbage collection, threads, as well as some aspects of the operating system [SPE05]. The system modelled by the benchmark is a wholesale company, with warehouses that serve a number of districts. Customers initiate a set of operations, such as placing new orders or requesting the status of an existing order. Additional operations are generated within the company, such as processing orders for delivery or entering customer payments [SPE05].

Context The system under test consists of the SPECjbb2005 benchmark (configured to run with 10 warehouses), Java HotSpot(TM) Client VM (build 17.0-b17), and Microsoft Windows XP Professional Version 2002 SP3. The software runs on a standard desktop dual-core machine with 3 GHz per CPU and 3.5 GB RAM. The performance metric of interest in this scenario is the average throughput of a benchmark run (*AvgThroughput*) measured in SPECjbb2005 bops (business operations per second). The input parameters are as follows (see [Ora12] for a detailed description of the parameters):

- the heap size (*HeapSize*) where we configured the possible variation from 300 MB to 950 MB in steps of 25 MB,

- the garbage collector (*GarbageCollector*) implementation which is either SerialGC, ParallelGC, or ConcMarkSweepGC,

- a boolean value that indicates whether biased locking (*Biased-Locking*) is enabled,

- the survivor ratio (*SurvivorRatio*) varied from 10 to 42 in steps of 8, and

- the new generation ratio (*NewGenerationRatio*) which is expressed in a share of the total heap size ranging from 10% to 40% and varied in steps of 10%.

Thus, we are looking for the function

$$f(HeapSize, GarbageCollector, BiasedLocking, SurvivorRatio,$$
$$NewGenerationRatio) = AvgThroughput. \tag{4.2}$$

The full parameter space consists of 3240 experiments. The range of values measured for the *AvgThroughput* is between 970 bops and 37000 bops. In this case study, the execution of a single experiment takes approximately five minutes (including required repetitions to control the measurement noise).

Results Table 4.6 outlines the five best and worst performing combinations in this case study.

The results show that this case study was the most complex in terms of inferring a prediction function without knowing the underlying model. Even the best combinations have a highest prediction error (HE) of 300 to 400 percent. However, the overall error as well as the efficiency of the prediction models built by the first three combinations is still acceptable, which demonstrates the robustness of these combinations. One reason for

Top 5						
Comb	NE	ET	MRE	HE	LT15	LT30
RB RVS MARS	276	23h	20.7	403.1	77.1	86.7
AEB RVS MARS	342	29h	20.3	301.4	73.6	87.0
RB RVS Kriging	365	30h	25.3	955.1	73.7	86.9
AEB DSG MARS	1076	90h	16.3	259.8	79.1	88.0
AEB DSL MARS	1325	110h	17.3	287.9	79.8	88.0
Worst 5						
Comb	NE	ET	MRE	HE	LT15	LT30
ARB DSG Kriging	1001	83h	73.0	964.0	46.7	65.0
ARB DSL Kriging	1011	84h	76.3	957.8	42.6	62.4
RB RVS GP	1388	116h	26.9	485.3	47.3	74.9
ARB DSL MARS	2027	169h	23.9	384.4	70.2	85.3
AEB RVS CART	3111	259h	26.4	432.5	68.8	82.3

Table 4.6.: Results for JVM tuning case study

the complexity of this scenario is that we included an enumeration variable (*GarbageCollector*) and a boolean variable (*BiasedLocking*) where we do not necessarily have monotonically increasing values which makes prediction harder for most of the statistical analyses techniques. Moreover, the large highest error values are an indicator that the granularity that we selected for the parameter variations was not fine-grained enough. Obviously, there are areas in the parameter space where we did not have enough information in order to build an accurate model. However, for these experiments we had to limit the parameter space to 3240 measurement points as we had to measure the full space upfront in order to compare the different strategies and validate the results. The case study also demonstrates that it is an important precondition that the performance analyst properly selects the input parameters and domains. Furthermore, it is important to note that the high relative prediction errors occur only in experiments where the measured throughput is low and the workload is high. In experiments with such heavy workloads, the system can get unstable and other effects might disturb the measurements. To avoid these situations, a performance analyst should conduct a set of preliminary experiments that determine the point where the workload gets to heavy for the given system configuration. Moreover, in such cases a rather small absolute deviation has a higher impact on the relative error metric (the range of values goes from 970 bobs to 37000 bops, the standard deviation of errors is for the **RB RVS MARS** combination 2826 bobs).

4.5.4. Evaluation

In this section, we discuss the results of the case studies presented in Section 4.5.2 and Section 4.5.3 as well as the conclusions that we can draw out of them. We start by evaluating the four statistical model inference techniques in isolation and then summarize the results.

Classification and Regression Tree (CART)   is a very fast method that built all the prediction models in the case studies in milliseconds. The prediction results were good for the simulated functions. However, in the real case studies the results were poor, especially with respect to the reliability of the predictions. According to our experiments, CART works best in combination with Adaptive Equidistant Breakdown (AEB) or Random Breakdown (RB) measurement point selection and Random Validation Set (RVS) validation. It does not work very well with the Dynamic Sector (DS) validation strategies.

Genetic Programming (GP)   achieved very good results in fitting the simulated functions as well as in the enterprise application customisation scenario. However, it was not able to efficiently derive a prediction function in the JVM tuning scenario. The best results have been achieved in combination with AEB measurement point selection and DSG or RVS validation, respectively. It did not work very well with the combination Adaptive Random Breakdown (ARB) and RVS. The biggest problem of the GP approach is its runtime. In average, it took the approach approximately 20 minutes to build a prediction model which adds up to a large amount of analysis time when using in it in our iterative process (see Figure 4.9).

Kriging   is in terms of runtime somewhere in the middle between CART and GP. It becomes slower with increasing number of measurement points which is mainly caused by the classical multidimensional scaling (CMDS) implementation that we run before the actual prediction model is built using the Kriging implementation (see Section 4.4.2.3). In general, the results of the simulated functions and in parts also the results of the JVM tuning scenario have shown that our approach with the CMDS in combination with Kriging is working and able to derive accurate prediction models. However, the best results could be achieved in the enterprise application customisation scenario, where we varied only two input variables and thus the dimension reduction step has not been executed. In this scenario, Kriging has been a very efficient method. Like GP, it worked best with the combinations AEB/DSG and AEB/RVS and delivered the worst results with ARB measurement point selection.

Multivariate Adaptive Regression Splines (MARS)   is the only method that achieved very good results in all case studies. From a runtime perspective MARS was also able to build prediction models within seconds (at least with the size of the training data in our scenarios). It worked most efficiently in combination with AEB measurement point selection and DSG validation. Good results have also been achieved with the combinations AEB/RVS and RB/RVS. The worst results with ARB measurement point selection.

In summary, MARS together with AEB measurement point selection and DSG validation has been the only combination that achieved very good results in all case studies. Only for the enterprise application customisation case study, GP and Kriging performed slightly better (but also in combination with AEB/DSG). CART turned out to be the worst method, and is based on our experiences not suited for black-box inference of Software Performance Curves. Kriging and GP are in general able to fit black-box models and can be good alternatives to MARS. Especially, if there is only one or two input parameters but a large number of measurement points Kriging can be an efficient option. The main problem with GP is the time it takes to create a prediction model which makes it not the perfect option for an iterative approach with repeated generation of prediction models. Regarding the measurement point selection algorithms and validation strategies there is a clear tendency that AEB is the most efficient algorithm that provides especially in combination with DSG and RVS validation the best results independent of the analysis method. The prediction models derived by the simple RB are in most cases very accurate and reliable. However, compared to AEB it required in most cases more measurement points to build the model.

4.5.5. Threats to Validity

For the function inference approach presented in this section, we see the following threats to validity:

Internal Validity

- Due to the large space of potential experiments and the complexity of the studied software systems, we cannot measure all possible experiments in reasonable time. Hence, we restricted the domains of the input parameters to a space that is completely measurable. This restriction influences the results.

- We are also aware that the non-determinism of performance measurements can cause false interpretations [GBE07]. For the different scenarios, we repeated experiment executions until we reached a proper confidence interval for the mean values.

- Most advanced analysis methods can be configured by different parameters. This configuration of an analysis method influences the function fitting process (e.g. in case of Multivariate Adaptive Regression Splines). In our case studies, we applied the default configurations of the respective analysis method implementation as we do not aim at an optimized solution.

External Validity

- To increase external validity we used real-world software systems in our validation case studies. The investigated benchmark applications represent a large set of practical applications and it has been shown that our approach provides good results independent of the considered system. However, the evaluation results are not automatically transferable to all software systems. As described in Section 4.5.4, the assumptions made by the analysis method have to match the model that is to be fitted in order to be able to derive a good estimator.

4.6. Discussion of Assumptions and Limitations

In the following, the limitations and assumptions of the SoPeCo approach that is presented in this chapter will be discussed.

Test System Availability   A precondition for the measurement-based approach of this work is that a test system is available on which the experiments can be conducted. This includes the system under test as well as additional software and tools required to execute experiments. For example, our approach does not provide load drivers or monitoring software. The focus of the SoPeCo approach is only on the experimentation process. In contrast to other approaches, we abstract from the concrete scenario by providing a flexible extension mechanism in our SoPeCo framework (see Section 4.3).

Parameter Availability   We can only include those parameters in our experiments that can be controlled by a piece of software or that can be measured at runtime without adding too much overhead to the system. For example, it might not always be possible to measure the CPU utilisation of a system under test as this requires access to the operating system or difficult sampling mechanisms [CG05]. In such cases, other metrics have to be used to achieve the goal of the performance evaluation. Kraft et al. [KPSCD09] use for example response time measurements to estimate CPU resource demands.

Abstraction of Test System   In most cases, experiments are not executed on the actual real-world system. Instead a dedicated test instance is used to run the experiments. The test system is often a smaller abstraction of the real system. This has to be taken into account when interpreting the experiment results and deriving conclusions.

Drawing Conclusions from Incomplete Data   Another core assumption of our approach is that it is possible to draw proper conclusions from incomplete data. Hence, we assume that it is possible to estimate a large set of unknown points correctly if the subset of measured points and the analysis method is properly chosen.

4.7. Summary and Contributions

In this chapter, we introduced a novel approach for automating software performance evaluations. The approach implements a systematic experimentation process and enables performance analysts to run performance evaluations more structured, more efficient, and in a more goal-oriented way. Moreover, the approach allows researchers and engineers to apply and compare different experimental design and analysis strategies.

The contributions of this chapter are the following:

- An experiment specification language that forms the basis for capturing information required to conduct goal-oriented performance evaluation experiments. The language supports a broad range of scenarios and allows for flexible scenario-specific extensions.

- A framework architecture that enables automated experiment execution based on our experiment specification language. Key characteristics of the architecture are the iterative combination of experimental design and analysis and the flexible introduction and use of components.

- A method that automatically classifies parameters in performance-relevant and -irrelevant based on state of the art experimental designs.

- Combination and evaluation of multiple experimental design and statistical inference techniques for deriving functional relationships efficiently and without making assumptions on the underlying model.

The presented approach provides a basis for different performance engineering tasks. In the remainder of this thesis, we demonstrate how the approach can be used for deriving software performance models. Moreover, the approach has already been applied for automated exhaustive performance regression testing [WWHM13] or to automatically detect performance anti-patterns [WHH13].

5. Industrial Case Study on Deriving Goal-Oriented Performance Models

In this chapter, we present an end-to-end industrial case study that we conducted in cooperation with performance analysts and development groups at SAP. We apply the goal-oriented performance modelling approach introduced in this thesis in a real-world context in order to demonstrate its applicability, accuracy and efficiency. Hence, we aim at answering two main questions:

1. Can we derive an accurate performance model that solves a real-world problem?

2. What are the efforts to apply the approach in a real-world scenario?

The remainder of this chapter is organized as follows. We introduce the context and the design of the study in Section 5.1. In Section 5.2, we present the scenario that we address in the course of the study. Section 5.3 describes how we implemented the process described in Chapter 3 using the methodologies introduced in Chapter 4. In Section 5.4 we outline and discuss the results. In Section 5.5, threats to validity are discussed and finally Section 5.6 summarizes the chapter.

5.1. Context

The study has been conducted at SAP AG [SAP13a], one of the largest providers of enterprise software and software-related services worldwide. The stakeholders in the study are coming from three different groups. The first group is the performance engineering team of the research department of SAP, which includes the author of this thesis. The second group is a team of performance analysts. The team acts as a service team to development groups, and is the main contact for performance-related tasks in the company. The third group is a team that develops an HTML5/JavaScript-based UI library named SAPUI5 [SAP13b]. The library is used by other development groups to build web application front-ends.

The stakeholders as well as the scenario of the case study arose from the context in which this thesis has been created. Performance engineering research at SAP aims at supporting software developers in avoiding or fixing performance problems while minimizing the required efforts and expert knowledge. SAPs performance analysts observed that very often the reason for bad front-end performance of enterprise web applications is an overloaded design of the screen (e.g. too many UI elements). Existing approaches were not able to deal with the complexity of the involved technology, the frequent changes in the system under test, or the large amount of developers that need to be supported. This led to the application of our work in the scenario introduced in the following section.

5.2. Scenario

For the development of web-based enterprise applications, companies often rely on JavaScript libraries that provide a uniform appearance, as well as a set of UI elements and utility functions commonly used in this kind of applications. At SAP, one of these libraries is the HTML5/JavaScript-based UI library named SAPUI5 [SAP13b]. Besides the classical challenges of web performance optimisation [Sou07, Sou09], UI developers and designers need to evaluate the impact of the design of a screen on front-end performance. This involves questions like „How many columns and rows can I add to a table of type X in my web application without violating performance requirements?“ or „What is the impact of back-end call Y on front-end performance?". Theoretically, these questions could also be answered with the existing performance measurement and analysis tools. However, practically the effort for applying measurement-based approaches to these kind of questions is too high which hinders the flexible, performance-aware construction and evaluation of screen designs. Moreover, the development of a screen's design is usually conducted before the screen is actually implemented (e.g. using wireframe or mockup tools). As a consequence, early performance feedback (prior to implementation) is essential to drive the deployment of fast web applications.

In the presented case study, we applied our approach to derive a performance model that predicts the expected performance of a screen. Based on the structure of the page, the UI elements used, and the service calls, our performance model estimates the expected front-end performance for the three major browsers (Internet Explorer, Firefox, Chrome). The predictions are used to give designers and developers early feedback about the expected front-end performance of their design. The approach does neither require that the application is implemented, nor that the developers conduct performance measurements. See Chapter 3.2 for a detailed introduction of the scenario using the proposed template for specifying goal-oriented performance models.

5.3. Execution

In this section, we describe how we derived a performance model for the scenario described in Section 5.2. The construction of the performance model has been a joint project of the research team, performance analysts, and SAPUI5 library developers. In the remainder of this section, we present the results from implementing the process introduced in Chapter 3 (see 3.4).

5.3.1. Define Context

The first step of the process is to define the evaluation goal and the experimentation landscape as well as to document the known issues in the context of the scenario.

5.3.1.1. Performance Evaluation Goal

To describe the performance evaluation goal, we follow the *Purpose, Consumption, Construction* approach introduced in Chapter 3.2.

Purpose

In today's web applications front-end performance contributes significantly to the overall user experience [Sou07] and thus affects business-critical metrics like conversion rate. Often, performance problems are caused by flawed screen designs [Fro13]. Changing the design of a screen in late development cycles implies large efforts and high costs. Hence, the effect of the screen design should be considered as early as possible. At SAP there are hundreds of developers using the SAP UI5 JavaScript library to build web application front-ends. Having a performance model that allows developers to easily evaluate the performance of their screen design, would significantly reduce the need for setting up and running performance tests by each individual developer. Moreover, it would significantly reduce the number of performance problems that are casued by flawed screen designs. Hence, the efforts to construct and maintain the performance model by an expert team are relatively small compared to the efforts that are necessary to achieve the same test coverage without the performance model (i.e., each developer needs to setup and run performance tests for each screen).

Consumption

The performance model should support developers in designing responsive web application screens by warning them when the design contains potential performance problems. Therefore, the model should predict the influence of different UI elements, their configuration and their interference on performance. The focus of the model is on screens developed with the SAP UI5 library, influences of custom coding or other libraries can be neglected. Furthermore, the model should be derived for a reference client machine and current versions of the most common browsers (Internet Explorer, Firefox, and Chrome). Thereby, it is important that the model reflects performance influences accurately for the reference setup. The transferability to other machine sizes or browser versions is neglectable. For the given scenario, we identified two potential consumption channels: a web-based prediction tool and an integration in a screen design editor. The web-based tool allows designers to quickly evaluate different screen designs by varying the screen configuration based on check boxes, sliders and input fields. It is a valuable tool for making rough estimations about front-end performance before actually starting the screen design. It helps answering questions like „How many columns and rows can I add to a table of type X in my web application without violating performance requirements?"or „What is the impact of back-end call data size on front-end performance?". Moreover, the web-based prediction tool can be used in developer trainings to clarify the impact of bad screen designs on front-end performance. The second consumption channel is the integration of the prediction model in a screen design editor used by developers to create SAP UI5 based web applications. Having the prediction integrated in the editor allows us to give immediate feedback on the expected performance while the screen is under development. Developers can get a warning when the screen design does not meet SAP's performance requirements and detailed views.

Construction

To derive the prediction model an experimental, measurement-based process is applied. The experiments are conducted using a screen generator software that allows to generate screens with different SAP UI5 library elements and configurations. The performance of the generated screens is measured on the latest versions of the main browsers on a test client machine.

5.3.1.2. Metric

The requirements for a metric that describes front-end performance are that i) it relates to the actual user experience, ii) it is measurable, iii) it is reproducible, iv) it is predictable, v) and it is influenced by the design of the screen. Previous measurements at SAP have shown that more than 70% of the end to end response time for typical enterprise web applications are spent in the browser. Standard web performance literature backs this assumption [Sou07]. This 70% of the end-to-end response time, include all client-side activities performed by the browser. For example parsing activities, JavaScript execution, DOM construction, and rendering [Sou07, Sou09]. Recently, the W3C Web Performance working group [W3C13] has published a standardisation recommendation that defines an interface for web applications to access timing information related to navigation and elements from the browser [W3C12b]. While the metrics that can be derived by this information (e.g. DOM processing time or total page load time) provide fine-grained insights in which browser tasks the time is spent, none of these metrics fulfils the requirements stated above. The metrics either leave parts out (e.g. the DOM processing time does not include the influence of back-end connection establishment) or include influences, such as network latency, that are not controllable and may disturb our measurements. Instead, we decided to use the *browser CPU time* as an indicator for front-end performance. We define the browser CPU time (short: CPU time) as the CPU time of the browser process consumed after a request has been sent to the application server until the full web application is displayed (see Figure 5.1). This includes all front-end activities performed by the browser and can be considered as the fastest achievable front-end performance, as it excludes disturbances caused by network latency and blocking requests. However, it is important to note that although the browser CPU time is a proper metric to determine the impact of design decisions on front-end performance and thus an excellent candidate for the prediction scenario, it does not replace the measurement of other metrics when aiming at, for example, optimizing the performance of an existing screen.

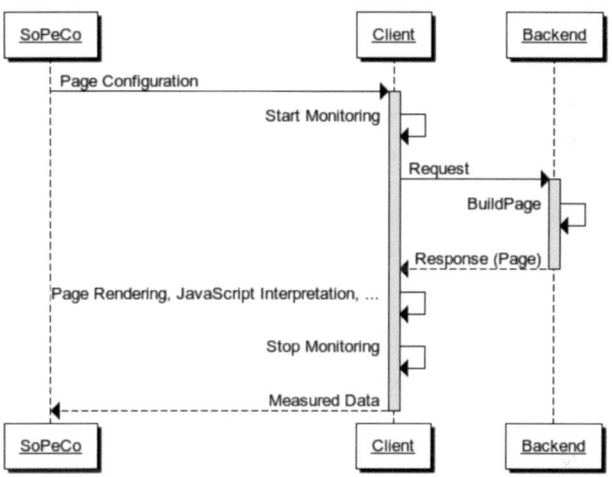

Figure 5.1.: Browser CPU time metric

5.3.1.3. Test Environment

In order to execute the experiments, we used the following components (see Figure 5.2):

- A test client machine that has the browser versions installed for which the performance models are to be constructed. Our experiments were performed on a Lenovo Laptop with an Intel(R) Core(TM)2 Duo CPU T7300 @2GHz processor, 4 GB

RAM, and the Windows 7 Enterprise operating system. We conducted all experiments on the three major browsers: Chrome 22.0.1229.94 (CH), Firefox 16.0.2 (FF) and Internet Explorer 9.9.0.8112.16421 (IE). Moreover, the client machine has to provide the capabilities (i) to control the browsers (start, stop, call url) via a parametrizable interface and (ii) to monitor the CPU time consumed by the browser between a request has been sent to the server and the point where the complete screen is loaded and displayed. Therefore, we installed a satellite component of the SoPeCo framework (see Chapter 4.3), that uses the Java libraries *Selenium* and *Sigar* to perform these tasks.

- Furthermore, a second machine is required that runs an instance of the SoPeCo framework. This instance allows us to define, execute and analyse experiments and handles the connection to the components on the test client.

- Finally, we need a web server that hosts a screen generator component. This screen generator has to have the capability to create screens based on the parameters transferred via the url. For our experiments, we developed a screen generator that creates SAPUI5 based screens with the UI element type manifestations and quantities given in the url (e.g. the url

  mygen.org/?table.rows=5&table.cols=5&table.quantity=2

  would create a screen with two tables both with five columns and five rows).

The SoPeCo instance transfers the information about the experiment (e.g. which browser to use, how many repetitions, parameter values for screen generation) to the test client. The test client prepares the experiment (e.g. killing all unnecessary processes, starting the browser, constructing the url that defines the screen) and triggers its execution by calling the url that transfers the screen specification to the screen generator component on

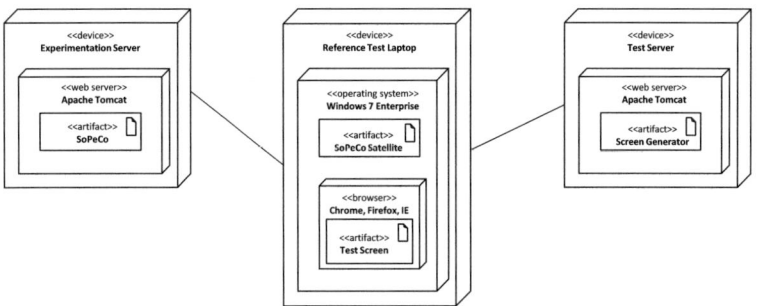

Figure 5.2.: Experimentation landscape

the web server. The screen generator generates the HTML and JavaScript files based on predefined code snippets. Then, the files that make up the screen are transferred to the client browser, which starts the rendering process. Once the screen is fully loaded, the experiment results are transferred back to the SoPeCo instance. This loop is repeated for each screen that is tested in an experiment series.

Furthermore, each screen is measured multiple times as performance measurements are of a stochastic nature and thus always include a certain error [Jai91]. To deal with this error, measurements are usually repeated until a certain confidence band has been reached that is considered as sufficient for the corresponding scenario. However, although a larger number of repetitions means that the calculate mean value is more stable, it also causes additional measurement time. As measurement time is in most cases a limited resource, we have to find a trade-off between the accuracy and measurement time. Therefore, we conducted a series of test runs with different screens and calculated the 95% confidence intervals for the mean value using different sample sizes. Figure 5.3 depicts an example that demonstrates how the confidence interval changes when the number of repetitions is increased. The graph shows that the improvements in the confidence band are getting smaller, with an increasing sample size. We decided to conduct 50 repetitions for each run and remove the outliers so that we end up between 30 and 50 valid samples per experiment. This results in an average measurement time of approximately 10 minutes for each experiment.

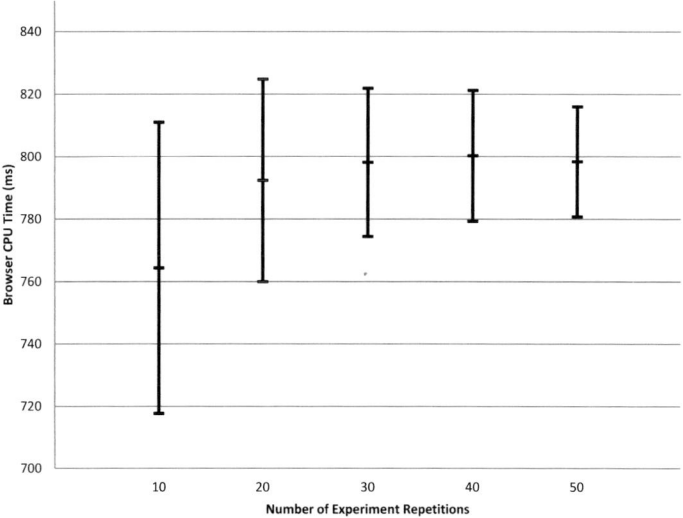

Figure 5.3.: 95% confidence intervals for different sample sizes

5.3.1.4. Known Issues

The following issues have been identified by the different stakeholders and should be considered in the modelling process:

- *Overloaded Screens:* Developers sometimes tend to place too much information on a single screen. This results in complex page structures and way too many UI elements. To render such screens, the browser requires multiple seconds. Figure 5.4 shows a real example of such an overloaded screen.

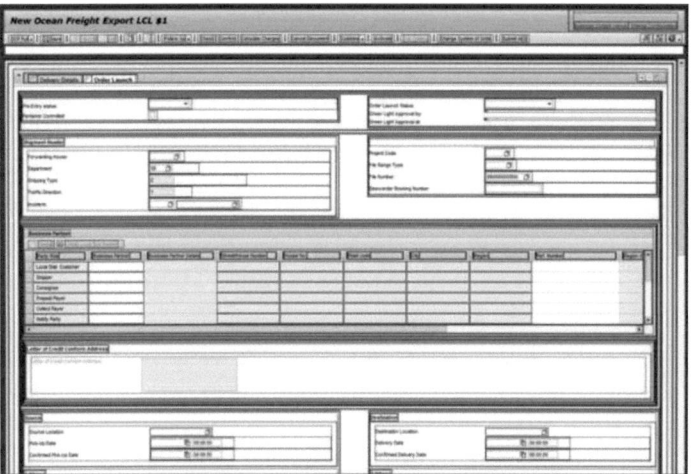

Figure 5.4.: Overloaded screen

- *Nesting:* Nested structures are created by layout containers in order to arrange the UI elements of a page. The analysis of screens with bad performance characteristics has indicated that often a high nesting level has been responsible for bad performance.

- *Data Transfer:* Performance measurements on service calls have shown that the amount of data that is transferred from the server to the client does not only influence the network delay but also the browser CPU activity.

- *Configuration:* A good example on how misconfiguration of a UI element can affect front-end performance has been published in [Lep12]. There, a rotating banner has been configured to load the images in parallel, instead of loading the visible image first. This was one reason for the bad performance of the web application screen. But also simple configuration options such as how many visible columns and rows are added to a table can affect the performance of a screen.

- *Browser:* The performance of the rendering engines of different browsers differs significantly [KH11]. Moreover, browser vendors strive to constantly improve their performance. Hence, performance characteristics of screens might change between different browsers and browser versions. Moreover, optimisation effects such as caching can influence performance measurements and have to be considered.

5.3.2. Understand Performance Behaviour

The next main block in the goal-oriented performance modelling process (illustrated in Figure 3.4) is to get an understanding of the performance influences in the scenario. In the following sections, we describe the assumptions that we defined with respect to relevant performance influences (Section 5.3.2.1) as well as the experiments that we conducted in order to test the assumptions (Section 5.3.2.2).

5.3.2.1. Initial Assumptions

Table 5.1 lists the assumptions that we investigated in order to get a profound understanding of the performance characteristics of SAP UI5-based web application screens. The assumptions are based on the known issues outlined in Section 5.3.1.4 and address the major aspects that vary from one web application to another: the number and type of UI elements used (A1, A2, and A3), the configuration of UI elements (A4), the type and number of service calls (A5), and the structure of the screen (A6 and A7). Understanding and quantifying the effect of these influencing factors, allows predicting the expected front-end performance of a web application.

ID	Assumption
A1	Performance worsens with an increasing number of UI elements on the screen.
A2	There is only a small subset of UI elements that affects performance significantly.
A3	Different UI elements do not interfere with respect to performance.
A4	For some UI elements the configuration can affect performance.
A5	The number of service calls and the amount of data that is transferred by a service call affect front-end performance.
A6	Deeply nested structures have a negative effect on the performance of a screen.
A7	The performance influence of a UI element depends on its placement in the layout structure.

Table 5.1.: Initial assumptions on relevant performance influences

5.3.2.2. Experiments to Test Assumptions

In this section, we present the experiments that we defined, executed and analysed in order to test the assumptions on performance relevant influences. Moreover, we tested how we can quantify the relevant influences in order to integrate them in a performance model.

A1: Performance worsens with an increasing number of UI elements on the screen. In order to test this assumption, we executed a series of experiments where we investigated how the CPU time changes if we only increase the number of UI elements. Figure 5.5 displays the browser CPU time for a screen containing 1 to 5 tables in all three major web browsers. Analysing the results we can make two main observations:

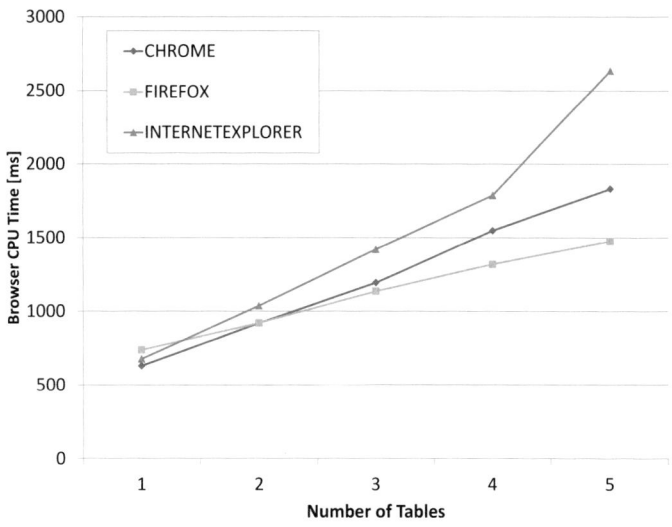

Figure 5.5.: Browser CPU time for 1 to 5 tables in different browsers

the browser CPU time increases (almost) linearly with the number of tables, i.e., each table requires the same amount of browser CPU time. The slope of the curve is different for each browser, i.e., the front-end performance heavily depends on the browser (and its version).

While in this first set of experiment series we placed only UI elements of the same type on a screen, Figure 5.6 illustrates the effect of combining different UI elements. In the depicted example, we varied the number of buttons from 0 to 500 and the number of tables from 0 to 5. Again, we can observe the same behaviour as in the previous experiments: CPU time increases almost linear (indicated by the smooth plane in the three dimensional space).

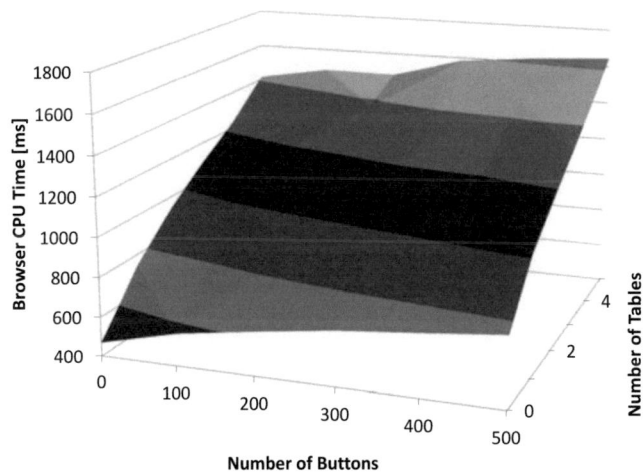

Figure 5.6.: CPU time for button/table mixes (Firefox)

In fact, we observed a similar behaviour for all UI elements that we tested. Hence, to quantify these influences we could derive the functional relationship between the number and type of UI elements on the screen and the CPU time consumed by the browser to display the screen. However, varying the quantity of all UI elements and the potential combinations in a single experiment series would not be feasible due to the exploding parameter space. Therefore, we need to test if we can apply heuristics that allow us to limit the parameter space that is to be measured. Assumptions A2 and A3 aim at finding such heuristics.

A2: There is only a small subset of UI elements that affect performance significantly. In the previous series of experiments, we could observe that different UI elements have a different influence on performance. Figure 5.7 illustrates these different influence. To derive the influence, we executed an experiment series where we placed for each type of UI element a single instance on a plain screen. The numbers in Figure 5.7 are calculated by subtracting the CPU time for the plain screen from the CPU time for the screen with the single UI element.

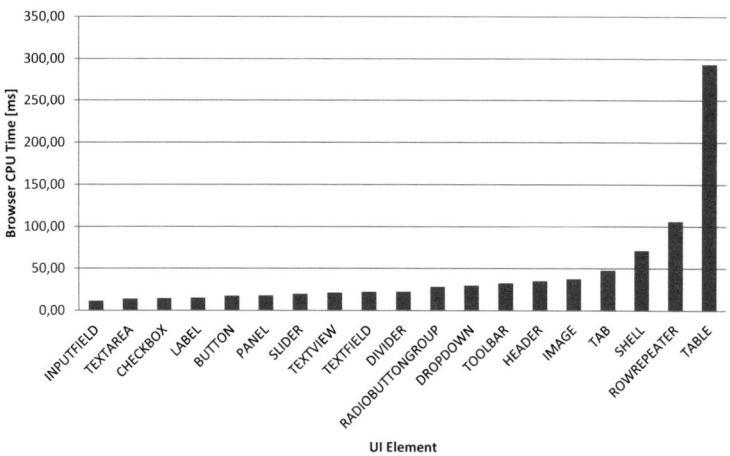

Figure 5.7.: CPU time cost for adding a single UI element on a plain screen

Furthermore, the slope for increasing, for example, the number of buttons has been very small. Hence, we make the assumption that the performance influence of such simple UI elements is quite small and thus does not need to be investigated in detail. Figure 5.7 shows that the bulk of elements has a rather small impact. Hence, to simplify the model construction process and to reduce the number of required measurements, we make the assumption that UI elements that do not have a large influence can be regarded as a group that we call simple UI elements. To quantify the influence of a simple UI element, we define a single, fixed cost value for all the UI elements in this group. We derive this cost value for each browser by measuring the performance costs introduced by one representative (e.g. button) of those simple UI elements group.

A3: Different UI elements do not interfere with respect to performance. To further limit the number of measurements that are to be conducted in the performance model construction activity, we test the assumption that different UI elements do not interfere with respect to performance. If this assumption holds, the relationship between the performance influence of different UI elements would be additive. Thus, we could derive the functional relationship between number of UI elements and CPU time separately for each UI element (i.e., without measuring all possible combinations) and then simply add up the different functions. In order to test the assumption, we conducted a set of experiment series using fraction factorial designs with resolution 5 (i.e.,main effects and two-factor interaction effects are not confounded (see Chapter 2.2.2.1)). We analysed the measurement results using Factorial ANOVA (see Chapter 2.2.2.2). Figure 5.8 shows the results for a selected set of UI elements. The figure shows for each factor and two-factor interaction, whether there is a significant main or interaction effect, respectively. Thereby, the null hypothesis is always that there is no significant effect. The $1 - p$ value indicates the probability that the hypothesis can be rejected. The values in Figure 5.8 reveal that all main effects are significant with a high probability. For the two-factor interactions the null hypothesis can not be rejected with a significant probability. Hence, the results show that making the assumption that different

	Df	Sum Sq	Mean Sq	F value	Pr(>F)	
BUTTON	1	59914	59914	11.6077	0.000685	***
RADIOBUTTONGROUP	1	708941	708941	137.3506	< 2.2e-16	***
TABLE	1	7200617	7200617	1395.0510	< 2.2e-16	***
DROPDOWN	1	360143	360143	69.7742	2.404e-16	***
IMAGE	1	652397	652397	126.3956	< 2.2e-16	***
BUTTON:RADIOBUTTONGROUP	1	13380	13380	2.5923	0.107724	
BUTTON:TABLE	1	5	5	0.0010	0.974920	
RADIOBUTTONGROUP:TABLE	1	9188	9188	1.7802	0.182455	
BUTTON:DROPDOWN	1	7673	7673	1.4865	0.223068	
RADIOBUTTONGROUP:DROPDOWN	1	1628	1628	0.3153	0.574562	
TABLE:DROPDOWN	1	5684	5684	1.1013	0.294260	
BUTTON:IMAGE	1	368	368	0.0712	0.789647	
RADIOBUTTONGROUP:IMAGE	1	2325	2325	0.4505	0.502287	
TABLE:IMAGE	1	1373	1373	0.2660	0.606171	
DROPDOWN:IMAGE	1	327	327	0.0633	0.801427	
BUTTON:RADIOBUTTONGROUP:TABLE	1	901	901	0.1745	0.676198	
BUTTON:RADIOBUTTONGROUP:DROPDOWN	1	297	297	0.0575	0.810467	
BUTTON:TABLE:DROPDOWN	1	1949	1949	0.3777	0.538999	
RADIOBUTTONGROUP:TABLE:DROPDOWN	1	6998	6998	1.3559	0.244553	
BUTTON:RADIOBUTTONGROUP:IMAGE	1	1	1	0.0002	0.989250	
BUTTON:TABLE:IMAGE	1	5264	5264	1.0199	0.312815	
RADIOBUTTONGROUP:TABLE:IMAGE	1	1	1	0.0002	0.988533	
BUTTON:DROPDOWN:IMAGE	1	984	984	0.1907	0.662461	
RADIOBUTTONGROUP:DROPDOWN:IMAGE	1	1804	1804	0.3495	0.554534	
TABLE:DROPDOWN:IMAGE	1	3768	3768	0.7301	0.393078	
BUTTON:RADIOBUTTONGROUP:TABLE:DROPDOWN	1	202	202	0.0391	0.843351	
BUTTON:RADIOBUTTONGROUP:TABLE:IMAGE	1	66	66	0.0128	0.909891	
BUTTON:RADIOBUTTONGROUP:DROPDOWN:IMAGE	1	6000	6000	1.1624	0.281240	
BUTTON:TABLE:DROPDOWN:IMAGE	1	18	18	0.0034	0.953442	
RADIOBUTTONGROUP:TABLE:DROPDOWN:IMAGE	1	3089	3089	0.5984	0.439374	
BUTTON:RADIOBUTTONGROUP:TABLE:DROPDOWN:IMAGE	1	8967	8967	1.7373	0.187809	
Residuals	928	4789913	5162			

```
---
Signif. codes:  0 '***' 0.001 '**' 0.01 '*' 0.05 '.' 0.1 ' ' 1
```

Figure 5.8.: ANOVA result for testing UI element additivity

UI elements do not interfere with each other is valid and thus can be applied when constructing the performance model. However, so far we used only UI elements in its standard configuration when conducting our experiments. In the following, we investigate the performance influence of different configuration options of a UI element.

A4: For some UI elements the configuration can affect performance. Many UI elements provide different configuration options. For example, a developer can set the number of columns and rows of a table, or the height, width and color of a button. While some of these configuration options will not affect performance (such as the color of a button), others are more likely to have a significant influence (e.g. the number of rows in a table). In the following, we describe the experiment series that we conducted in order to test this assumption and to quantify the influence of different UI element configuration parameters on performance. As an excerpt from the experiment series that we conducted, we present the results for the UI elements table and image.

For the tables we investigated the following configuration parameters:

- *ROWS* - the number of table rows
- *COLS* - the number of table columns
- *EDIT* - indicates if the fields of the table can be edited by the user
- *SEL* - indicates how rows of the table can be selected (one at a time, multiple at a time, or none)

To determine which configuration parameters affect performance, we chose to apply a full factorial design with the four parameters described above. Figure 5.9 shows the result of the visual analysis.

The box plots indicate for each configuration parameter whether its effect is significant or not. One can see that changing the row selection mode does not change the consumed CPU time significantly. Making the table

153

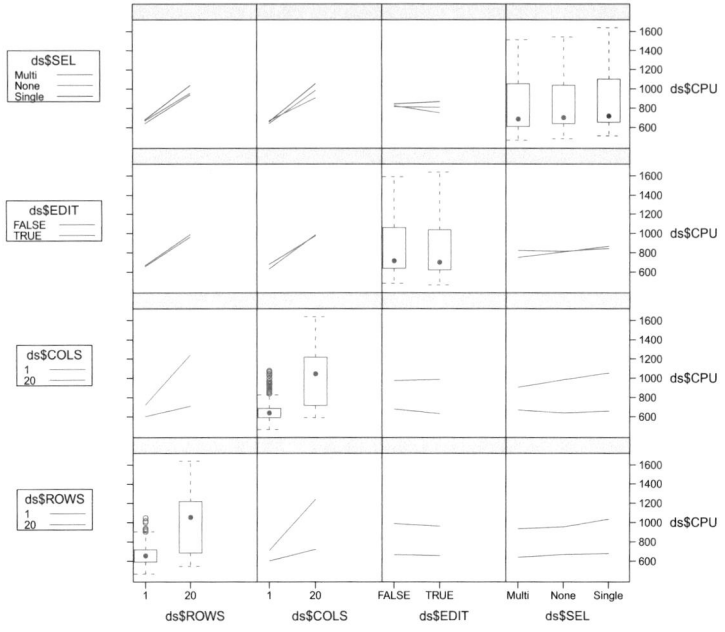

Figure 5.9.: Effect of table configuration parameters on CPU time

editable does also not affect CPU time significantly. However, changing the number of columns and rows affects CPU time significantly. When looking at the interaction plots for these two parameters one can also see that there is a significant interaction effect between the number of rows and the number of columns (i.e., the higher the number of columns in a table, the higher is the effect of the number of rows on CPU time).

Moreover, we investigated how different cell types affect performance. Therefore, we executed an experiment series were we placed a single table with a single column on a plain screen and varied the type of the cells in the column. The cell types that we investigated are *TextField*, *TextView*, *Link*, *Rating*, and *Check*. Figure 5.10 shows the result of the experiment series in a boxplot.

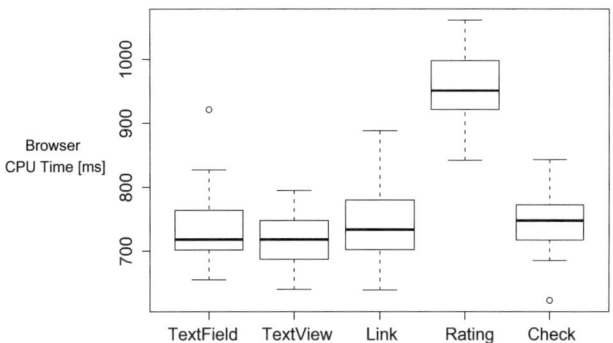

Figure 5.10.: Effect of table cell types on CPU time

The results reveal that only the CPU time costs for the column with the *Rating* cell type are significantly different from the CPU time costs for the other cell types.

In summary, the experiment series on understanding the effect of configuration parameters on the CPU time costs for displaying a table have shown that we need to include the number of rows, the number of columns and the cell type in our prediction function as these parameters significantly affect performance.

For the images, we investigated the following configuration parameters:

- *Height* - the visible height of the image
- *Width* - the visible width of the image
- *Size* - the data size of the image

Again, we conducted an experiment series using a full factorial design with two levels (high and low) for each parameter and analysed the result using Factorial ANOVA. We varied the parameters *Height* and *Width* between 100 px and 1000 px and the parameter *Size* between 104 KB and 955 KB. Figure 5.11 shows the measurement results in a box plot.

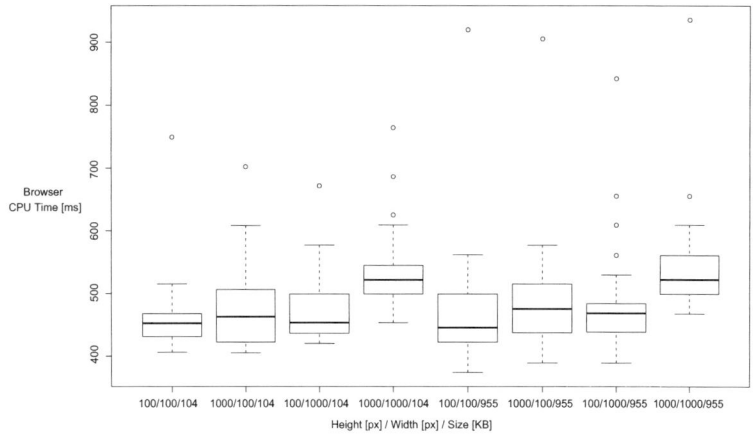

Figure 5.11.: Effect of image configuration parameters on CPU time

The plot reveals that the image size does not affect CPU time, while the height and width of an image do affect CPU time. The ANOVA result shown in Figure 5.12 confirms the result of the visual analysis. There is a significant main effect for the configuration parameters *Height* and *Width*

```
                    Df   Sum Sq  Mean Sq  F value     Pr(>F)
HEIGHT               1    94010    94010  14.7908 0.0001552 ***
WIDTH                1    78409    78409  12.3362 0.0005338 ***
SIZE                 1    12298    12298   1.9349 0.1655600
HEIGHT:WIDTH         1    28471    28471   4.4794 0.0353721 *
HEIGHT:SIZE          1      421      421   0.0663 0.7970431
WIDTH:SIZE           1     1206     1206   0.1897 0.6635346
HEIGHT:WIDTH:SIZE    1       12       12   0.0019 0.9651640
Residuals          232  1474595     6356
---
Signif. codes:  0 '***' 0.001 '**' 0.01 '*' 0.05 '.' 0.1 ' ' 1
```

Figure 5.12.: Effect of image configuration parameters on CPU time (ANOVA)

on CPU time. Moreover, there is a significant interaction effect between these two parameters. The parameter *Size* does not affect performance on a significant level. However, please note that although the image size does not affect the CPU time metric that we use to build the front-end performance model, it has to be considered carefully as it definitely affects the end-to-end response time of a screen.

In summary, the assumption that some configuration parameters influence the performance cost of a UI element significantly can be considered as valid. In our case study, we determined for each UI element that is not considered as simple (see experiment results for assumption A2), which configuration parameters actually influence its performance cost and how these costs can be quantified.

A5: The number of service calls and the amount of data that is transferred by a service call affect front-end performance. In the previous experiments, we used data that has been hard coded in the JavaScript source file. However, in real scenarios the data usually comes from a back-end system. To retrieve this data from the back-end system, OData [OAS13] and JSON [Cro13] are two common data representation alternatives for enterprise applications that are both supported by the investigated SAPUI5 library. In the following, we describe the experiment series that we conducted in order to understand the effect of OData and JSON service calls on browser CPU time. For all experiments, we used the publicly available Northwind service provided by odata.org [OAS13]. The service is accessible via a REST interface and supports both, JSON and OData format.

In the first set of experiment series, we investigated if the number of service calls affects performance. Therefore, we conducted experiments where we systematically increased the number of service calls executed by a screen. Figure 5.13 shows the results for the two data formats.

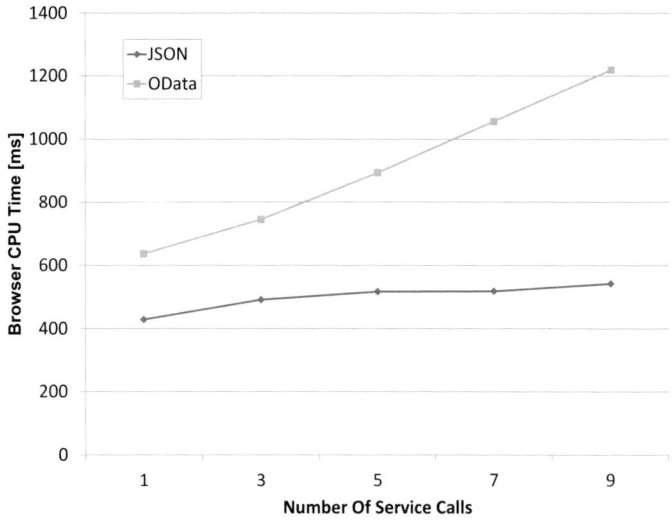

Figure 5.13.: Effect of service calls on browser CPU time

The graph shows that for both data formats the CPU time increases with the number of service calls. Although both service calls used the same query, there is a significant difference in performance. We assume that the reason for this difference is that the OData format requires much more data to describe the same content than the JSON format.

In the next set of experiment series, we investigated whether the increase in CPU time is actually caused by the number of service calls or by another metric. The metrics that we investigate in the following experiment series are the following.

- *CALLS:* the number of service calls that are executed when a screen is loaded

- *DATA:* the total amount of data (in KB) that is transferred to the client (i.e., the sum of data transferred by each service call)

- *RT:* the total number of round trips between client and server in order to transfer the data for all service calls on a screen

Table 5.2 lists the screens that we used in our experiment series for the OData calls. Screens A to E contain a single service service call, while screens F to R contain different combinations of the service calls from screen A to E. Hence, we test a broad set of screens with different manifestations of the three metrics that we want to investigate.

The measurement results for the screens listed in Table 5.2 are illustrated as box plots in Figure 5.14.

When comparing the measured CPU times for the different screens, we can make the following observations:

- The measured CPU time of screens B, C and D, reveal the influence of the amount of data that is transferred by a service call. All three screens contain the same number of service calls (1) and a similar number of round trips (2 to 5), but differ in the amount of data (B: 146 KB, C:84 KB, D:34 KB). One can see that the CPU time correlates with the amount of data as screen B required the most CPU time and screen D the least.

SCREEN	CALLS	RT	DATA
A	1	10	599
B	1	5	146
C	1	2	84
D	1	3	34
E	2	10	292
F	6	16	304
G	4	12	136
H	8	24	273
I	12	36	408
J	16	48	544
K	20	60	680
L	24	72	816
M	2	4	168
N	4	8	336
O	6	12	504
P	8	16	672
Q	10	20	840

Table 5.2.: Screens used for OData service call experiments

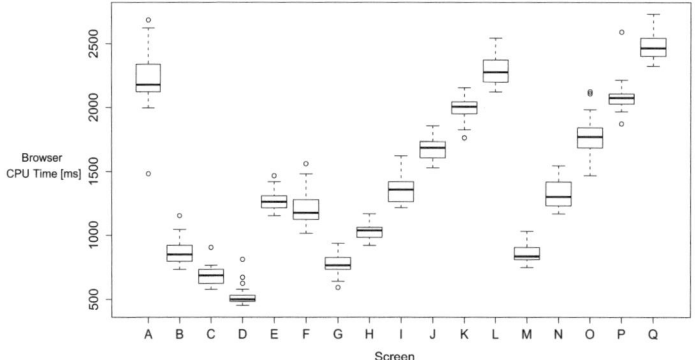

Figure 5.14.: Effect of service calls on browser CPU time (detailed)

- With respect to the number of service calls and the number of round trips, the results do not reveal a significant influence on CPU time. To the contrary, when we compare the measured CPU time for the screens E, F, N and I, we can assume that the number of calls and the number of round trips do not affect CPU time. All of the four screens transfer a similar amount of data while the number of calls (2 to 12) and the number of round trips (8 to 36) vary significantly between the four screens. Hence, if the number of calls or the number of round trips would have an effect on performance, the measured CPU time for the four screens should differ significantly. However, as illustrated in Figure 5.14, the measured CPU times for the four screens do not differ at a significant level.

In summary, the measurement results revealed that the number of calls is not a sufficient metric to describe the influence of OData-based service calls on front-end performance. Instead, the total amount of data transferred by the service calls of a screen is actually the metric that properly describes the influence of OData-based service calls on front-end performance.

In the next set of experiment series, we analysed if we get the same results for JSON-based service calls. Table 5.2 lists the screens that we used for the JSON calls. Screens A to H contain a single service service call, while screens I to R contain different combinations of the service calls from screen A to H. The measurement results for the screens listed in Table

SCREEN	CALLS	DATA
A	1	4
B	1	50
C	1	37
D	1	535
E	1	62
F	1	93
G	1	501
H	1	1071
I	2	99
J	4	95
K	15	93
L	2	8
M	4	16
N	8	32
O	16	64
P	2	186
Q	3	279
R	4	372

Table 5.3.: Screens used for JSON service call experiments

5.3 are illustrated as box plots in Figure 5.15.

When comparing the measured CPU times for the different screens, we can make the following observations:

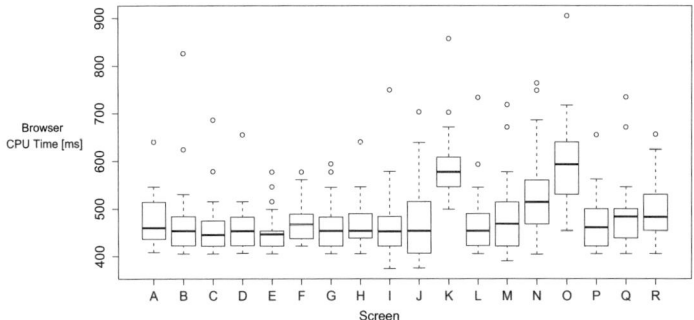

Figure 5.15.: Effect of JSON-based service calls on browser CPU time (detailed)

- The number of round trips for the single service calls A to H is always one, i.e., the JSON calls are not split in multiple round trips. Thus, we can skip the number of round trips metric in further experiments.

- The measured CPU time of screens A to H also indicate that the amount of data that is transferred by a JSON-based service call does not affect browser CPU time. Screens A to H contain the same number of service calls (1), but differ in the amount of data (ranging from 4 KB to 1071 KB). One can see that the CPU time does not correlate with the amount of data as screens A to H require almost the same browser CPU time.

- To test if the number of calls has a significant influence on browser CPU time, we compare the measured CPU time of screens I, J and K. The three screens consume nearly the same amount of data (between 93 KB and 99 KB), but differ in the number of calls that are executed by the screens (I: 2, J:4, K:15). When looking at the measurement results shown in Figure 5.15, one can see that the CPU time consumed by screen K is significantly higher than the CPU time consumed for screens I and J. Thus, we assume that the cause for the higher CPU time for screen K is the higher number of calls.

In summary, the measurement results revealed that in order to describe the influence of JSON-based service calls on the browser CPU time, it is sufficient to consider the relationship between CPU time and the number of calls on a screen. The results of a Factorial ANOVA analysis which are listed in Figure 5.16 confirm these assumptions. Based on the findings of

```
              Df  Sum Sq Mean Sq  F value      Pr(>F)
CALLS          1 30258.9 30258.9 314.8829 1.772e-11 ***
DATA           1    70.6    70.6   0.7351    0.4047
Residuals     15  1441.4    96.1
---
Signif. codes:  0 '***' 0.001 '**' 0.01 '*' 0.05 '.' 0.1 ' ' 1
```

Figure 5.16.: ANOVA result for testing performance-relevant parameters of JSON-based service calls

these experiment series, we assume that we can quantify the influence of JSON-based service calls by deriving a prediction function that describes the relationship between the total number of JSON-based service calls on a screen and the browser CPU time.

A6: Deeply nested structures have a negative effect on the performance of a screen.

In this set of experiment series, we analysed the effect of nested structures (e.g. nested tables and div containers) on browser CPU time. Nested structures are usually created by layout containers in order to arrange the UI elements of a page. For example a Matrix Layout is mapped to an HTML table with rows and cells. In our experiments, a nesting level of two conforms to two Matrix Layouts A and B where B is contained in a cell of A. The analysis of existing applications suggested that especially nesting is important. Nesting is critical if its width and height relate to the size of the browser (also known as percent sizing).

In other words, the layout is elastic as it scales with the size of the browser window. Such scaling can be especially computation intensive. Figure 5.17 shows the browser CPU time for Chrome, Firefox and Internet Explorer for a critical nesting level varying from 0 to 14.

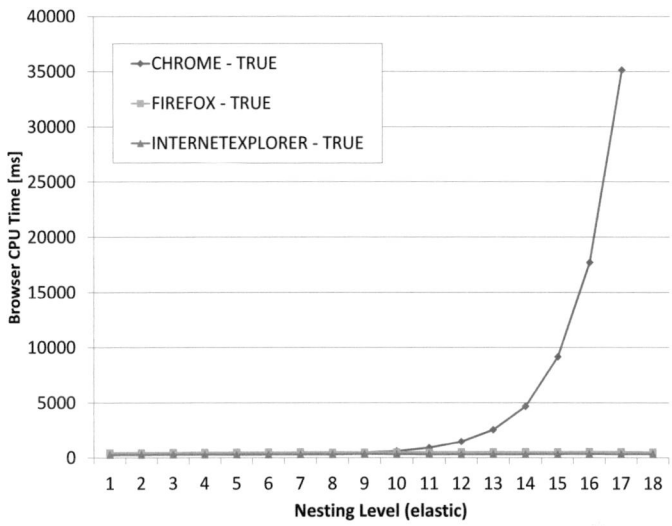

Figure 5.17.: Effect of critical nesting on browser CPU time

While critical nesting does not affect the browser CPU time in Internet Explorer and Firefox, Chrome's browser CPU time grows exponentially for a nesting level larger than 10. As it is a general best practice to keep the critical nesting of a screen below 10, and as only Chrome seems to have an issue with critical nesting, we decided to ignore the nesting level when creating a performance model.

A7: The performance influence of a UI element depends on its placement in the layout structure. With the experiment series introduced in the following, we aim at testing the assumption that the placement of the UI element in the structure of the screen affects its CPU time costs. Therefore, we need to understand the effect of placing a UI element in a leaf node compared to any other node in the UI tree. The placement may affect the layout computation of the browser and thus can be important for browser CPU time. In our experiments, we analysed the effect of three strategies for distribution:

1. all UI elements are placed in one leaf node of the UI tree (Leaf),

2. all UI elements are equally distributed among all UI containers on the screen (Round Robin), and

3. all UI elements are randomly distributed among all UI containers (Random).

Figure 5.18 illustrates the results of the experiments. The results show

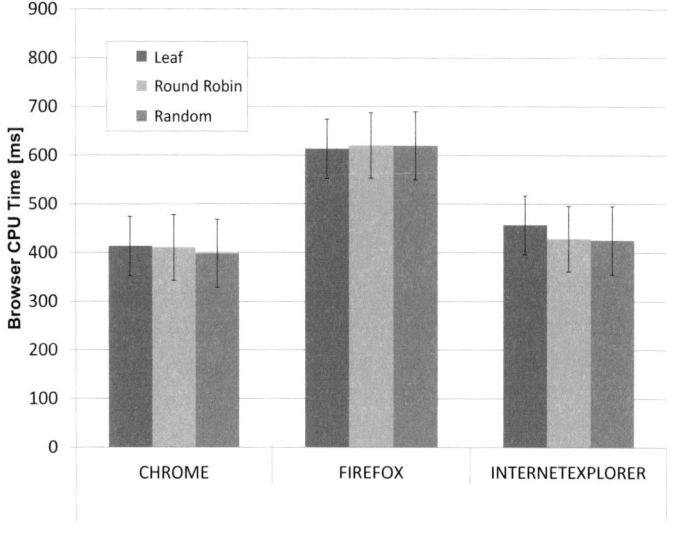

Figure 5.18.: Effect of UI element placement on browser CPU time

only little variation between the different distribution strategies. Also the confidence intervals are stable. This behaviour suggests that placement has no significant effect on browser CPU time. Hence, we do not consider the placement of the UI elements when creating the performance model.

5.3.2.3. Results

Based on the experiment series that we executed in order to test our initial assumptions (see Table 5.1), we could improve our understanding of the front-end performance characteristics of different SAPUI5-based UI elements. The experiment series as well as the results are properly documented and can be easily repeated if, for example, the performance team wants to test the assumptions again for a new set of browser versions. In summary, the systematic experimentation process led to the validated assumptions listed in Table 5.4.

These validated assumptions, as well as the other findings from the conducted experiment series form the input for the next process step which is the construction of a performance model. How we implemented this activity in the case study is presented in the following section.

ID	Assumption
A1	Performance worsens with an increasing number of UI elements on the screen.
A2	There is only a small subset of UI elements that affects performance significantly.
A3	Different UI elements do not interfere with respect to performance.
A4	For some UI elements the configuration can affect performance.
A5	Depending on the type of service call, either the amount of data (OData) or the number of calls (JSON) affect front-end performance.
A6	Deeply nested structures have a negative effect on the performance of a screen in some browsers.
A7	The performance influence of a UI element is independent of its placement in the layout structure.

Table 5.4.: Validated assumptions on relevant performance influences

5.3.3. Derive Performance Model

The performance model introduced in this section quantifies the relationship between the construction of a web application screen and the browser CPU time for different browsers. The model is created based on two inputs:

1. the assumptions and heuristics yielded from the experiments introduced in the previous section, and

2. a set of additional experiments for the derivation of functional dependencies.

In the following, we define a performance model for web application screens as well as a process to derive a concrete instance of this model for applications built using the SAP UI5 library.

If a screen S of a web application consists of the UI elements $e_1, ..., e_n$, we write: $S = e_1 \cdot ... \cdot e_n$ where $\cdot$ denotes the composition of UI elements (e.g. a screen that consists of tables, buttons, and text fields). Hence, when a UI developer creates a screen S, he evaluates $e_1 \cdot ... \cdot e_n$. We assume this composition as associative and commutative (i.e., the UI elements can be arbitrarily placed on the screen).

Furthermore, we define $\phi(S)$ as the front-end performance of screen S which is in our case expressed as the browser CPU time consumed to load the full screen (see also Section 5.3.1). Following the additivity and placement assumptions, we state that the performance of the UI element composition is the sum of the performance values of the individual UI elements $(\phi(e_1), ..., \phi(e_n))$ and a constant offset (ε_S).

$$\phi(S) = \phi(e_1 \cdot ... \cdot e_n) + \varepsilon_S = \phi(e_1) + ... + \phi(e_n) + \varepsilon_S \qquad (5.1)$$

The offset ε_S describes the browser CPU time consumed to load an empty screen. This includes for example the CPU time required to load the UI libraries and the CSS files (i.e.,all components of a screen that are independent of a certain UI element).

Depending on its properties $p_1, \ldots, p_k$ (e.g. number of columns and rows of a table), a UI element e yields different front-end performance characteristics. We estimate the performance value of UI element e as

$$\phi_{type}(p_1, \ldots, p_k) \tag{5.2}$$

Moreover, we derive an offset value ε_{type} for each UI element type that has a performance relevant property. This offset value captures the basic performance costs of a UI element when a first instance is placed on a screen (e.g. caused by loading and interpreting the JavaScript code that contains the sources for the UI element).

In order to derive an instance of such a prediction model for the SAP UI5 library and the three major browsers, we followed our systematic process introduced in Chapter 3.3.3. In the following, we give a detailed description of how we implemented this process in our industrial case study.

5.3.3.1. Define, Run and Analyse Experiments for Model Derivation

In this section, we describe the experiment series that we conducted in order to derive the performance value estimators required for Equation 5.1. Leveraging the result of the validated assumption that only a subset of all UI elements affects performance significantly (see A2 in Table 5.4), we group them in simple types and complex types.

For the simple elements, we do not conduct a detailed evaluation of the properties. Instead, we just determine a general performance value estimator based on an experiment series conducted with a representative element from this group. Examples for such simple UI element types in our study are buttons, text views, or labels.

As a result of the experiments conducted in the previous process step (see Section 5.3.2), we consider the following UI elements as complex: *Table*, *RowRepeater*, *Image*, *Toolbar*, *Shell*, *TabStrip*, and *Header*. For each complex UI element, we derive a prediction function that describes the relationship between the performance-relevant parameters of a UI element and the browser CPU time (i.e., we derive $\phi_{type}(p_1, \ldots, p_k)$ for those properties that are considered as performance-relevant). In order to deal with the large parameter space, we derive these multidimensional functions using the Adaptive Equidistant Breakdown (AEB) exploration strategy in combination with a Dynamic Sector validation with Local scope (DSL) and Multivariate Adaptive Regression Splines (MARS) analysis (see Chapter 4.4.2). This combination has been proven to produce reliable estimators using only a small subset of potential experiments (see Chapter 4.5). Figure 5.19 shows a screenshot of the SoPeCo UI, where the configuration of the exploration strategy and the analysis strategy is displayed.

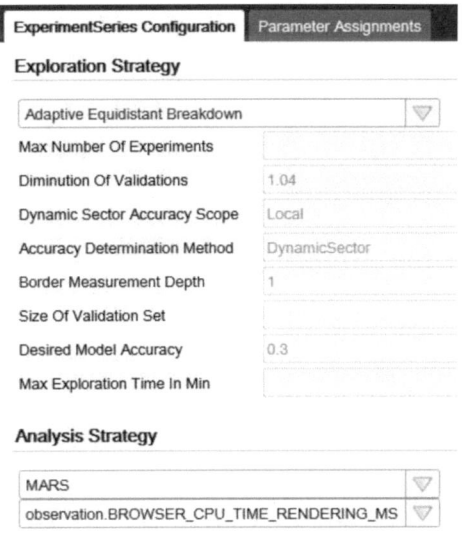

Figure 5.19.: Configuration of parameter space exploration for function derivation

In the following, we describe the experiment series as well as the analysis results for the simple element representative, the complex UI elements and the screen offset. Like in Section 5.3.2, we focus on the Firefox browser when describing the experiments and results.

Screen Offset (ε_S): As a first step, we determine the CPU time consumed by the browser to process the basic screen layout in which we place the different UI element types for our experiments. Therefore, we define and run an experiment that measures an empty screen. As a result we get the screen offset $\varepsilon_S = 420ms$. Figure 5.20 shows the distribution of the measured values in a box plot diagram. As discussed in Section 5.3.1, the variance is quite high, which is why we repeat each measurement at least 30 times.

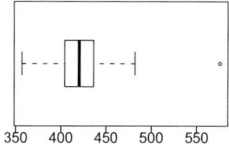

Figure 5.20.: Range of measured values for screen offset

Simple Elements (ϕ_{Simple}): To determine the estimator for the UI elements that we consider as simple, we conduct an experiment series in which we use the UI element Button as a representative for this group. The only performance-relevant parameter of simple elements is the number of elements placed on a screen. The parameter space for this experiment is listed in Table 5.5.

Varied Parameter	Variation
Button.Quantity	Linear: Min(1), Max(100), Step(1)
	Total Number of Experiments: 100

Table 5.5.: Parameter space for derivation of ϕ_{Simple}

To select the experiments for model fitting, we used our adaptive equidistant breakdown algorithm, which executed 9 experiments. As a result we got the linear function shown in Equation 5.3 that describes the relationship between the number of buttons (or in general simple UI elements) on a screen and the CPU time required by the browser to display the screen.

$$CPU = 440 + 1.943456 * Quantity \qquad (5.3)$$

The coefficient of determination for the linear regression is $R^2 = 0.92$. Figure 5.21 shows the 9 data points and the fitted function. The prediction error is in most cases less than 5%.

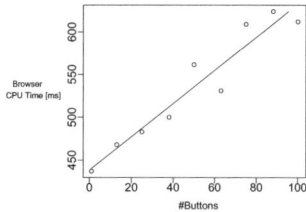

Figure 5.21.: Linear regression for Button (i.e., SimpleElement) performance

To derive the offset value for simple elements (ε_{Simple}), we calculate the CPU time required for a single simple element using Equation 5.3 and subtract the offset of the blank screen (ε_S). To determine ϕ_{Simple}, we subtract the the sum of the two offsets $\varepsilon_{Simple} + \varepsilon_S$) from the linear function listed in Equation 5.3.

Table (ϕ_{Table}):   .

The first complex UI element for which we derive a prediction function is the Table element. The Table element is one of the most often used elements in enterprise applications, and in our study also the one with the highest impact on front-end performance (see Figure 5.7). As a result of

173

the previous process step (see Section 5.3.2.2), we know that three configuration parameters affect performance: the number of rows, the number of
simple columns (represented in the following by text field columns), and
the number of rating columns. Hence, in our experiment series we varied
the parameters as listed in Table 5.6. When selecting the ranges in which

Parameter	Variation
Table.Quantity	Linear: Min(1), Max(5), Step(1)
Table.Rows	Linear: Min(1), Max(30), Step(1)
Table.SimpleCols	Linear: Min(0), Max(30), Step(1)
Table.RatingCols	Linear: Min(0), Max(1), Step(1)
	Total Number of Experiments: 9.300

Table 5.6.: Parameter space for derivation of ϕ_{Table}

we vary the parameters, we considered in all experiment series that we
do not create screens that are unlikely to occur in practice (e.g. tables with
more than one rating column) and that exceed a certain CPU time (as we are
not interested in predicting CPU time behaviour under extreme load situations). The step size is chosen to be as fine-grained as necessary in order to
allow our adaptive parameter space exploration algorithm to gather enough
points in areas where the prediction model needs more data to provide an
accurate result (see Chapter 4.4.2). When considering the parameters and
the variation granularity shown in Table 5.6, the potential parameter space
for deriving a prediction function consists of 9.300 potential experiments.
However, using our automated combination of experiment selection and
statistical analysis allows us to derive prediction functions with only a small
fraction of these experiments (see Chapter 4.5). For the Table UI element,
we could derive the following multidimensional linear prediction function
using only 52 experiments (i.e., 0,56%).

$$CPU = 630.6861$$

$-\,0.9837964 * Rows$

$-\,1.451458 * SimpleCols$

$-\,706.4417 * RatingCols$

$+\,5.741513 * Quantity$

$+\,0.005112995 * Rows * SimpleCols$

$+\,48.38323 * Rows * RatingCols$

$+\,46.90708 * SimpleCols * RatingCols$

$+\,1.603063 * Rows * Quantity$

$+\,3.421011 * SimpleCols * Quantity$

$+\,237.0174 * RatingCols * Quantity$

$-\,3.089817 * Rows * SimpleCols * RatingCols$

$+\,1.069729 * Rows * SimpleCols * Quantity$

$-\,12.56101 * Rows * RatingCols * Quantity$

$-\,14.18982 * SimpleCols * RatingCols * Quantity$

$+\,0.9006174 * Rows * SimpleCols * RatingCols * Quantity$

$$(5.4)$$

The calculated coefficient of determination R^2, is 0.99 for the linear function shown in Equation 5.4 which indicates that the prediction function fits the data well. In addition to the coefficient of determination, we validated the accuracy of the prediction function already during its derivation using our iterative process introduced in Chapter 4.4.2. Figure 5.22 shows the residual plot from the generalized cross validation which also confirms that the function provides accurate predictions. Finally, to determine the offset value for table elements (ε_{Table}), we calculate the CPU time required for a single table element using Equation 5.4 and subtract the offset of the blank screen (ε_S). To determine ϕ_{Table}, we subtract the the sum of the two offsets $\varepsilon_{Table} + \varepsilon_S$) from the linear function listed in Equation 5.4.

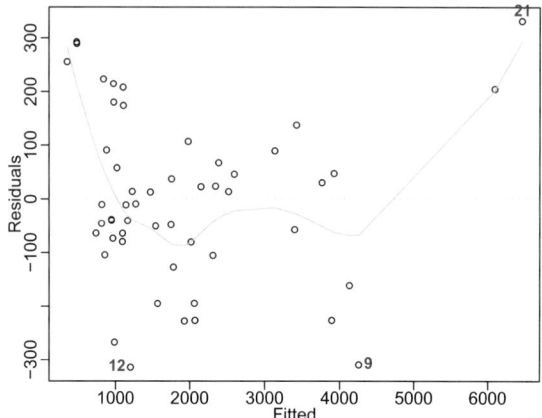

Figure 5.22.: Residuals vs. fitted values for linear function on Table performance

Image (ϕ_{Image}): To derive a performance prediction function for images, we vary the parameters listed in Table 5.7. As our experiment series ex-

Parameter	Variation
Image.Quantity	Linear: Min(1), Max(10), Step(1)
Image.Width	Linear: Min(1), Max(1000), Step(10)
Image.Height	Linear: Min(1), Max(1000), Step(10)
	Total Number of Experiments: 10.000

Table 5.7.: Parameter space for derivation of ϕ_{Image}

ecuted in the previous process step have shown that the size of an image does not affect browser CPU time (see Section 5.3.2.3), we only include the performance-relevant configuration parameters height and width in the prediction function. With the chosen variation granularity this results in 10.000 potential experiments. However, due to our automated combination of experiment selection and statistical analysis, we could derive the following MARS prediction function using only 21 experiments (i.e., 0,21%).

$$CPU = 483.5$$
$$+ 0.03131313 * max(0, Width - 505)$$
$$- 0.04292929 * max(0, 505 - Width)$$
$$+ 0.026 * max(0, Height - 500)$$
$$- 0.04387755 * max(0, 500 - Height)$$
$$- 0.9642857 * max(0, Quantity - 5)$$
$$- 3.669643 * max(0, 5 - Quantity)$$
$$+ 2.020202e - 05 * max(0, Width - 505) * max(0, Height - 500)$$
$$- 7.070707e - 06 * max(0, 505 - Width) * max(0, Height - 500)$$
$$- 0.0001752216 * max(0, Width - 505) * max(0, 500 - Height)$$
$$+ 5.462791e - 05 * max(0, 505 - Width) * max(0, 500 - Height)$$
$$+ 0.01189033 * max(0, Width - 505) * max(0, Quantity - 5)$$
$$+ 0.01038961 * max(0, Width - 505) * max(0, 5 - Quantity)$$
$$- 0.001528571 * max(0, Height - 500) * max(0, Quantity - 5)$$
$$+ 0.003160714 * max(0, Height - 500) * max(0, 5 - Quantity)$$

$$(5.5)$$

The coefficient of determination for the derived MARS function is $R^2 = 0.97$. Figure 5.23 shows the residual plot from the generalized cross validation which also reveals that the model fits the data well. To determine ϕ_{Image}, we calculate the offset values ε_{Image} and ε_S and subtract the sum of the two values from the function outlined in Equation 5.5 in order to get only the estimation for the performance costs of additional images added to the screen.

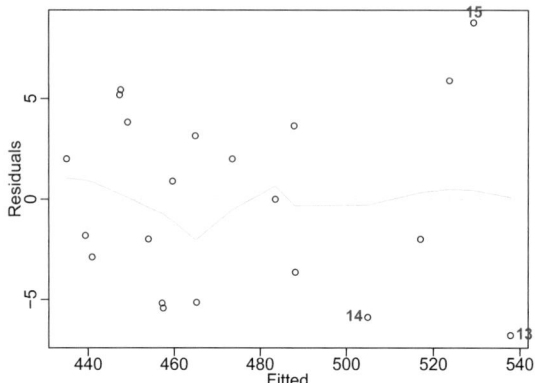

Figure 5.23.: Residuals vs. fitted values for MARS function on Image performance

RowRepeater ($\phi_{RowRepeater}$): The next complex UI element is called RowRepeater. Besides the quantity of the RowRepeater, the number of rows that are displayed by a RowRepeater have a significant effect on the performance of a screen. Hence, in our experiment series to derive a prediction function for screens containing RowRepeaters, we vary these parameters as listed in Table 5.8. As the number of potential appropriate values for

Parameter	Variation
RowRepeater.Quantity	Linear: Min(1), Max(10), Step(1)
RowRepeater.Rows	Linear: Min(1), Max(30), Step(1)
	Total Number of Experiments: 300

Table 5.8.: Parameter space for derivation of $\phi_{RowRepeater}$

the two varied parameters is not very high, the parameter space consists of only 300 potential experiments. However, running 300 experiments would take already 2 days. With our adaptive breakdown methodology, we derived the MARS function shown in Equation 5.6 using only 86 experiments which could be executed in 12 hours.

$$CPU = 742.6767$$
$$+ 12.6454 * max(0, Rows - 9)$$
$$- 25.48596 * max(0, 9 - Rows)$$
$$+ 24.57518 * max(0, Quantity - 6)$$
$$- 31.63405 * max(0, 6 - Quantity)$$
$$+ 2.622546 * max(0, Rows - 9) * max(0, Quantity - 5)$$
$$- 2.301101 * max(0, Rows - 9) * max(0, 5 - Quantity)$$
$$- 1.45611 * max(0, 9 - Rows) * max(0, Quantity - 8)$$
$$+ 2.422541 * max(0, 9 - Rows) * max(0, 8 - Quantity)$$

$$(5.6)$$

The coefficient of determination $R^2 = 0.99$ for the derived MARS function indicates a good prediction accuracy. The residual plot (Figure 5.24) from the generalized cross validation also shows that the model fits the data well. As with the other UI elements, we determine $\phi_{RowRepeater}$ by calculating the offset values $\varepsilon_{RowRepeater}$ and ε_S and subtract the sum of the two values from the function outlined in Equation 5.6 in order to get only the estimation for the performance costs of additional RowRepeater elements added to the screen.

TabStrip ($\phi_{TabStrip}$): The TabStrip UI element does not have any performance-relevant configuration parameters. We tested if the number of tabs has a significant influence on CPU time, which is not the case as can be seen in the box plot depicted in Figure 5.25. Hence, we varied only the number of TabStrips on a screen (from 1 to 5 in steps of 1) and derived the

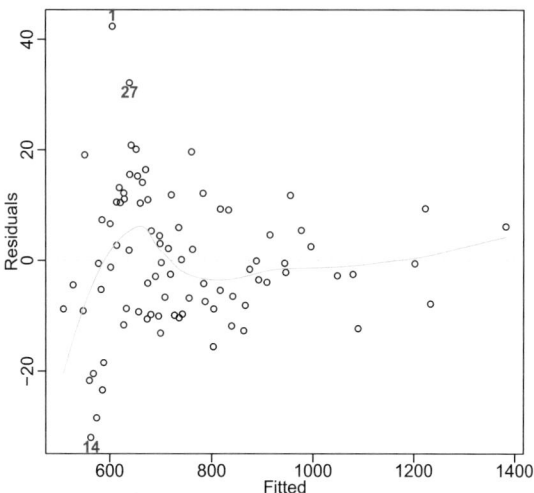

Figure 5.24.: Residuals vs. fitted values for MARS function on RowRepeater performance

linear function shown in Equation 5.10.

$$CPU = 467.4 + 16 * Quantity \tag{5.7}$$

The coefficient of determination for the linear regression is $R^2 = 0.99$. Figure 5.26 shows the five data points and the fitted function. To determine $\phi_{TabStrip}$, we calculate the offset values $\varepsilon_{TabStrip}$ and ε_S and subtract the sum of the two values from the linear function in Equation 5.10.

Toolbar ($\phi_{Toolbar}$): The UI element Toolbar does not have any performance-relevant configuration parameters. Hence, we conducted an experiment series were varied only the number of Toolbars on a screen (from 1 to 10 in steps of 1) and derived the linear function shown in Equation 5.8.

$$CPU = 457.1333 + 7.484848 * Quantity \tag{5.8}$$

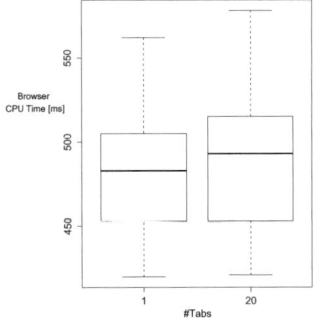

Figure 5.25.: Influence of the number of tabs on browser CPU time

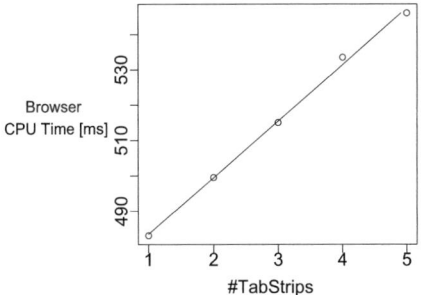

Figure 5.26.: Linear regression for TabStrip performance

The coefficient of determination for the linear regression is $R^2 = 0.94$. Figure 5.27 shows the ten data points as well as the fitted function. As with the other UI elements, we calculate the offset values $\varepsilon_{Toolbar}$ and ε_S and subtract the sum of the two values from the linear function in Equation 5.8 in order to determine $\phi_{Toolbar}$.

Header (ϕ_{Header}) and Shell (ϕ_{Shell}):   Header and Shell are UI elements that occur only once on a screen. Moreover, none of their configuration parameters has a significant influence on performance. Hence, ϕ_{Header} and ϕ_{Shell} are constant values derived by simply measuring a screen that con-

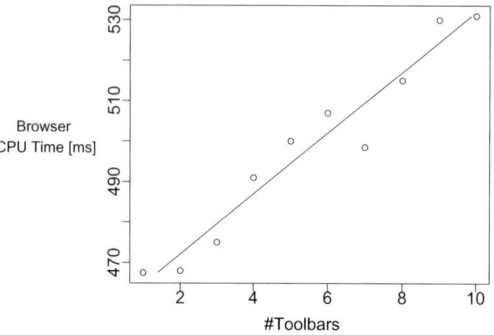

Figure 5.27.: Linear regression for Toolbar performance

tains a Header or a Shell, respectively, and subtract the screen offset ε_S from the measured values. Figure 5.28 shows the measurement results for the two experiment screens in a box plot diagram. This results in the fol-

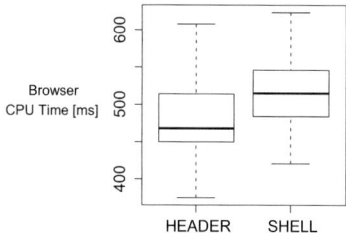

Figure 5.28.: Measured browser CPU times for Header and Shell

lowing values for ϕ_{Header} and ϕ_{Shell}:

$$\phi_{Header} = 28 \tag{5.9}$$

$$\phi_{Shell} = 75 \tag{5.10}$$

OData-based Service Call (ϕ_{OData}):   In Section 5.3.2.2, we presented our experiment series for understanding the performance influence of OData-based service calls. The results revealed that the total amount of data that is transferred by the service calls is the only service call parameter that affects front-end performance. Hence, to build a prediction function for OData-based service calls and derive ϕ_{OData}, we consider only this parameter. We use the measurement results (Figure 5.14) derived for the screens listed in Table 5.2 as training data for the MARS analysis. The resulting MARS function is listed in Equation 5.11.

$$
\begin{aligned}
& 1181.766 \\
& + 2.317290 * max(0, DATA - 336) \\
& - 2.336814 * max(0, 336 - DATA)
\end{aligned}
$$

$$(5.11)$$

The coefficient of determination for the function is $R^2 = 0.97$ and indicates a good prediction accuracy. The residual plot derived by a generalized cross validation is depicted in Figure 5.29 and confirms the quality of the MARS model.

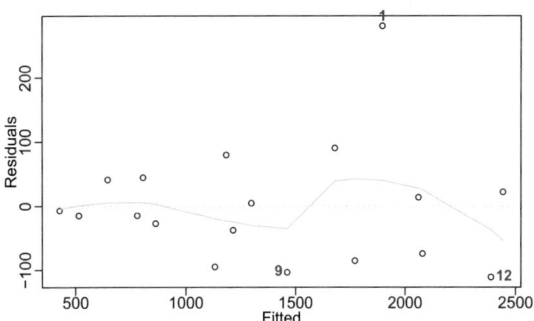

Figure 5.29.: Residuals vs. fitted values for MARS function on OData-based service call performance

Finally, we calculate the offset value ε_S and subtract it from the MARS function shown in Equation 5.11 in order to determine ϕ_{OData}.

JSON-based Service Call (ϕ_{JSON}): In Section 5.3.2.2, we also presented our experiment series for understanding the performance influence of JSON-based service calls. In contrast to OData-based service calls the only parameter that affects the front-end performance of a screen that includes JSON-based service calls is the number of calls on the screen. Hence, to build a prediction function for JSON-based service calls and derive ϕ_{JSON}, we consider only this parameter. We use the measurement results (Figure 5.15) derived for the screens listed in Table 5.3 as training data for a Linear Regression analysis. The resulting regression function is listed in Equation 5.12.

$$CPUtime = 440.9531 + 9.147735 * CALLS \qquad (5.12)$$

The coefficient of determination for the function is $R^2 = 0.94$ which indicates a good prediction accuracy. Figure 5.30 shows the measured data points as well as the fitted function. The plot also reveals that the function fits the data well. Like with the other elements, we calculate the offset

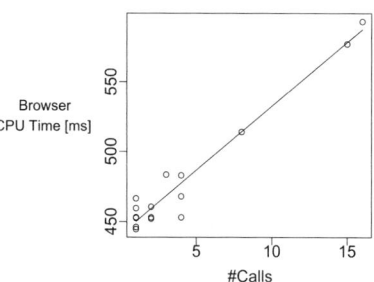

Figure 5.30.: Linear regression for JSON-based service calls

values ε_{JSON} and ε_S and subtract the sum of the two values from the linear function in Equation 5.12 in order to determine ϕ_{JSON}.

5.3.3.2. Construct Prediction Functions

In the previous section, we introduced the experiment series that we conducted in order to derive the performance estimators $\phi_{type}(p_1,\ldots,p_k)$ as well as the offset value for the different UI element types ε_{type} and the screen offset value ε_S. Now, we can compose these terms to a prediction function that predicts the browser CPU time for a screen S as shown in Equation 5.1. As the function $\phi_{type}(p_1,\ldots,p_k)$ returns the performance cost of a certain UI element type in a particular configuration, we need to add up the performance costs of the different configurations of each UI element type. Hence, we define two additional variables: *#Type* denotes the total number of UI elements of a certain type on a screen, and *#TypeConfigs* denotes the number of different configurations of a certain UI element type on a screen. Equation 5.13 shows how we derive the prediction functions in our scenario.

$$\phi(S) = \varepsilon_S + min(1, \#Simple) * (\varepsilon_{Simple} + \phi_{Simple}(Quantity)),$$

$$+ min(1, \#Image) * \left(\varepsilon_{Image} + \sum_{i=1}^{\#ImageConfigs} \phi_{Image}(Height, Width, Quantity)\right)$$

$$+ min(1, \#Table) * \left(\varepsilon_{Table}\right.$$

$$+ \sum_{i=1}^{\#TableConfigs} \phi_{Table}(\#SimpleCols, \#RatingCols, \#Rows, Quantity))$$

$$+ min(1, \#RowRepeater) * (\varepsilon_{RowRepeater}$$

$$+ \sum_{i=1}^{\#RowRepeater} \phi_{RowRepeater}(\#Rows, Quantity))$$

$$+ min(1, \#TabStrip) * (\varepsilon_{TabStrip} + \phi_{TabStrip}(Quantity))$$

$$+ min(1, \#Toolbar) * (\varepsilon_{Toolbar} + \phi_{Toolbar}(Quantity))$$

$$+ min(1, \#Header) * \phi_{Header}()$$

$$+ min(1, \#Shell) * \phi_{Shell}()$$

$$+ min(1, \#OData) * \phi_{OData}(Data)$$

$$+ min(1, \#JSON) * \phi_{JSON}(\#Calls)$$

$$(5.13)$$

Since different browsers show different behaviours with respect to front-end performance, we derived the performance model shown in Equation 5.13 for three important browsers (Firefox, Chrome, and Internet Explorer). We listed the concrete values and functions for the corresponding implementations of Equation 5.13 in Appendix C. As all experiments introduced in Section 5.3.3.1 and Section 5.3.3.2 have been defined using our experiment specification language (see Chapter 4.3.1), we can automatically run the same experiments for other browsers. Having this set of automatically executable experiments has the benefit that it limits the effort for creating or updating the functions for new browsers browser versions or UI library versions.

5.3.4. Validate Performance Model

The constructed prediction function instances are abstractions of the real behaviour that is based on assumptions, heuristics and statistical inference. Hence, it has to be validated that the estimated performance values sufficiently reflect the behaviour of real screens. The goal of our validation is to judge prediction accuracy and thus the utility of our heuristics and the practicability of our approach. Therefore, we compare our predictions with actual performance measurements.

We selected twelve real-world screens built with the SAP UI5 library. Six screens are taken from demo applications provided by the SAP UI5 development team. These screens cover a broad spectrum of different manifestations of the two most important control types in business applications, namely tables and service calls. The other six screens are taken from a real application called Networking Lunch. Networking Lunch is a social enterprise application where people can search for other people interested in the same topic and setup a joint lunch meeting. Figure 5.31 outlines the content of the twelve validation screens which is also the the input to our performance prediction functions.

demo1	demo2	demo3	demo4	demo5	demo6
1 ODataCall (10KB)	1 ODataCall (106KB)	1 ODataCall (72KB)	1 ODataCall (38KB)	1 ODataCall (542KB)	1 ODataCall (380KB)
1 Header	1 Table (5SC,10R)	1 Table (4SC,10R)	1 AppHeader	2 Table (14SC,10R + 5SC,1R)	1 Table (10SC,10R)
7 Simple	1 AppHeader	1 AppHeader	7 Simple	1 AppHeader	1 AppHeader
	2 Simple	22 Simple		2 Simple	25 Simple

nwlunch1	nwlunch2	nwlunch3	nwlunch4	nwlunch5	nwlunch6
3 JsonCalls (4KB)	1 Shell	1 Shell	1 Shell	2 JsonCalls (1KB)	1 Shell
1 Shell	2 JsonCalls (1KB)	2 JsonCalls (1KB)	2 JsonCalls (2KB)	1 Shell	1 Table (2SC,1R)
2 RowRepeater (1R)	2 Tables (4SC,1R + 2SC,1R)	1 Table (3SC,1R)	1 RowRepeater (1R)	4 Simple	1 JsonCall (1KB)
1 Image (W:440,H:300)	12 Simple	2 RowRepeater (1R)	22 Simple		3 Simple
7 Simple		7 Simple			

Figure 5.31.: Overview of the control types on the validation screens

We measured the browser CPU time of all screens on the same test client and with the same browser versions for which we derived our prediction model. We also ensured that the validation screens use the same version of the SAP UI5 library as our screen generator. Generally, the process for measuring the real screens was equal to the process for measuring the generated screens during our experiments (see Section 5.3.1). To make sure that we compare only the browser CPU times for processing the controls that are added to the basic layout of an application, we also measured the offset values for the two web applications, i.e.,we measured the browser CPU time consumed by a blank screen in the corresponding application frame ($\varepsilon_{P_{validation}}$). To determine the offset value for our predictions $\varepsilon_{P_{prediction}}$, we add the difference between the offset value used for a blank screen constructed by our screen generator ($\varepsilon_{P_{pagegen}}$) and the offset value measured for a blank screen in the validation application to the prediction offset value $\varepsilon_{P_{validation}}$. With this adjustment of the offset value, we avoid that influences like login procedures or loading of additional libraries affect the prediction result.

To determine the prediction accuracy, we calculate the absolute prediction error (i.e., the difference between actual and predicted performance) in ms and the relative prediction error in percent:

$$error = \frac{actual - predicted}{actual} * 100\%.$$

Following standard literature [MA01], we consider a relative prediction error of less than 30% as acceptable.

Page	Chrome				Firefox				InternetExplorer			
	Measured	Predicted	Abs. Error	Rel. Error	Measured	Predicted	Abs. Error	Rel. Error	Measured	Predicted	Abs. Error	Rel. Error
nwlunch1	881 ms	1050 ms	169 ms	19%	934 ms	1065 ms	131 ms	14%	722 ms	763 ms	41 ms	6%
nwlunch2	1123 ms	1043ms	-81ms	7%	952 ms	945 ms	-7 ms	1%	760 ms	785 ms	25 ms	3%
nwlunch3	1341 ms	1194 ms	-147 ms	11%	1217 ms	1251 ms	34 ms	3%	1026 ms	900 ms	-126 ms	12%
nwlunch4	952 ms	1026 ms	74 ms	8%	936 ms	1045 ms	109 ms	12%	795 ms	746 ms	-49 ms	6%
nwlunch5	788 ms	851 ms	63 ms	8%	769 ms	687 ms	-82 ms	11%	650 ms	579 ms	-71 ms	11%
nwlunch6	1067 ms	992 ms	-75 ms	7%	1019 ms	899 ms	-120 ms	12%	830 ms	720 ms	-111ms	13%
demo1	646 ms	721 ms	75 ms	12%	523 ms	471 ms	-52 ms	10%	430 ms	402 ms	-28 ms	7%
demo2	1018 ms	1189 ms	170 ms	17%	861 ms	972 ms	111 ms	13%	695 ms	821 ms	126 ms	18%
demo3	1014 ms	1128 ms	114 ms	11%	842 ms	918 ms	76 ms	9%	735 ms	750 ms	15 ms	2%
demo4	661 ms	758 ms	96 ms	15%	546 ms	536 ms	-10 ms	2%	495 ms	473 ms	-22 ms	4%
demo5	2058 ms	2057 ms	-1 ms	0%	1841 ms	2123 ms	282 ms	15%	2045 ms	2131 ms	86 ms	4%
demo6	1482 ms	1702 ms	220 ms	15%	1503 ms	1719 ms	216 ms	14%	1356 ms	1633 ms	277 ms	20%

Figure 5.32.: Validation results

In Figure 5.32 we show the results for the twelve validation screens. The average relative prediction error across all screens and browsers is 10% (i.e., an average absolute prediction error of 82 ms). For 88% of the predictions, the relative prediction error is less than 15% and there is no real outlier with an error higher than 30%. The prediction accuracy is similar between all three investigated browsers (between 9% and 11% average error). Also between the two applications, we could not observe a general difference with respect to prediction accuracy (average relative prediction errors are 9% for Networking Lunch and 10% for the Demo Application).

For the screen *demo6*, we overestimate the CPU time in all three browsers relatively high. The same is true for screen *demo5* in the Firefox browser. These overestimations are most likely caused by the estimation function for the OData service calls as these contribute largely to the estimated overall CPU time for these screens. Hence, in order to further improve the prediction accuracy of the performance model, we could run further experiments to improve the regression function for OData calls. For the screen *nwlunch1*, we also overestimate the CPU time in Chrome and Firefox, which in this case is caused by the image predictions. Again, more training data can help to improve these predictions in the future. However, in general the predictions are very accurate and we do not tend towards a general over- or underestimation. We assume that the prediction errors are in most cases cÂ´caused by the statistical nature of the measurement results.

5.4. Discussion of Results

Based on the results and experiences gathered through the execution of the industrial case study, we discuss in the following the questions stated at the beginning of this chapter.

Can we derive an accurate performance model that solves a real-world problem? The models that we derived for the front-end performance prediction in three different browsers, have an average relative prediction error of 10% which can be considered as very accurate (see also Section 5.3.3 for a detailed discussion of the model accuracy). Having these models allows SAP to solve the problem that UI developers or designers create web application screens without being aware of the influence of their design decisions on front-end performance. The existing approach to deal with this problem is that developers have to measure the front-end performance of their implemented screens in order to ensure that the design meets SAP's performance requirements. However, this approach has several disadvantages:

- Measuring each screen causes a lot of overhead to the already tight schedules in software development projects. Especially if developers are not familiar with performance measurement tools and practices, the overhead is too large and the screens are only rarely tested for performance.

- If a performance problem is caused by an inappropriate design of the screen, the costs for fixing the problem in late development cycles can be very high. It might be necessary to change the implementation of multiple screens to solve an issue while still providing the same functionality or information.

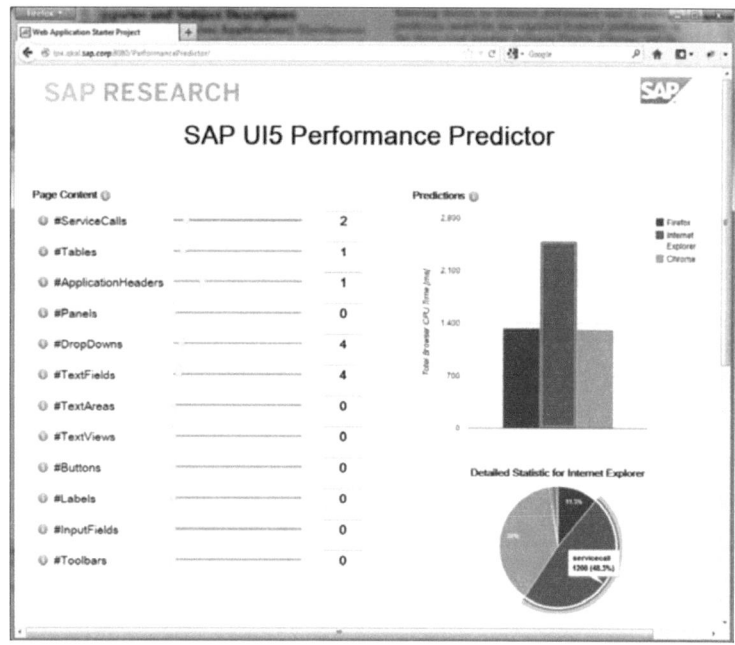

Figure 5.33.: Front-end performance prediction tool

We identified two ways how UI developers can leverage the results provided by the models to create responsive web application screens with only very limited overhead. The first way is through a web application that allows to easily evaluate the front-end performance of different design alternatives. Figure 5.33 shows a screenshot of the web-based prediction tool.

Using the web interface, developers can provide the intended design of a screen and get a prediction of the expected front-end performance for the three major browsers. It is also possible to get a detailed pie chart for each browser that shows which UI elements and UI element configurations contribute the most to the eventually bad performance. The web application is hosted internally and provides an easy acccssible means for developers of SAP UI5 based web application screens to assess if their screen design meets SAP's performancc requirements. Moreover, it is used in developer trainings at SAP in order to increase the performance awareness of developers.

The second way of using our performance models at SAP is the integration of performance predictions in the SAP UI5 UI editor tooling. The tool call SAP UI5 App Designer is a „what you see is what you get"editor for the development of SAP UI5 based web applications. The predictions can be integrated into the tool so that the developers get an alert if their design does not meet the performance requirements.

We believe that the application of our performance models in the two presented ways will improve the front-end performance of SAP's SAP UI5 based web application screens. However, only an empirical study, which is out of the scope of this thesis, could validate this causal relationship.

What are the efforts to apply the approach in a real-world scenario? The industrial case study that has been presented in this chapter shows that it is possible to derive an accurate performance model to predict the front-end performance of web application screens. In the following we discuss the efforts necessary to implement the approach, i.e., to create and maintain the performance models. These efforts are the metric that we use derive a conclusion for the practical applicability. Although we did not conduct a controlled experiment to track the actual efforts, we can provide rough estimates that allows the reader to classify the necessary efforts.

In the following, we discuss the efforts necessary to implement the different usage variants outlined in Table 5.9. To provide rough estimates on the efforts, we assign to each variant whether its implementation is a matter of days, weeks or moths.

ID	Variant	Effort
V1	Creating a model for a further UI library.	months
V2	Creating a model for a further device.	weeks
V3	Creating a model for a further browser.	weeks
V4	Updating the model for a new library version	days
V5	Updating the model for a new browser version	days

Table 5.9.: Usage variants

V1: Creating a performance model for a further UI library. Often, software development organisations use multiple libraries for the development of web application screens. Extending the measurement environment to support a new library requires already much less efforts than creating a performance model for a completely new scenario. Most parts of the measurement environment can be reused (e.g. devices and measurement tooling). Also many experiment definitions can be reused and automatically executed for the new library. The largest efforts in that variant is the adjustment of the screen generator for the new library and the verification if the assumptions and heuristics defined for library A are also true for library B.

V2: Creating a performance model for a further device. Web applications have to run on multiple devices with different characteristics (e.g. desktop, laptop, or tablet). When testing the front-end performance of a web application, different client setups should be considered. If a performance model has to be derived for a new device, one main effort is the installation of the measurement tooling and the preparation of the device to minimize factors that disturb measurements (e.g. killing unnecessary processes, configuring browsers). All the experiment definitions can be reused and executed automatically. In some cases it might be necessary to adjust the domains of some parameters due to the changed hardware capabilities.

Another main effort is again the verification if the assumptions and heuristics also hold for the new device.

V3: Creating a performance model for a further browser. If a performance model should be derived for a new browser, the measurement environment has to be extended in order to support the new browser (e.g. automatically control the browser via Selenium, disable all disturbing browser configurations). While all the experiment definitions can be reused and executed automatically, the assumptions and heuristics have to be verified for the new browser.

V4: Updating a performance model for a new library version. If the version of the UI library for which a performance model has already been derived is updated, performance analysts can simply rerun all experiments and test if the assumptions and heuristics are still valid. In case the library update includes new UI elements or new configuration options, the screen generator has to be extended and the corresponding experiments have to be defined or updated. As a side effect, the experiments can also identify performance regressions introduced by library changes. In cases where the library is developed in-house (such as the SAP UI5 library at SAP), this is another benefit of the approach that justifies the efforts.

V5: Updating a performance model for a new browser version. Besides the updates caused by new library versions (V5), an update due to a new browser version is one of the most frequently occurring task. As with V5, the manual efforts required to perform this task is kept at a minimum by our approach. Performance analysts can simply rerun the defined experiments and verify if the assumptions and heuristics are still valid.

In summary, creating an initial performance model for a scenario requires some effort. However, as this effort is mainly in understanding the performance behaviour of the system it is in most cases well worth to be spent. Moreover, our approach shifts the efforts to a small team of performance analysts and domain experts while the large bulk of developers can just leverage the results to evaluate performance with nearly no effort. A big problem of most existing performance modelling approaches is the large effort to maintain the models and update them due to frequent system changes. In our approach, a model update is mainly automatically conducted by simply rerunning the predefined experiments which has been a major argument for the performance analysts at SAP to apply the approach in future. In general, the fact that our measurement-based approach is close to the existing practice increased the acceptance and trust among practitioners. As the performance analysts at SAP are going to adopt the approach for their daily work, we conclude that the approach is efficient enough to be applied in practice.

5.5. Threats to Validity

The results presented in Section 5.4 demonstrate that our approach can accurately predict the front-end performance of enterprise web applications and is efficient enough to be applied in practice. However, it is important to note the threats to validity of our approach in order to understand its applicability.

5.5.1. Internal Validity

The selection of the case study was given by the context in which the thesis has been conducted. The author of the thesis has been employed by the research department of SAP and the case study has been initiated by a trigger from SAP's performance analysts team that identified the need to support UI developers and designers in assessing the performance effect of their screen designs. Moreover, the author of the approach has been part of the team that executed the case study which can affect the quality of the results in a positive way (Experimenters Bias).

5.5.2. External Validity

Small Validation Set   The screens evaluated in Section 5.3.3 are only part of two web applications. Both are very different in type and front-end performance. One represents a typical enterprise web application for processing data, the other a social enterprise application. Even though the predictions complied to measurement for the presented web applications, a broader set of validation scenarios is required, to ensure its general applicability.

Custom JavaScript Code   Our prediction focuses on the influence of UI elements and service calls on front-end performance. This is a reasonable assumption for typical enterprise applications. However, developers often add custom JavaScript code to process data, to create new controls or to change configuration. This custom code will add to the browser CPU time and thus to front-end performance. While such custom code played only a minor role in the web applications used for our model validation, it may have huge effects on front-end performance in other cases. However, our goal is to give early feedback on front-end performance, thus, we cannot consider such effects in our prediction.

Single Library   In our industrial case study at SAP, developers of web applications usually use only the SAP UI5 library to build a web application front-end. The library encapsulates other common JavaScript libraries. In other development environments, especially non-enterprise web application development, it is often the case that multiple libraries are combined to develop the front-end code. Moreover, additional style definitions can affect front-end performance in standard web sites [Sou07] which could have been neglected for the enterprise web applications developed with the SAP UI5 library and the corresponding pre-defined styles.

195

No All-in-One Solution The purpose of the performance model derived in the course of the case study is to help designers and developers of SAP UI5 based web application screens to assess the effect of different design alternatives prior to implementation. However, the approach is no replacement for continuous performance tests to measure and evaluate the actual performance of an application and avoid common performance problems such as those described by Souders [Sou07, Sou09].

5.6. Summary and Contributions

In this chapter, we presented an industrial case study that we conducted at SAP. In the case study, we applied our approach to derive a goal-oriented performance model for predicting the front-end performance of SAPUI5-based web applications. The derived performance models supports hundreds of UI designers and developers at SAP in building responsive screens. Hence, we showed that performance analysts can derive a performance model that solves a real-world problem using our approach. The average relative prediction error of the derived performance model was below 10%. Due to the automatically executable experiments, our approach requires only limited manual effort for updating a performance model to system changes.

In summary, the contributions of this chapter are

- An industrial experience report on applying the approach introduced in this thesis including a discussion of model accuracy and modelling efforts.

- A performance model for front-end performance predictions that allows developers and designers of enterprise web applications to assess the effect of different UI design alternatives on front-end performance prior to implementation.

6. Related Work

In this chapter, we present related research work in the field of software performance engineering [SW01, Smi07, WFP07]. Our approach contributes to two main areas:

1. measurement-based performance evaluation (Section 6.1), and

2. combining measurements with performance modelling (Section 6.2).

Accordingly, we group the related approaches discussed in this chapter. For each group of related work, we define a set of criteria based on which we classify the existing approaches and outline the distinction to the approach presented in this thesis.

6.1. Measurement-based Performance Evaluation

In this section, we discuss state of the art approaches in the field of measurement-based performance evaluation that are related to our work presented in Chapter 4. Section 6.1.1 focuses on approaches that support experimental performance evaluation. In Section 6.1.2 we present approaches that apply statistical inference methods to evaluate the performance of software systems.

6.1.1. Experimental Performance Evaluation

The need for a systematic and holistic performance evaluation process has been first described by Raj Jain in his book about the art of computer systems performance analysis [Jai91]. Jain emphasizes that proper experimental designs can help to reduce analysis costs and introduces a systematic process. Similar process definitions have been introduced by Smith and Williams [SW01] and Menasce and Almeida [MA01]. In the following, we discuss research approaches that deal with supporting the practical implementation of such systematic processes by providing proper frameworks, tools and methodologies for experimental performance evaluation.

Table 6.1 provides an overview on the discussed approaches by classifying them based on the following criteria:

- [ExpDef] Indicates if the approach provides a means to define experiments in a standardized way.

- [Auto] Indicates if the approach supports the automated execution of experiments.

- [FlexDes] Indicates if the approach allows performance analysts to flexibly add new experimental designs.

- [Indep] Indicates if the approach is independent of a concrete technology or scenario.

In summary, none of the related approaches outlined in Table 6.1 can be classified in the same way like the SoPeCo approach presented in Chapter 4 of this thesis. To the best of our knowledge we are the first that enable the flexible introduction of experimental designs for automated experiment executions in a wide range of scenarios.

In the following, we provide a description of the approaches listed in Table 6.1.

Thakkar et al. [THHF08] provide a conceptual description of a framework that aims at supporting performance analysts in deriving measurement-based performance models. The authors describe seven steps that are to be executed by the performance analyst in the lifecycle of measurement-

Approaches	ExpDef	Auto	FlexDes	Indep
Thakkar [THHF08]	✗	✓	✗	✓
Woodside [WVCB01], Vetland [VW97]	✓	✓	✗	✓
Prodan [PF05, PF04]	✓	✓	✗	✗
Abramson [ASGH95, AGK00]	✓	✓	✗	✗
Ioannidis [ILGP96]	✓	✗	✗	✓
Jung [JPS07]	✗	✓	✗	✗
Miller [MCC+95], Karavanic [KM97]	✓	✓	✗	✗
Hauck [HKHR11]	✓	✓	✗	✗
Worringen [Wor05]	✓	✓	✗	✗

Table 6.1.: Related work for experimental performance evaluations

based performance modelling: test enumeration, test reduction, environment setup, test execution, test transition, test analysis, and model building. In order to reduce the required number of actually needed test runs the authors suggest to use domain knowledge or statistical analyses technique s such as Main Screen Analysis [YKM+05] and two-way ANOVA [SM05]. Moreover, the authors highlight the need for application-specific extensibility. The authors also estimate the effort necessary to customize the framework to for other applications. However, the authors remain open how to design such a framework and how their solution can be actually customized to other applications. Moreover, the approach does not consider the formal definition of experiments.

Woodside et al. [WVCB01] and Vetland et al. [VW97] describe a workbench that supports the automated execution of experiments to derive resource functions. A resource function describes the demands of a software component with respect to the infrastructure that runs it, in dependence of the configuration and the usage of the component. The authors use the resource functions to parametrise performance models. The workbench allows performance analysts to define experiments based on a simple language. Parameter variations can be, for example, specified in a list or in a sequence. The workbench also executes the experiments automatically by calling test scripts that trigger the measurement tools and the system under test. Finally, the results are stored in a central repository and a function fitting component derives the resource functions from the measured data. However, the approach lacks the capability to introduce experimental designs that optimize the trade-off between the number of experiments and the accuracy of the resource function. Moreover, the workbench does not provide the capabilities to add custom parameter types, parameter variations, or analysis methods.

ZEN [PF05] is a directive based experiment specification language that aims at supporting performance analysts in specifying and controlling the execution of large number of experiments. ZEN defines four types of directives. Substitute and assignment directives for the flexible specification of parameter values through string substitution semantics or value assignments, respectively. Constraint directives to restrict the number of experiments and thus define the experimental design, and performance behaviour directives to specify the performance metrics that are to be observed in an experiment. The authors also provide an experiment management system called ZENTURIO [PF04] that employs the ZEN language for performance studies of parallel applications on cluster and grid architectures. The drawback of such a directive-based language is that the experiment metainformation is defined in the application source code. This limits the scope to studies where the source code is (i) available and (ii) easy to compile and deploy, as for every experiment a recompilation and redeployment is necessary. Moreover, the reusability of experiment definitions is limited.

Nimrod [ASGH95] and its successor Nimrod/G [AGK00] are tools that allow performance analysts to perform parametrised simulations over networks of loosely coupled workstations. Performance analysts describe experiments in a declarative plan file that is then used to run experiments in parallel on a grid environment. The corresponding specification language allows to define input parameters and different types of value assignments (such as value ranges). However, the language also includes parts that are very specific to the execution of simulation models in grid environments. Moreover, the tool does not support the definition of experimental designs and data analysis methods that allow for more sophisticated experiment selection strategies.

Ioannidis et al. [ILGP96] introduced an experiment management environment called ZOO. Although the authors mainly developed the tool for the physical and life sciences domain, they report on the very similar life-cycle of experimental studies in different domains. And indeed, the architecture of their approach is very close to the architecture described in this work. With respect to the experiment specification language, Ioannidis et al. introduce a meta-schema that has to be used by a scientist to create a schema for the experiment. It allows scientists to define parameters, parameter values and relationships between parameters. However, the language lacks features to describe properties for the automated control of experiments such as experimental designs and analysis methods.

In [JPS07], Jung et al. introduce an approach for the automatic instrumentation of applications called Mulini that is based on AOP and code generation techniques. They weave non-functional specifications into staging implementations in order to explore large configuration parameter spaces. They apply their approach to bottleneck detection of a reference application called RUBiS [OW209]. Mulini automatically monitors, collects, and analyses a significant number of performance metrics in iterative staging executions. For the bottleneck detection scenario, multiple tools and software have been integrated, many different performance metrics have been measured, and a large number of staging trials with changes of configuration parameters has been executed. To achieve this, they used Mulini to generate the necessary workload drivers, monitors and deployment scripts and to connect to monitoring utilities. While the approach of Jung et al. allows the collection of large amounts of data and the evaluation of the influence of different parameters, the authors neither perform any further analysis on the collected data (such as symbolic regression or machine learning techniques) nor do they optimise the number of required measurements using sophisticated experimental designs.

Hauck et al. [HKHR11] provide an infrastructure for the definition and execution of experiments that aim at deriving performance-relevant properties and behaviours of the runtime environment of an application (e.g. operating system or virtualisation software). The authors use the results of the measurements to enhance an existing architecture-based performance model [BKR09]. Their approach, called Ginpex, includes a meta-model that allows performance analysts to define experiments and a set of predefined experiment templates based on which executable experiment applications are generated. These experiment applications conduct automated performance measurements that automatically detect and quantify the performance-relevant parameters of the runtime environment. Unlike our approach, Hauck et al. focus on a very specific scenario. Moreover, the experiment definition is closely coupled with the measurement environment.

Miller et al. [MCC$^+$95] propose Paradyn, a tool for the automatic diagnoses of performance problems. They apply dynamic instrumentation to control the instrumentation in search of performance problems. Paradyn starts looking for high-level problems for a whole application and, once the general problem is found, inserts further instrumentations to find more specific causes. Karavanic and Miller [KM97] developed an experiment management system for their work on performance problem diagnosis based on different executions over the lifetime of an application. The authors introduce a language that allows to specify the parameters that characterize an execution in a *Program Event*. However, Karavanic and Miller focus on the detection of performance problems from execution traces and do not measure parameter spaces systematically.

Worringen [Wor05] also introduced an approach to manage and analyse the results of experiment executions. The tool called perfbase supports the definition of experiments in an XML file that conforms to a perfbase-specific document type definition (DTD). The DTD allows performance analysts to specify experiment meta-information, like the analysts name and data usage restrictions, as well as a description of parameters and their types. However, as the goal of the approach is to extract experiment information from past executions in order to search for performance problems in the historical data, the tool lacks capabilities to define parameter value variations and experimental designs for the systematic control and execution of experiments.

6.1.2. Function Inference

Inferring functional relationships from measured data using statistical analyses and machine learning techniques is a commonly applied methodology in a variety of disciplines [HTF09]. In the following, we present and classify research approaches that deal with inferring functional relationships between the configuration and workload parameters of a software system and a performance metric of interest (i.e., response time, throughput, or resource utilisation). To classify the approaches, we apply the following criteria:

- [ConExp] Indicates if the approach uses controlled experiments to derive the measurement data used for the function inference, i.e., if the configuration and workload parameters are varied in a systematic way.

- [MultDim] Indicates if the approach supports the inference of multi-dimensional functions.

- [Opt] Indicates if the approach supports optimizing the trade-off between the number of measurement points and the accuracy of the inferred function.

- [Assump] Indicates to what extend the approach requires assumptions on the kind of functional dependency (e.g. it being linear).

Table 6.2 provides an overview on the related research presented in this section.

Approaches	ConExp	MultDim	Opt	Assump
Courtois [CW00]	✓	✓	✓	few
Reussner [RSPM98]	✓	✗	✓	many
Wang [WAA+04]	✗	✓	✗	few
Nadeem [NYPF06]	✓	✓	✓	many
Pacifici [PSST06]	✗	✓	✗	many
Kraft [KPSCD09]	✓	✓	✗	many

Table 6.2.: Related work for measurement-based function inference

Two of the presented approaches formed the starting point for our research, and influenced the methodologies presented in Chapter 4.4.2. One of them is the approach introduced by Courtois and Woodside [CW00], the other one is the approach introduced by Reussner et al. [RSPM98]. The approach of Courtois and Woodside is also the only one that can be classified in the same way as our approach. In the following, we give a detailed presentation of the two foundational approaches as well as other related research.

Courtois and Woodside [CW00] highlight the need for sophisticated experimental designs to automatically infer performance prediction functions. The goal of their research is to derive the resource demands of a software component by systematically measuring performance metrics in dependence of configuration and input parameters. The authors provide examples where simple linear regression techniques are not sufficient to model the performance behaviour measured in a real software system. In order to fit such complex functions without human intervention, they use their experiment automation workbench [WVCB01] in combination with the Multivariate Adaptive Regression Splines (MARS) [Fri91] method. Moreover, Courtois and Woodside introduce a heuristic calculation for the accuracy of the resource function that is based on a measure provided by MARS as well as a heuristic strategy to select new experiments with the goal to get a resource function with a certain target accuracy using as few experiments as possible. The accuracy and the robustness that can be achieved by the approach is demonstrated in two case studies. The methodology allows performance analysts to automatically fit non-linear and even discontinuous functions while considering the trade-off between the number of experiments and the accuracy of the prediction model. The promising results described by Courtois and Woodside motivated the research presented in this thesis. In our work, we extended their research by providing a means to flexibly combine different strategies for the automated and iterative experiment selection, function inference and function validation.

Reussner et al. [RSPM98] introduce an approach to benchmark and compare different OpenMPI implementations. Their approach combines performance metrics with linear interpolation techniques to assess the implementation's overall performance behaviour. To maximise the information gain of subsequent experiments, they identify those points with the (potentially) largest error in the current prediction model. While this approach presents another starting point for our work, it is limited to the evaluation of a single parameter and simple linear interpolation techniques that are not suited for multi-dimensional scattered data.

Wang et al. [WAA$^+$04] predict the performance of storage devices based on functions that they derived using the Classification and Regression Tree (CART) [HTF09] method. The approach allows to predict the performance of a device depending on the input workload and does not require any knowledge of the device internals. The input workload is described by four parameters: arrival time, logical block number, request size in number of disk blocks, and read write type. To train the CART model the authors used a set of real-world traces. Hence, the input parameters are not varied systematically. In the presented case study the approach yields models with a median relative prediction error between 15% and 47%. The authors conclude that the training workloads play a critical role in model accuracy and highlighted the need for proper synthetic workload generation techniques. Due to the promising results presented by Wang et al. and the fact that CART does not require assumptions on the underlying functional relationship, we decided to include CART in the list of methods for our function inference approach.

An approach for the prediction of application execution times in grid environments has been introduced by Nadeem et al. [NYPF06]. The predictions are used to support decision making with respect to the efficient usage of grid resources. The authors introduce an experimental design that allows to extrapolate the prediction function derived on a single grid resource to other grid resources. First, one experiment is executed on each grid resource. Then, the fastest grid resource is chosen and a full factorial design with all performance-relevant input parameter values of the application is executed on this basis resource. The resulting measurement data is used as the training set for the predictions. To minimize the number of experiments, the approach normalizes the performance behaviour derived on the basis resource and assumes that the normalized performance behaviour of an application for different input parameter values on different grid resources are similar. Based on this assumption the training data for other grid resources is simply calculated. The actual prediction is conducted via a lookup in the training data or an estimation based on the nearest reference value. The optimisation of the number of experiments that are to be executed is very specific to grid environments. The authors do not try to minimize the number of experiments necessary to derive a proper training set for prediction the application performance on a single grid resource.

Pacifici et al. [PSST06] introduce an approach for dynamic estimation of resource demands by analysing multiple kinds of web traffic using CPU utilisation and throughput measurements. They formulate and solve the problem using linear regressions. In order to deal with practical issues that lead to unstable measurement data (e.g. insignificant flows, colinear flows, background noise), the authors introduce mechanism like flow rejection, flow combining, noise reduction and smoothing. The technique produces estimates with an accuracy of factor 2. However, the approach aims at fitting resource demands dynamically from data observed at system runtime and thus differs significantly from the systematic experimental function inference proposed in this thesis. The challenges that are to be solved by the approach of Pacifici et al. are rather on how to prepare existing data for optimal function fitting than on systematically finding a minimal set of measurement points for fitting a function with a certain accuracy target.

The approach presented by Kraft et al. [KPSCD09], deals with the problem of determining resource demand functions for system where utilisation measurement is difficult or unreliable, for example virtualised systems or third-party services. They apply a linear regression method and the maximum likelihood technique for estimating resource demands of different workload classes based on response time measurements. While especially the Maximum Likelihood methodology provided robust accurate results in multiple scenarios, the approach requires assumption on scheduling strategies and the general form of the distribution before starting the estimation activity. Furthermore, the authors do not consider the trade-off between the number of measurements and the accuracy of the estimation.

6.2. Performance Prediction Models

The use of performance prediction models to assess the performance behaviour of a software system has been established by Connie Smith under
the term Software Performance Engineering (SPE) [Smi81, Smi82]. Since
then a lot of research has been conducted in this field and several authors
surveyed the progress and defined outstanding problems [Smi86, UH97,
Poo00, Smi01, DRSS01, BDIS04]. The most recent overviews are provided by Woodside et. al [WFP07], Smith [Smi07], and Koziolek [Koz10].
A common conclusion is that although the modelling methods and tools
have evolved and it has been proven that the resulting models can provide accurate predictions for real-world software systems, there is a need to
„[...] make SPE more accessible to software developers rather than requiring modelling gurus, and to make SPE more likely to be adopted and used
in development organisations." [Smi07]. Woodside et al. [WFP07] highlight the need for a convergence between measurement-based and model-
based approaches towards more practicable and maintainable performance
prediction models. Our approach aims at filling this gap between research
and practice or between measurement-based and model-based performance
evaluation, respectively. A main challenge with respect to practical scenarios is to find proper mechanisms for determining the performance behaviour of systems or parts of a system (e.g. legacy systems or third-party
components) that cannot be modelled formally (or only with large manual
effort). In the following, we focus on discussing performance prediction
approaches that also apply measurement-based techniques to reduce the
manual modelling effort. A more general discussion of model-based approaches is provided by Balsamo et al. [BDIS04] and Koziolek [Koz10].
To classify the approaches we use the following criteria (see also the research challenges outlined in Chapter 3.1):

- [ProcDef] Indicates if the approach contains a process definition
  that guides practitioners through the modelling process.

- [ModExist] Indicates if the approach addresses the problem of efficiently modelling already existing software systems.

- [Maint] Indicates if the approach addresses the problem of efficiently maintaining performance models of existing software systems that are subject to frequent changes.

- [ToolInd] Indicates if the approach is independent of a certain type of modelling tool or technique.

- [ScenInd] Indicates if the approach is independent of a specific scenario.

Table 6.3 gives an overview on the approaches that are discussed in this section. In general, none of the approaches can be classified in the same way as the approach presented in this thesis. The approach introduced by Avritzer et al. [AW04] is the most related as it proposes a similar procedure for constructing performance models in practice. In the following, we provide a detailed discussion of the related works.

Avritzer and Weyuker [AW04] present an approach that uses performance measurement results to build a simulation model for performance prediction. The introduced process suggests a goal-oriented modelling approach. Based on systematic measurements potential bottlenecks are identified and the according performance-relevant parameters are defined. To construct the prediction model, the authors propose the use of state transition diagrams [CD94] for modelling the software system. The resulting state transition models are then automatically transferred in a simulation model. The basic process defined by the authors is similar to the process introduced in this thesis. The work presented in this thesis could be used to support the performance analyst in conducting the measurement required to build the simulation model in the process defined by Avritzer and Weyuker. However, in complex software systems it might be hard for performance analysts to create and maintain the manually constructed state transition diagrams.

Approaches	ProcDef	ModExist	Maint	ModInd	ScenInd
Avritzer [AW04]	✓	✓	✓	✗	✓
Jin [JTHL07]	✓	✗	✓	✓	✓
Wu [WW08]	✓	✗	✓	✓	✓
Krogmann [KKR10]	✓	✓	✗	✗	✗
Mos [MM02]	✓	✗	✓	✗	✗
Sandeep [SSN$^+$08]	✗	✓	✓	✗	✗
Thereska [TDZN10]	✗	✓	✓	✗	✗
Tariq [TZV$^+$08]	✓	✓	✓	✗	✗

Table 6.3.: Related work for performance prediction models

Jin et al. [JTHL07] introduce an approach called BMM that combines benchmarking, production system monitoring, and performance modelling. Their goal is to predict the performance characteristics of real-world legacy systems that are subject to exorbitant growth. In the planning phase of the presented process, the performance analyst has to identify the factors that affect the applications' performance. Moreover, the performance analyst has to select a proper modelling method (e.g. analytical or simulation) and build the model. Then, to calibrate the model goal-oriented production system monitoring and test system benchmarking is conducted and the measured results are correlated. The correlation aims at validating the measured data and removing or normalising data peculiarity. After that, the model is validated in an iterative process until a sufficient accuracy has been reached. While the approach supports performance analysts in properly calibrating an existing performance model during system evolution, it still requires the upfront definition of a performance model. Therefore, the approach could be complemented by the approach presented in this thesis in order to further reduce the manual efforts in building prediction models for already existing software.

Wu and Woodside [WW08] present an approach similar to Jin et al. [JTHL07] aiming at calibrating existing performance models while the system evolves. The work of Wu and Woodside specifically deals with two problems. The first is estimating service demands that cannot be measured directly. The authors propose the use of Kalman Filters [Jaz70], to estimate such hidden parameters. The second problem is to decide automatically when a model is properly calibrated. To solve this issue they introduce an extended version of a Kalman Filter that controls the model calibration loop and stops when a certain condition is satisfied. However, as with the model calibration approach of Jin et al. [JTHL07], the performance analyst is not supported in building the initial model of the existing software system.

Krogmann et al [KKR10] introduce an approach that uses a genetic search algorithm to reverse engineer architecture-based performance models from existing source code. The reverse engineered performance models are instances of the Palladio Component Models (PCM) [BKR09] and aim at supporting software architects in their design decisions (e.g. by estimating the impact of using caches on performance). The approach uses benchmarks to characterize the performance behaviour of different runtime environments so that a single performance model can be used to predict the performance on different runtime environments. To map the runtime environment capabilities with the resource demands of the software components, Krogmann et al. use bytecode analysis. The benchmark that is executed on the runtime environment determines the performance of Java bytecode instructions. To determine the resource demands of the existing application components they use symbolic execution and a tool called By-Counter [KKR08] that identifies the bytecode instructions executed by the component. While the authors validated that the approach can provide accurate predictions, it is limited to Java-based applications and not suitable for heterogeneous environments. Furthermore, deriving and maintaining the models for large software systems can require large manual efforts.

Mos and Murphy [MM02] introduce the COMPAS framework which targets the identification of performance issues in component based software systems. COMPAS is based on three modules. A monitoring module captures performance data by inserting proxy components into the architecture of the target system. The gathered data is then used by a modelling module that builds various UML models. These models are further enhanced by a performance prediction module that allows to simulate and analyse the models. Based on this approach, Parsons and Murphy [PM08] built a framework for the detection of performance anti-patterns in component based systems. In addition to the COMPAS framework, they use byte code analysis as monitoring technique. Although the approach simplifies the model building process, it is focused on component-based applications that are developed from scratch using a rather homogeneous technology stack such as the Java Enterprise Edition platform [Ora13]. Hence, porting the approach to a different scenario requires a lot of effort. Moreover, the derived performance models can become very large and thus hard to calibrate and maintain in a real-world environment.

The CLUEBOX toolkit introduced by Sandeep et al. [SSN+08] supports performance analysts in deriving performance prediction models by only analysing performance log data gathered at runtime. The authors apply several machine learning techniques (e.g. Principal Feature Analysis [LCZT07] and Random Forest [Bre01]) on runtime logs to derive the performance-relevant parameters and the prediction model. Moreover, the approach aims at reducing the effort for system administrators to identify the root-cause of a performance anomaly. However, as the target scenario of this approach is early performance anomaly detection on productive systems, it lacks capabilities to create performance models that support, for example, software architects or software developers in proactively evaluating design decisions.

Thereska et al. [TDZN10] present an approach that uses data gathered from a large set of client installations to create a performance model. The goal of the model is to help answering what-if performance questions with respect to a reconfiguration of a client system (e.g. upgrading from Windows Vista to Windows 7 or doubling the amount of memory). To create the models the authors apply the Classification and Regression Tree (CART) [HTF09] technique in combination with a similarity search algorithm. The CART model is trained with the large data set gathered from Microsoft client installations. This is also the major limitation of this approach, as it is only applicable on popular applications that are installed on many observable client systems with different configurations.

Another approach that aims at creating performance models for answering what-if deployment and configuration questions is introduced by Tariq et al. [TZV+08]. Their performance prediction tool called WISE includes an algorithm that learns the functional dependencies between performance-relevant parameters and service response times and represents these dependencies in a Causal Bayesian Network (CBN) [Pea00]. The training data is derived from traces that are obtained from existing installations. Moreover, WISE provides a simple query interface that allows to describe what-if question based on their scenario specification language. While WISE is applicable to a larger set of scenarios than the approach introduced by Thereska et al. [TDZN10]., it also lacks the capabilities to build prediction models in scenarios where the runtime data is not available or not sufficient.

6.3. Summary

In this chapter, we introduced research that is closely related to the approach presented in this thesis. We introduced the state of the art regarding (i) measurement-based performance evaluation and (ii) performance modelling in combination with measurements.

In the field of measurement-based performance evaluation, we presented approaches that showed the value of systematic, experimental processes and the importance of an appropriate experiment specification language for a specific domain. However, none of the presented approaches enables the flexible introduction of experimental designs for automated experiment executions independent of the concrete scenario. Hence, the experiment specification language and the corresponding framework presented in Chapter 4 extend the state of the art presented in this chapter. Moreover, we introduced state of the art approaches with respect to the inference of performance prediction functions. Two of the presented approaches [RSPM98, CW00] formed the starting point for our research, and influenced the methodologies presented in Chapter 4. We extended this and the other related research work by systematically evaluating methodologies for the automated, iterative combination of experiment selection, statistical model inference, and model validation for the derivation of multidimensional performance prediction functions.

Out of the existing performance modelling approaches [BDIS04, Koz10], we discussed those approaches in detail that deal with evaluating and modelling performance of existing software systems. The main difference between our approach presented in Chapter 3 and the state of the art approaches is the abstraction level on which the models are derived. Existing approaches are in most cases extensions to classical architecture- or simulation-based performance modelling and thus are bound to the abstraction level and the capabilities of the underlying modelling techniques.

7. Conclusion

In this chapter, we conclude this thesis by summarising the main contributions and validation results in Section 7.1, describing the benefits for performance engineers, software developers and software development organisations in general (Section 7.2), and finally introducing ideas and directions for future work in Section 7.3.

7.1. Summary

In this thesis, we presented a method for experimental, measurement-based performance modelling. The implementation of the method required the definition, execution, and analysis of a large number of experiment series. In order to support performance engineers in conducting these tasks, we introduced (i) a language and a framework for the specification and execution of automatable experiment series and (ii) presented and compared different strategies for the automated, adaptive generation of experimental designs for statistical model inference. The accuracy and the efficiency of our approach has been validated in a number of case studies using standard industry benchmarks such as SAP Sales & Distribution [SAP12] and SPECjbb2005 [SPE05]. Furthermore, we demonstrated the applicability of our approach in a real-world scenario, where we derived a performance model that supports UI designers and developers at SAP in designing high-performance enterprise web application front-ends. In the following, we give a brief summary of the main contributions and validation results of our work.

A Method for Experimental, Measurement-based Performance Modelling We developed a performance modelling methodology that combines measurements with statistical modelling in an iterative, experimental process. In order to find a suitable abstraction level for the performance model, we proposed a goal-oriented specification procedure that adopts existing best practices[BCR94, Jai91, SW01, Hap08, Sin09, Rie11]. The actual modelling process allows performance engineers to efficiently derive and maintain performance models of complex software systems. Based on a well-defined test environment and a set of initial assumptions on performance-relevant influences, performance engineers start an iterative definition and execution of experiment series in order to understand and quantify all performance-relevant influences. Then, a performance model is derived using statistical model inference and extensively validated. In the scope of this thesis, we applied this method for the design of a performance model of SAP enterprise web application front-ends.

Language and Framework for the Specification and Execution of Automatable Experiment Series To support performance engineers in conducting large amounts of experiments, we developed a novel experiment specification language. In order to find a suitable abstraction level for the design of the language and to ensure that the language is independent of concrete domains, technologies or applications, we applied it across a wide-range of different scenarios. In addition to the language, we developed a framework that uses the specified experiment information to automate the execution of experiments and to iteratively combine experimental design and analysis.

Automated, Adaptive Generation of Experimental Designs for Statistical Model Inference The capabilities of the experiment specification language and the experiment automation framework introduced before, allowed us to develop and compare a set of strategies for the automated derivation of multidimensional performance prediction functions. We designed an iterative process that combines experiment selection, function inference and function validation in order to automatically derive experimental designs that optimize the trade-off between the number of executed experiments and the accuracy of multidimensional performance prediction functions. We validated the approach by applying the different combinations in two case studies using industry standard benchmarks (SAP Sales & Distribution, SPECjbb2005). In general, the best results have been achieved by the combination Adaptive Equidistant Breakdown (AEB) measurement point selection, Dynamic Sector validation with Global prediction error (DSG), and Multivariate Adaptive Regression Splines (MARS) model inference. The case studies have shown that our approach allows performance engineers to automatically derive performance prediction functions with a mean relative prediction error of less than 20% using only up to 10% of the potential measurement points.

Performance Model for Enterprise Web Application Front-ends

To demonstrate the applicability of the overall approach in an end-to-end case study, we derived a performance model for web application screens developed with the SAP UI5 JavaScript library. The industrial case study has been conducted in cooperation with performance analysts and development groups at SAP. We validated the accuracy of the performance model by comparing predictions to measurements for screens of two real-world enterprise web applications in three browsers (Internet Explorer, Firefox, and Chrome). The results show that the approach is applicable to a real world scenario and that the derived performance models can predict the front-end performance with an average prediction error of 11% across all studied browsers. Due to the automatically executable experiments, our approach requires only limited manual effort for updating a performance model to system changes (e.g. new versions of the browser or the UI library).

7.2. Benefits

The results of this thesis support three main roles: Performance Engineers, Software Architects/Developers, and Researchers. In the following, we describe how each of these roles benefits from our work.

Performance Engineers Our goal-oriented performance modelling method introduced in Chapter 3, helps performance engineers to focus their modelling effort on performance influences that are actually relevant for the consumers of the performance model (e.g. software architects or developers). The close upfront communication between performance engineers and model consumers makes it more likely that the models are actually adopted in the software development process. Moreover, it helps performance engineers in finding a suitable abstraction level for the performance models and thus in avoiding to model too many unnecessary details.

Compared to existing architecture-based modelling approaches, there is no need to re-engineer the internals of existing, complex software system (e.g. the rendering engines of different browsers). This can save a lot of effort for performance engineers when creating and maintaining performance models. Moreover, it allows performance engineers to build performance models even for those systems where information about the internal architecture and behaviour is not available at all (e.g. third-party software).

The experiment specification language as well as our framework to automate the execution of experiments presented in Chapter 4 support performance engineers in several ways. The clear separation between technical tasks, and the experimentation and analysis process allows performance engineers to focus on understanding the performance behaviour of the system. There is no need to write custom scripts to automate experiment execution or gather measurement data. Moreover, they can share experiment specifications and knowledge in order to create a performance knowledge base [WFP07].

Our methodology for automatically deriving experimental designs for fitting multi-dimensional performance prediction functions helps performance engineers in deriving more accurate functions with less effort and in less time. There is no need to manually select the data points used for function fitting. Such a manual selection often leads to either too many data points with little information gain or not enough data points in areas where the analysis method requires more information in order to fit an accurate model. The automated, iterative combination of experiment selection, function inference and function validation, introduced and validated in Chapter 4, reduces the probability of badly fitted areas and optimizes the trade-off between the number of experiments and accuracy of the prediction function.

Software Architects/Developers   Tailoring a performance model to the needs of the stakeholders that consume the the information provided by the model as suggested in Chapter 3, helps these stakeholders (usually software architects or developers) in getting the information they actually need in the granularity they need it. It also helps software developers to better understand the model output as well as the general value of having a performance model. Often, the use of performance models can significantly reduce the overhead for quality assurance which allows developers to design better software with less effort (see for example our case study presented in Chapter 5). Moreover, as performance models are usually applied in the design phase of a product, performance problems can be detected early, and thus are easier to fix.

Researchers   The framework that we introduced in Chapter 4 has been published as an open source project [WHW$^+$13]. Researchers in the performance engineering community frequently conduct measurements and analyses. Examples are case studies for their work, resource demand estimations for a modelling approach or running benchmarks to demonstrate scalability of a developed system. There are already common scenarios that are used by a wide range of researchers e.g. the SPEC benchmarks [SPE12], CoCoME [RRMP08] or the Dell DVD Store [JM11]. However, controlling and analyzing these scenarios is done by each researcher every time anew, although it is often the same procedure. If the components to control these scenarios (or any other kind of application) as well as components for data analysis and data exports would be available as part of an open source project, researchers could benefit from the work of others and save a lot of time when conducting measurements and thus focus on their actual research. Hence, we provide a platform for interested researchers to cooperate and share their work.

The flexible extensibility of our iterative approach for automatically fitting multidimensional performance prediction functions (see Chapter 4), allows researchers to compare different existing algorithms and analysis methods with minimal effort. Moreover, novel algorithms and analysis methods can be benchmarked against state of the art methodologies using the same scenario (e.g. as shown in [FH12]).

In general, our work provides new capabilities to develop novel performance engineering approaches that are based on executing large sets of experiment series. See Section 7.3 for a number of examples.

7.3. Future Work

In the following, we provide pointers for research extending the work conducted in this thesis.

Experimental Function Inference   In the scope of this thesis, we developed and compared a set of experiment selection algorithms and analysis methods for deriving multidimensional performance prediction functions. However, as this set is not complete, further algorithms and analysis methods can be developed and compared based on our work. Moreover, the different algorithm/analysis combinations should be applied to more case studies in order to get a better understanding on their suitability for different performance evaluation scenarios.

Performance-Aware Development of Web Application Screens
With respect to our case study presented in Chapter 5, we plan the following enhancements in future work. The derived performance model will be validated with more SAP UI5 based applications and possibly extended with additional performance-relevant UI elements. Moreover, the prediction function will be integrated in a web-based „what you see is what you get" editor for SAP UI5 based applications and thus rolled out to a larger group of developers. A future direction that requires more in-depth research is the extension of the front-end performance predictions towards an end-to-end performance feedback which includes network and back-end performance. Here, we might have to combine our measurement-based performance modelling approach with simulation- or architecture-based approaches.

Further Developer Feedback Scenarios In existing case studies, performance models are often used to evaluate architectural design decisions and thus, mainly targeting software architects in the design phase. However, as we have shown in our industrial case study, performance models can also be valuable during software development. At SAP an additional developer feedback scenario has already been initiated that follows the ideas presented in this thesis. There, the approach is applied to derive a performance model that predicts the response time of database queries based on the structure of the query and the size of the database. The model aims at providing immediate feedback to developers of database queries with respect to the expected performance characteristics of the query. In this context, several additional research challenges need to be solved. As an example, it is subject to research how to determine the workload that is to be used for model building as it has to be representative for a large set of applications. Another example that is subject to research is how the workload used for model building can be mapped to the workload that is provided by the developers as an input to the model.

A Generic Model For Developer Feedback Scenarios Once more experience in building performance models for developer feedback has been gathered, one can start to identify common objects and patterns across the scenarios and further simplify the performance model construction process of such scenarios. We envision a generic meta-model that allows performance engineers (in collaboration with domain experts) to formally describe different domains (e.g. web application UIs or database queries). This comprises the development artifact (e.g. a web page or a query) and its properties (e.g. the type of stylesheet or type of database connection), individual elements of an artifact (e.g. a button or select statement) and its properties (e.g. the maximum number of buttons on a page or the expected number of rows returned by a select query), the relationships between components (e.g. that tables or queries can be nested) as well as the properties of the relationship (e.g. the maximum nesting depth). Moreover, performance engineers can specify different execution platforms (e.g. the browser type or the database version) for which he or she wants to derive the prediction functions. Based on the resulting model instance, a set of standard experiment series can be derived by a model to model transformation. In these experiment series, it is checked which elements, relationships, and properties influence the performance metric of interest how the parameters interact with each other. The automated generation of experiment series definitions saves time and ensures that the most important aspects are considered by the performance engineer.

Industrial Experience Reports The goal-oriented specification of performance models prior to the actual modelling process (proposed in Chapter 3) has been derived based on our experience of applying performance modelling in an industrial context at SAP. Many industry reports from applying approaches like Design Thinking [Bro09] and The Lean Startup [Rie11] have shown that early and continuous hands-on discussions with target groups can increase the adoption of products and reduce development efforts. It would be interesting to see more industrial experience reports on how a goal-oriented procedure in the context of performance modelling can affect the adoption of the models among developers and the effort to create the models.

Combination with Architecture-based Performance Modelling

In some scenarios, it can be beneficial to combine our measurement-based modelling approach with existing architecture-based approaches like the Palladio Component Model (PCM) [BKR09]. In such approaches architectural models of a software system are annotated with performance-relevant information such as resource demands and branching probabilities. Then, the architectural models are transformed to analytical models, such as stochastic Petri nets, stochastic process algebras, and queueing models [BH07] or to discrete-event simulations [PK05, LB05].

For the integration of architecture-based and measurement-based performance analysis, we assume that some parts of the system are already available (for example, 3rd party services or software artefacts) and other parts are to be designed. Then, the performance analysis could follow the process shown in Figure 7.1.

Software architects specify the system's components, behaviour, deployment, and usage (*System Modelling*). This activity results in a *System Model* that describes the newly developed parts as well as its usage. In order to consider the effect of existing parts in performance analysis, we include them in the prediction model using the approach presented in this thesis. From a set of *Measurements*, we get *Performance Data* of the system which is used for *Model Inference*. The resulting statistical performance models

225

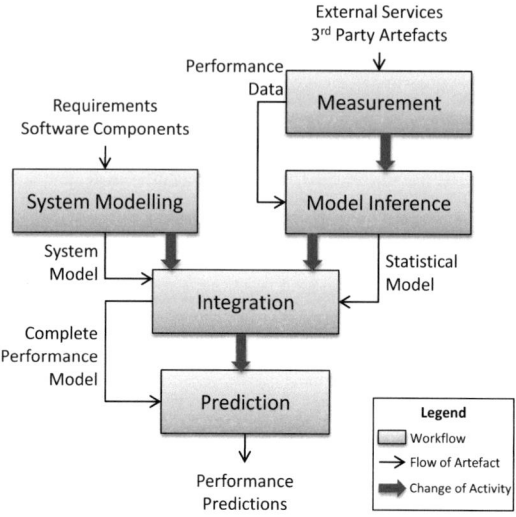

Figure 7.1.: Overview of integrating goal-oriented performance models with architecture-based approaches [WHW12]

have to be integrated with or made available in architecture-based prediction approaches (*Integration*). This step merges both model types and creates a common basis for further performance analysis (*Prediction*). Based on the *Performance Predictions*, software architects and performance analysts can then decide about design alternatives, plan capacities, or identify critical components.

The presented process has already been applied in two case studies which have been introduced in [HWSK10, WHW12]. A more detailed description of the technical integration is provided in [WHW12].

Exhaustive, Tailored Performance Regression Testing   The capability to efficiently define and run a large set of experiments, is also valuable for performance engineering tasks other than performance modelling. In performance regression testing, the probability of actually observing an issue as well as the effort for identifying its root cause is highly dependent on the number and quality of performance tests executed on a regular basis [HHF13]. Applying a systematic, experimental approach can help to increase the number and quality of performance regression test significantly. At SAP our approach has already been applied to conduct systematic performance regression tests for the persistence service of the SAP HANA Cloud platform [WWHM13]. Our experimental approach helps performance engineers to identify performance-critical test cases that can be automatically executed on a nightly basis. Figure 7.2 shows a performance regression that we observed after having the automated tailored experiments in place.

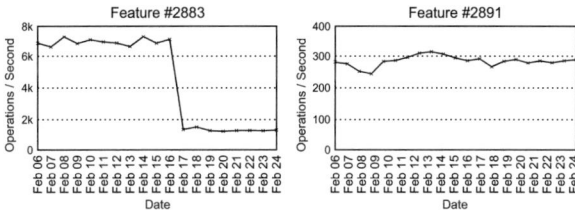

Figure 7.2.: Identified regression [WWHM13]

The graphs show the measured throughput for two experiments over a certain period of time. The experiment on the left side executes a named query that retrieves all instances of an entity in a certain data model. The experiment on the right side executes a query that stores a number of instances of the same entity to the database. The graph on the left side of Figure 7.2 shows that for this experiment a performance regression of factor 4 has been introduced. As the tests run on a nightly basis, we have been able to identify the root cause for the issue very quickly which happened to be an update of the database version that has been conducted at that day. An interesting observation is that the regression has only been observed in one test out of the set of experiments. The experiment shown on the right side of Figure 7.2 does, for example, not show a performance regression. This observation underlines the assumption that more and tailored performance tests increase the probability of detecting a performance issue. Moreover, knowing the exact conditions under which a problem occurs and under which not can be very helpful in fixing a performance issue.

Performance Problem Diagnosis   In scenarios where an existing software system already contains performance and scalability issues, performance models might not help to find the root cause of the problem. However, the capability of efficiently running a large set of systematic experiments supports approaches that target such scenarios. Wert et al. [WHH13, Wer13] introduce such an approach that uses the systematic experimentation capabilities presented in this thesis, in order to detect performance and scalability issues in existing software systems and identify the root cause. The approach is based on the observations that particular performance problems share common symptoms, and many performance problems described in literature are defined by a particular set of root causes [WHH13]. Based on a hierarchical structure of performance problems, their symptoms, and their root causes, the approach executes a series of systematic experiments that first test for symptoms and then search for more specific performance problems and their root cause.

Systematic Guidance in Solving Performance and Scalability Problems   The approach introduced by Heger [Heg13], applies the experimental, measurement-based performance modelling approach presented in this thesis in order to (i) evaluate different solutions to a given performance problem and (ii) recommend the best solution to a developer. The approach is illustrated by an example where a developer discovered a software performance bottleneck manifested in the resource pool for database connections [Heg13]. The known solutions of performance experts are (1) to increase the amount of resources available in the connection pool, (2) to replace the connection pool implementation, or (3) to reduce holding times of database connections. Based on a generic evaluation plan for each solution, a set of systematic experiment series are executed for the specific scenario. In these experiment series, the influence of connection pool parameters on performance is determined (1), prediction functions for alternative connection pool implementations are derived (2), and code statements that can be moved to reduce holding times are identified (3). Finally, the results of the experiments presented to developers which can make trade-off decisions if necessary.

A. Software Performance Cockpit

We developed a framework called Software Performance Cockpit (SoPeCo) [WHHH10, WH11, WHW+13] to implement the approach presented in this thesis. It allows performance engineers to define, execute and analyse experiment series very efficiently. Moreover, it is designed to be flexibly adapted to different performance evaluation scenarios and to flexibly add new experimental design and analysis strategies.

A.1. Motivation

Today's software often builds upon a large stack of runtime and middleware components. Examples are virtual machines, operating systems, or browsers, as well as application, messaging, or database servers. Moreover, applications run on different hardware like desktop PCs, laptops, or mobile devices. Thus, performance analysts have to assess data from various distributed locations and interfaces. Moreover, performance analysts can choose from a wide range of sophisticated tools for instrumenting and monitoring applications (e.g. Compuware dynaTrace [Com13] or NewRelic [New13]), as well as for simulating usage behaviour (e.g. HP LoadRunner [HP13] or Apache JMeter [Fou13]). As a result, test environments for performance evaluations are usually very heterogeneous. However, a performance analyst requires a unified view on the measurement data in order to analyse them properly. In general, having a common interface to control and monitor the components of any test environment, allows performance analysts to reuse automation and analysis strategies in different scenarios.

A.2. Goals

SoPeCo pursues the following goals:

- Automation: A typical performance evaluation project requires the execution of a large set of experiments. Manually triggering the measurements and gathering the measured data is very time-consuming and inefficient. Hence, SoPeCo aims at automating this process.

- Separation of Concern: A typical scenario in scientific or industrial performance evaluation projects is that the performance analyst spends a lot of time setting up the test environment or looking for appropriate analysis or data visualisation tools. To enable the performance analyst to focus on the problem to be studied, we target a clear distinction between the different tasks in the performance evaluation process. This distinction facilitates that for example the system administrator sets up the test Environment, a component expert instruments a component, and a statistics expert provides an analysis method.

- Adaptability: The goals of performance evaluations are also very diverse. While, for example, in some scenarios the performance analyst wants to identify a list of performance-relevant parameters, he might want to determine a functional relationship between a set of parameters in other scenarios. To support these goals a variety of methodologies and strategies exist or are developed by scientists or engineers. For example, different goals require different strategies to select experiments (i.e., the combination of input parameter values to be measured), terminate them, or analyse their results. A goal of SoPeCo is to facilitate the flexible introduction and use of such strategies by performance analysts. Moreover, SoPeCo should allow scientists and engineers to easily benchmark novel strategies against the state of the art.

- Reusability: Although test environments and evaluation projects are very diverse, there is still potential to reuse components and knowledge developed by others. With SoPeCo, we aim at supporting reusability at different points in the evaluation process. Examples are components that control or monitor a certain piece of software, or appropriate analysis methods to solve a certain problem type.

A.3. Architecture

Based on the objectives described above, we developed a framework architecture that provides the basis for the practical implementation of the approach presented in this thesis. Figure A.1 shows the basic architecture of SoPeCo.

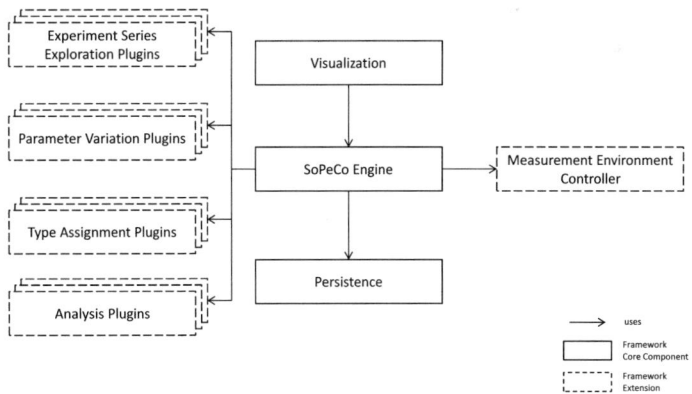

Figure A.1.: SoPeCo Architecture

The central component is the SoPeCo Engine which orchestrates the other components and constitutes the main entry point for the application logic of the framework. The Visualisation component, on top of the SoPeCo Engine, is the user-friendly interface to the performance analyst that wants to conduct performance evaluation experiments. The Persistence component is responsible for storing and loading experiment definitions, measurement data, and analysis results. In order to trigger an experiment, the SoPeCo Engine passes the parameter values for this specific experiment to the Measurement Environment Controller. As its name implies, this component controls the execution of single experiments on the actual measurement environment. This includes tasks like setting configuration parameters in the system under test, starting the load driver, and gathering monitoring data via different channels. Hence, the Measurement Environment Controller is the interface between the generic and the scenario-specific part of a performance evaluation.

The decision which experiments are to be executed on the measurement environment is taken by an Experiment Series Exploration Plugin. These plugins implement different experimental design strategies that select a set of experiments from the complete experiment space spanned by the experimentation parameters and its values (see Chapter 4.4). The strategies also decide on the order in which experiments are executed and determine when an experiment series can be terminated.

The basic definition of a parameter (i.e., name, description, type, potential values) depends on the scenario-specific measurement environment on which the experiments are to be executed. As our goal is to provide a scenario-independent approach, we also use an extension mechanism for the definition of parameter types and potential values. Which values a single parameter can take, can be specified via the parameter variation strategies provided by different Parameter Variation Plugins. Examples are a linear variation defined by a minimum value, a maximum value and a step size, or a variation based on a set of values specified in a comma separated string. The Type `Assignment Plugins` map type names to source code objects which allows the flexible introduction of new types if this is required by a specific measurement environment.

The interface that connects the framework to the scenario-specific measurement environment comprises the following actions:

- *Initializing Measurement Environment:* When a new measurement environment controller is registered at the framework its initialisation method is called. The concrete action performed by this method depends on the concrete scenario. Possible actions are setting of tool configurations, starting monitoring software, or generating test data.

- *Preparing Experiment Series:* In this step, the controller prepares the measurement environment for a series of experiments with a collection of value assignments that remain constant in the series.The corresponding method call can for example be used to set configuration parameters of system components or measurement tooling components.

- *Run Experiment:* In this step, the conroller runs a single experiment on the measurement environment. The parameter values that should be used in the experiment are provided by the framework based on the experiment definition of the performance analyst. The result of this method call is a list of measured values for each observed performance metric.

- *Finalize Experiment Series:* Once all experiments of an experiment series are executed, this method is called by the framework to enable the measurement environment controller to clean up the measurement environment. Depending on the scenario, this can for example include cleaning caches, resetting test data, or stopping monitoring software.

In order to analyse the data derived by a set of experiments, the SoPeCo framework provides different `Analysis Plugins`. These plugins provide, for example, methods to determine statistical metrics such as a confidence level or methods to derive the functional relationship between parameters. Moreover, the analyses can be used by sophisticated exploration strategies (such as those presented in Chapter 4.4) in order to support a specific evaluation goal.

The flexible architecture presented above has the following benefits:

1. It separates the scenario-specific measurement environment from the general experimentation tasks.

2. It allows researchers and engineers to implement and test novel experimental design or analysis strategies.

3. It allows performance analysts to select a proper experimental design and analysis strategy for their specific experiment goal.

4. It allows performance analysts to run performance evaluation experiments automatically and repeatedly.

In the following section, we demonstrate the usage of the framework based on the enterprise application customisation scenario introduced in Section 4.3.1.3.

A.4. Example

In this section, we continue the example introduce in Chapter 4.3.1.3. The goal of the performance analyst is to derive a functional relationship between the number of benchmark users, the number of work processes allocated to dialogue workload and the average response time for dialogue

steps. Using this function, the performance analyst can derive the performance-optimal configuration for an SAP ERP application installation in a
customer-specific setup. Figure A.2 sketches out a sample instantiation of
the SoPeCo framework.

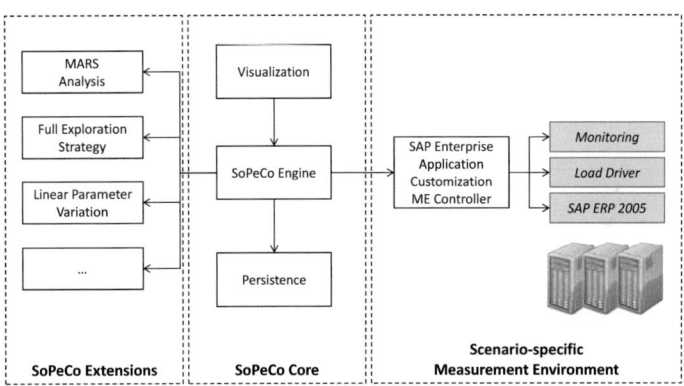

Figure A.2.: SoPeCo Example

The block to the right is the scenario-specific part which consists of a
set of hardware resources hosting the ERP application, a load driver that
simulates user behaviour and a monitoring tool that measures different
performance metrics (such as the average response time of the dialogue
steps). Moreover, the scenario-specific part contains a Measurement Environment Controller implementation that acts as the connector between SoPeCo and the measurement environment. The controller gets the
values of the input parameters for each experiment and triggers the respective components. If the experiment Exp{numSDUsers=100; numDialogue-
WPs=5} should be executed on the measurement environment, the controller configures the application server to allocate 5 work processes for
dialogue workload and triggers the load driver to run with 100 simulta-
neous users. When the measurement is finished, the controller reads the
measured response time from the log provided by the monitoring tool and

returns this as experiment result to the `SoPeCo Engine`. The `SoPeCo En-`
`gine` forwards the result to the persistence component which stores it for
example in database. The `Full Exploration Strategy` and the `Linear`
`Parameter Variation` shown on the left side of Figure A.2 are two example SoPeCo extensions responsible for determining which experiments
to execute. The `Linear Parameter Variation Plugin` provides an it-
erator for numeric parameter values that is configured by the experiment
definition of the performance analyst which specifies for example that the
number of users parameter can take values from 1 to 500 in steps of 1.
The `Full Exploration Strategy` is a simple experimental design strategy that triggers every possible combination of input parameter values as
experiment. Finally, the `MARS Analysis` extension derives the functional
dependency between the input parameters and an observed metric using
the Multivariate Adaptive Regression Splines [Fri91] technique. Using this
function, the performance analyst can derive the performance-optimal configuration for the customer's ERP application.

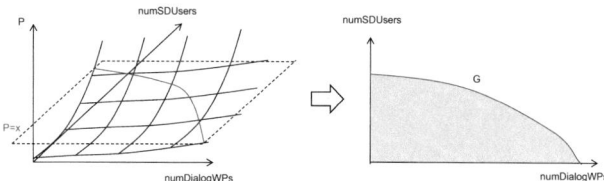

Figure A.3.: General Cutting Curve

Figure A.3 illustrates a straight-forward approach for the usage of the
function in that scenario. As the performance function

$$P = f(numSDUsers, numDialogWPs)$$

depends on two parameters, there is no single value defining the best configuration. Instead, the optimum is defined by the cutting curve, which is

calculated by fixing the average response time (P) to the target threshold x (e.g. one second). In other words, we calculate the function G as the cutting edge between P and the $P = x$ plane where x is the threshold we want to guarantee. The resulting function $G = f(numDialogWPs)$ defines a convex set for $numSDUsers > 0$, $numDialogWPs > 0$ and $numSDUsers <= G$. Hence, every point $< numSDUsers*, numDialogWPs* >$ within the convex set represents a feasible configuration for the given average response time threshold.

B. Complete Results for Automated Experiment Selection Validation

Field Interpretation: Mean Relative Error/ Highest Error/ Percentage of Validation Points with Prediction Error below 15% / Percentage of Validation Points with Prediction Error below 30% / Number of Executed Experiments

Scenario: NLSDF / Number of Possible Experiments: 8000

	AEB	DSL	DSG	RVS	ARB	RB
CART	0.088/0.110/1/1/307	0.273/2.286/0.582565/0.690476/83	0.088/0.221/0.853175/1/22	0.096/0.129/1/1/307	0.043/0.183/0.968379/1/212	0.043/0.157/0.992095/1/230
GP	0.018/0.074/1/1/216	NaN	0.053/0.150/1/1/22	0.016/0.054/1/1/574	0.014/0.079/1/1/909	0.038/0.133/1/1/334
Kriging	0.044/0.263/0.857143/1/288	1.030/79.375/0.375963/0.49444/1001	0.044/0.241/0.972332/1/96	0.050/0.191/0.944064/1/304	0.091/0.384/0.913043/1/214	0.059/0.172/0.992095/1/222
MARS	0.024/0.099/1/1/290	0.173/2.879/0.797884/0.87963/1076	0.024/0.099/1/1/22	0.003/0.008/1/1/306	0.002/0.007/1/1/213	0.003/0.007/1/1/218

Scenario: NLSSF / Number of Possible Experiments: 100000

	AEB	DSG	RVS	DSL	ARB	RB
CART	0.162/0.981/0.622951/0.8375/114	0.162/0.981/0.622951/0.8375/114	0.099/0.432/0.778154/0.982812/603	0.109/0.486/0.731460/0.967950/103		0.092/0.527/0.819672/0.982031/291
GP	0.063/0.315/0.923936/0.999219/376	0.150/0.742/0.631538/0.823875/88	0.099/0.269/0.905543/1/440	0.060/0.369/0.931304/0.997656/182		0.093/0.277/0.895161/291
Kriging	0.117/0.630/0.69477/0.934375/376	0.192/5.375/0.601562/0.903344/501	0.126/0.432/0.644028/0.946094/1002	0.097/0.272/0.786885/1/508		0.163/0.720/0.519513/0.874219/290
MARS	0.055/0.307/0.80484/0.998437/114	0.055/0.307/0.80484/0.998437/114	0.010/0.054/1/1/1002	0.014/0.087/1/1/134		0.008/0.039/1/1/290

Scenario: SOBENCH / Number of Possible Experiments: 360

	AEB	DSG	RVS	DSL	ARB	RB
CART	0.205/0.400/0.441590/0.723684/52	0.300/0.874/0.265714/0.539474/50	0.287/0.320/0.350649/0.578947/77		0.287/0.320/0.350649/0.578947/77	0.287/0.320/0.350649/0.578947/77
GP	0.082/0.416/0.883117/0.947368/49	0.087/0.260/0.833162/0.986842/21	0.077/0.260/0.883117/1/77		0.069/0.160/0.883117/0.937864/77	0.066/0.312/0.857143/0.986842/76
Kriging	0.028/0.380/0.948052/0.986842/50	0.060/0.430/0.883182/0.940526/38	0.083/0.292/0.844156/1/75		0.006/0.220/0.987013/1/71	0.002/0.071/1/1/74
MARS	0.076/0.313/0.857143/0.986842/50	0.074/0.317/0.870313/0.986842/53	0.083/0.292/0.844156/1/75		0.083/0.388/0.844156/1/74	0.083/0.291/0.844156/1/74

Scenario: SPECBENCH / Number of Possible Experiments: 3240

	AEB	DSL	DSG	RVS	ARB	RB
CART	0.364/4.325/0.688243/0.822751/3111	0.273/2.286/0.582565/0.690476/83	0.255/4.272/0.698811/0.832011/1736	0.273/4.755/0.702776/0.828542/847	0.259/4.305/0.723910/0.846561/1226	0.282/4.845/0.714653/0.82804/698
GP	0.287/3.819/0.422712/0.72222/874	NaN	0.205/4.056/0.557464/0.80158/1056	0.384/3.326/0.481260/0.79437/1117	0.221/2.695/0.655218/0.75799/1043	0.269/4.853/0.429359/0.78687/1588
Kriging	0.817/75.760/0.360790/0.62896/872	1.030/79.375/0.375963/0.49444/1001	0.393/9.440/0.466791/0.649471/1065	0.463/8.965/0.665478/0.90016/834	0.763/5.576/0.42857/0.623389/1011	0.253/3.551/0.717212/0.80934/365
MARS	0.203/3.014/0.735799/0.87037/742	0.173/2.879/0.797884/0.87963/1076	0.169/2.416/0.764861/0.879637/1420	0.195/4.224/0.763194/0.875461/855	0.239/3.444/0.78277/0.853177/2027	0.207/4.351/0.771446/3.867252/276

Figure B.1.: Complete Results for Validation presented in Chapter 4.5

C. Prediction Functions of Industrial Cased Study

In the following, we present the concrete values and functions used for predicting the screens in Chapter 5. The corresponding general prediction function is described in Equation 5.13 in Chapter 5.3.3.2.

C.1. Prediction Function for Firefox

$\varepsilon_S = 420$

$\varepsilon_{Simple} = 18.3$

$\phi_{Simple} = 1.943456 * QUANTITY$

$\varepsilon_{Image} = 15.3$

$$\phi_{Image} = 48.2 + 0.03131313 * max(0, WIDTH - 505)$$
$$- 0.04293 * max(0, 505 - WIDTH) + 0.026 * max(0, HEIGHT - 500)$$
$$- 0.04387 * max(0, 500 - HEIGHT) - 0.964 * max(0, QUANTITY - 5)$$
$$- 3.669 * max(0, 5 - QUANTITY) + 0.00002 * max(0, WIDTH - 505)$$
$$* max(0, HEIGHT - 500) - 0.000007 * max(0, 505 - WIDTH)$$
$$* max(0, HEIGHT - 500) - 0.000175 * max(0, WIDTH - 505)$$
$$* max(0, 500 - HEIGHT) + 0.000055 * max(0, 505 - WIDTH)$$
$$* max(0, 500 - HEIGHT) + 0.01189033 * max(0, WIDTH - 505)$$
$$* max(0, QUANTITY - 5) + 0.01038961 * max(0, WIDTH - 505)$$
$$* max(0, 5 - QUANTITY) - 0.001528571 * max(0, HEIGHT - 500)$$
$$* max(0, QUANTITY - 5) + 0.003160714 * max(0, HEIGHT - 500)$$
$$* max(0, 5 - QUANTITY)$$

$$\varepsilon_{Table} = 210.5$$

$$\phi_{Table} = 0.9837964 * ROWS - 1.451458 * SIMPLECOLS$$
$$- 706.4417 * RATINGCOLS + 5.741513 * QUANTITY$$
$$+ 0.005 * ROWS * SIMPLECOLS + 48.38 * ROWS * RATINGCOLS$$
$$+ 46.907 * SIMPLECOLS * RATINGCOLS + 1.603 * ROWS * QUANTITY$$
$$+ 3.4 * SIMPLECOLS * QUANTITY + 237 * RATINGCOLS * QUANTITY$$
$$- 3.08 * ROWS * SIMPLECOLS * RATINGCOLS$$
$$+ 1.06 * ROWS * SIMPLECOLS * QUANTITY$$
$$- 12.56101 * ROWS * RATINGCOLS * QUANTITY$$
$$- 14.18982 * SIMPLECOLS * RATINGCOLS * QUANTITY$$
$$+ 0.9006174 * ROWS * SIMPLECOLS * RATINGCOLS * QUANTITY$$

$$\varepsilon_{RowRepeater} = 322.7$$

$$\phi_{RowRepeater} = 12.6454 * max(0, ROWS - 9) -$$
$$25.48596 * max(0, 9 - ROWS) + 24.57518 * max(0, QUANTITY - 6)$$
$$- 31.63405 * max(0, 6 - QUANTITY) + 2.622546 * max(0, ROWS - 9)$$
$$* max(0, QUANTITY - 5) - 2.301101 * max(0, ROWS - 9)$$
$$* max(0, 5 - QUANTITY) - 1.45611 * max(0, 9 - ROWS)$$
$$* max(0, QUANTITY - 8) + 2.422541 * max(0, 9 - ROWS)$$
$$* max(0, 8 - QUANTITY)$$
$$\varepsilon_{TabStrip} = 47.4$$
$$\phi_{TabStrip} = 16 * QUANTITY$$
$$\varepsilon_{Toolbar} = 37.1$$
$$\phi_{Toolbar} = 7.484848 * QUANTITY$$
$$\phi_{Header} = 48$$
$$\phi_{Shell} = 95$$
$$\phi_{OData} = 761.766 + 2.317290 * max(0, DATA - 336)$$
$$- 2.336814 * max(0, 336 - DATA)$$
$$\phi_{JSON} = 20.9531 + 9.147735 * CALLS$$

$$(C.1)$$

C.2. Prediction Function for Chrome

$$\varepsilon_S = 300$$
$$\varepsilon_{Simple} = 6.3$$
$$\phi_{Simple} = 0.6180106 * QUANTITY$$
$$\varepsilon_{Image} = 9.95$$

$$\phi_{Image} = 0.0045 * WIDTH + 0.0076 * HEIGHT + 1.258 * QUANTITY$$
$$+ 0.000008 * WIDTH * HEIGHT + 0.001 * WIDTH * QUANTITY$$
$$+ 0.001 * HEIGHT * QUANTITY$$
$$+ 0.0000048 * WIDTH * HEIGHT * QUANTITY$$

$$\varepsilon_{Table} = 115.6$$

$$\phi_{Table} = 16.22777 * QUANTITY - 2.94197 * ROWS * SIMPLECOLS$$
$$- 26.7864 * ROWS * RATINGCOLS$$
$$+ 2.818925 * SIMPLECOLS * RATINGCOLS$$
$$+ 20.47580 * ROWS * QUANTITY$$
$$+ 5.270141 * SIMPLECOLS * QUANTITY$$
$$+ 5.667817 * RATINGCOLS * QUANTITY$$
$$+ 2.03301 * ROWS * SIMPLECOLS * RATINGCOLS$$
$$+ 5.654935 * ROWS * SIMPLECOLS * QUANTITY$$
$$+ 57.29617 * ROWS * RATINGCOLS * QUANTITY$$
$$+ 2.364257 * SIMPLECOLS * RATINGCOLS * QUANTITY$$
$$- 1.638865 * ROWS * SIMPLECOLS * RATINGCOLS * QUANTITY$$
$$- 13.35 * ROWS - 3.84 * SIMPLECOLS - 158.6 * RATINGCOLS$$

$$\varepsilon_{RowRepeater} = 162.3$$

$$\phi_{RowRepeater} = 401 + 18.25758 * max(0, ROWS - 13)$$
$$- 25.53951 * max(0, 13 - ROWS) + 46.31842 * max(0, QUANTITY - 5)$$
$$- 70.33231 * max(0, 5 - QUANTITY) + 0.9303674 * max(0, ROWS - 7)$$
$$* max(0, QUANTITY - 5) - 4.30947 * max(0, 7 - ROWS)$$
$$* max(0, QUANTITY - 5) - 1.20965 * max(0, 13 - ROWS)$$
$$* max(0, QUANTITY - 5) + 4.669123 * max(0, 13 - ROWS)$$
$$* max(0, 5 - QUANTITY) + 1.655087 * max(0, ROWS - 13)$$
$$* max(0, QUANTITY - 4) - 4.809822 * max(0, ROWS - 13)$$
$$* max(0, 4 - QUANTITY)$$
$$\varepsilon_{TabStrip} = 171$$
$$\phi_{TabStrip} = 10.55 * QUANTITY$$
$$\varepsilon_{Toolbar} = 3$$
$$\phi_{Toolbar} = 3.912121 * QUANTITY$$
$$\phi_{Header} = 185$$
$$\phi_{Shell} = 261$$
$$\phi_{OData} = 258.621 + 1.300211 * DATA$$
$$\phi_{JSON} = 194.306 + 5.295485 * CALLS$$

$$(C.2)$$

C.3. Prediction Function for Internet Explorer

$$\varepsilon_S = 280$$
$$\varepsilon_{Simple} = 6.95$$
$$\phi_{Simple} = 1.55 * QUANTITY$$
$$\varepsilon_{Image} = 29.2$$

$$\phi_{Image} = 0.00036 * WIDTH * HEIGHT + 0.0062 * WIDTH * QUANTITY$$
$$+ 0.006727862 * HEIGHT * QUANTITY$$
$$- 0.000011 * WIDTH * HEIGHT * QUANTITY - 0.02 * WIDTH$$
$$- 0.01517278 * HEIGHT - 3.404207 * QUANTITY$$

$$\varepsilon_{Table} = 118.7$$

$$\phi_{Table} = 11.46970 * ROWS + 13.54278 * SIMPLECOLS$$
$$- 28.058 * RATINGCOLS + 8.214 * QUANTITY$$
$$- 5.851 * ROWS * SIMPLECOLS - 7.10 * ROWS * RATINGCOLS$$
$$+ 11.96 * SIMPLECOLS * RATINGCOLS - 13.57 * ROWS * QUANTITY$$
$$- 3.55 * SIMPLECOLS * QUANTITY - 11.14 * RATINGCOLS * QUANTITY$$
$$- 2.072536 * ROWS * SIMPLECOLS * RATINGCOLS$$
$$+ 6.35768 * ROWS * SIMPLECOLS * QUANTITY$$
$$+ 12.73665 * ROWS * RATINGCOLS * QUANTITY$$
$$- 6.951127 * SIMPLECOLS * RATINGCOLS * QUANTITY$$
$$+ 1.773920 * ROWS * SIMPLECOLS * RATINGCOLS * QUANTITY$$

$$\varepsilon_{RowRepeater} = 132.1$$

$$\phi_{RowRepeater} = 214.93 + 27.61191 * max(0, ROWS - 11)$$
$$- 38.39952 * max(0, 11 - ROWS) + 47.56512 * max(0, QUANTITY - 4)$$
$$- 48.72615 * max(0, 4 - QUANTITY) + 4.391978 * max(0, ROWS - 11)$$
$$* max(0, QUANTITY - 7) - 3.974507 * max(0, ROWS - 11)$$
$$* max(0, 7 - QUANTITY) - 2.163148 * max(0, 11 - ROWS)$$
$$* max(0, QUANTITY - 9) + 3.861891 * max(0, 11 - ROWS)$$
$$* max(0, 9 - QUANTITY)$$

$$\varepsilon_{TabStrip} = 75.75$$

$$\phi_{TabStrip} = 3.05 * QUANTITY$$

$$\varepsilon_{Toolbar} = 8.5$$

$$\phi_{Toolbar} = 4.8 * QUANTITY$$

$$\phi_{Header} = 64$$

$$\phi_{Shell} = 111$$

$$\phi_{OData} = 8.1403 + 2.559657 * DATA$$

$$\phi_{JSON} = 96.13 + 3.278756 * CALLS$$

$$(C.3)$$

List of Figures

List of Tables

Bibliography

[ABC10]   A. Aldini, M. Bernardo, and F. Corradini, *A Process Algebraic Approach to Software Architecture Design.*   Springer, 2010.

[AGK00]   D. Abramson, J. Giddy, and L. Kotler, "High Performance Parametric Modeling with Nimrod/G: Killer Application for the Global Grid?" in *Proceedings of the 14th International Parallel & Distributed Processing Symposium (IPDPS'00).* IEEE Computer Society, 2000, pp. 520–528.

[App13]   Apple, "The WebKit Open Source Project," http://www.webkit.org/, 2013, last visited June 2013.

[AR10]   J. Allspaw and J. Robbins, *Web Operations: Keeping the Data On Time.*   O'Reilly Media, 2010.

[ASGH95]   D. Abramson, R. Sosic, J. Giddy, and B. Hall, "Nimrod: a tool for performing parametrised simulations using distributed workstations," in *Proceedings of the 4th IEEE International Symposium on High Performance Distributed Computing*, ser. HPDC '95.   Washington, DC, USA: IEEE Computer Society, 1995, pp. 112–.

[AW04]   A. Avritzer and E. J. Weyuker, "The Role of Modeling in the Performance Testing of E-Commerce Applications," *IEEE Transactions on Software Engineering*, vol. 30, no. 12, pp. 1072–1083, 2004.

[BCR94]   V. R. Basili, G. Caldiera, and H. D. Rombach, "The Goal Question Metric Approach," in *Encyclopedia of Software Engineering*. Wiley, 1994.

[BDIS04]   S. Balsamo, A. Di Marco, P. Inverardi, and M. Simeoni, "Model-Based Performance Prediction in Software Development: A Survey," *IEEE Transactions on Software Engineering*, vol. 30, no. 5, pp. 295–310, 2004.

[BGdMT06] G. Bolch, S. Greiner, H. de Meer, and K. S. Trivedi, *Queueing Networks and Markov Chains: Modeling and Performance Evaluation with Computer Science Applications*, ser. Wiley-Interscience publication.   Wiley, 2006.

[BH07]   M. Bernardo and J. Hillston, Eds., *Formal Methods for Performance Evaluation (Int. School on Formal Methods for Design of Computer, Communication, and Software Systems, SFM2007)*, 2007.

[Bix10]   J. Bixby, "Web Performance Today," http://www.webperformancetoday.com/2010/07/01/the-best-graphs-of-velocity/, 2010, last visited November 2012.

[BK02]   F. Bause and P. S. Kritzinger, *Stochastic Petri Nets - An Introduction to the Theory*.   Vieweg, 2002.

[BKK09]   F. Brosig, S. Kounev, and K. Krogmann, "Automated Extraction of Palladio Component Models from Running Enterprise Java Applications," in *Proceedings of the 1st International Workshop on Run-time Models for Self-managing Systems and Applications (ROSSA 2009). In conjunction with Fourth International Conference on Performance Evaluation Methodologies and Tools (VALUETOOLS 2009), Pisa, Italy, October 19, 2009*.   ACM, New York, NY, USA, 2009.

[BKR09]   S. Becker, H. Koziolek, and R. Reussner, "The Palladio component model for model-driven performance prediction," *Journal of Systems and Software*, vol. 82, pp. 3–22, 2009.

[Bre01]   L. Breiman, "Random Forests," *Machine learning*, vol. 45, no. 1, pp. 5–32, 2001.

[Bro09]   T. Brown, *Change by Design: How Design Thinking Transforms Organisations and Inspires Innovation.*   Harper-Collins, 2009.

[CC00]   T. F. Cox and M. A. A. Cox, *Multidimensional Scaling, Second Edition.*   Chapman & Hall/CRC, 2000.

[CD94]   S. Cook and J. Daniels, *Designing object systems: object-oriented modelling with Syntropy.*   Upper Saddle River, NJ, USA: Prentice-Hall, Inc., 1994.

[CG05]   L. Cherkasova and R. Gardner, "Measuring CPU Overhead for I/O Processing in the Xen Virtual Machine Monitor," in *USENIX Annual Technical Conference, General Track*, 2005, pp. 387–390.

[Com13]   Compuware, "Compuware dynaTrace - Enterprise," http://www.compuware.com/application-performance-management/dynatrace-enterprise.html, 2013, last visited June 2013.

[Cro12]   C. Crocker, "Real User Monitoring at Walmart," http://minus.com/msM8y8nyh/1e, 2012, last visited November 2012.

[Cro13]   D. Crockford, "Introducing JSON," http://www.json.org/, 2013, last visited February 2013.

[CW00]   M. Courtois and M. Woodside, "Using Regression Splines for Software Performance Analysis and Software Characterisation," in *Proceedings of the 2nd International Workshop on Software and Performance (WOSP)*.   N. Y.: ACM Press, 2000, pp. 105–114.

[DGL]   M. J. De Smith, M. F. Goodchild, and P. A. Longley, *Geospatial Analysis: A Comprehensive Guide to Principles, Techniques and Software Tools*.   Troubador Publishing.

[Dix09]   P. Dixon, "Shopzilla Site Redesign - We get what we measure," http://www.scribd.com/doc/16877317/Shopzillas-Site-Redo-You-Get-What-You-Measure,   2009,   velocity 2009, last visited November 2012.

[DRSS01]   R. R. Dumke, C. Rautenstrauch, A. Schmietendorf, and A. Scholz, Eds., *Performance Engineering, State of the Art and Current Trends*, ser. Lecture Notes in Computer Science, vol. 2047.   Springer, 2001.

[FH12]   M. Faber and J. Happe, "Systematic adoption of genetic programming for deriving software performance curves," in *Third Joint WOSP/SIPEW International Conference on Performance Engineering, ICPE'12*.   ACM, 2012, pp. 33–44.

[Fou13]   A. S. Foundation, "Apache JMeter," http://jmeter.apache.org/, 2013, last visited June 2013.

[Fri91]   J. H. Friedman, "Multivariate Adaptive Regression Splines." *Annals of Statistics*, vol. 19, no. 1, pp. 1–141, 1991.

[Fro13]   B. Frost, "Performance as Design," http://bradfrostweb.com/blog/post/performance-as-design/, 2013, last visited March 2013.

[Gar11]   T. Garsiel, "How browsers work," http://taligarsiel.com/
            Projects/howbrowserswork1.htm, 2011, last visited July
            2013.

[GBE07]   A. Georges, D. Buytaert, and L. Eeckhout, "Statistically rig-
            orous java performance evaluation," in *Proceedings of the
            22nd annual ACM SIGPLAN conference on Object-oriented
            programming systems and applications*, ser. OOPSLA '07.
            New York, NY, USA: ACM, 2007, pp. 57–76.

[GG05]   A. Grosskurth and M. W. Godfrey, "A Reference Architec-
            ture for Web Browsers," in *Proceedings of 21st IEEE In-
            ternational Conference on Software Maintenance (ICSM)*.
            IEEE Computer Society, 2005, pp. 661–664.

[Goo13]   Google, "V8 JavaScript Engine," https://code.google.com/p/
            v8/, 2013, last visited June 2013.

[Hap08]   J. Happe, "Predicting Software Performance in Symmetric
            Multi-core and Multiprocessor Environments," Dissertation,
            University of Oldenburg, Germany, 2008.

[Heg13]   C. Heger, "Systematic guidance in solving performance and
            scalability problems," in *Proceedings of the 18th interna-
            tional doctoral symposium on Components and architecture*,
            ser. WCOP '13.   New York, NY, USA: ACM, 2013, pp.
            7–12.

[HH04]   R. M. Heiberger and B. Holland, *Statistical Analysis and
            Data Display: An Intermediate Course with Examples in S-
            Plus, R, and SAS*.   Springer, 2004, iSBN 0-387-40270-5.

[HHF13]   C. Heger, J. Happe, and R. Farahbod, "Automated root cause
            isolation of performance regressions during software devel-
            opment," in *Proceedings of the 4th ACM/SPEC Interna-*

tional Conference on Performance Engineering, ser. ICPE '13. New York, NY, USA: ACM, 2013, pp. 27–38.

[Hil96] J. Hillston, *A Compositional Approach to Performance Modelling*. Cambridge University Press, 1996.

[HKHR11] M. Hauck, M. Kuperberg, N. Huber, and R. Reussner, "Ginpex: deriving performance-relevant infrastructure properties through goal-oriented experiments," in *7th International Conference on the Quality of Software Architectures, QoSA 2011 and 2nd International Symposium on Architecting Critical Systems, ISARCS 2011. Proceedings*, I. Crnkovic, J. A. Stafford, D. C. Petriu, J. Happe, and P. Inverardi, Eds. ACM, 2011, pp. 53–62.

[Hol08] A. T. Holdener, *Ajax: the definitive guide*. O'Reilly, 2008.

[HP13] HP, "HP Load Runner," http://www8.hp.com/us/en/software-solutions/software.html?compURI=1175451\#.UP-q7ydEHpw, 2013, last visited June 2013.

[HTF09] T. Hastie, R. Tibshirani, and J. Friedman, *The Elements of Statistical Learning: Data mining, Inference ,and Prediction*, 2nd ed., ser. Springer Series in Statistics. Springer, 2009.

[HWSK10] J. Happe, D. Westermann, K. Sachs, and L. Kapová, "Statistical Inference of Software Performance Models for Parametric Performance Completions," in *Research into Practice - Reality and Gaps, 6th International Conference on the Quality of Software Architectures, QoSA 2010. Proceedings*, ser. Lecture Notes in Computer Science, vol. 6093. Springer, 2010, pp. 20–35.

[ILGP96] Y. E. Ioannidis, M. Livny, S. Gupta, and N. Ponnekanti, "ZOO : A Desktop Experiment Management Environment," in *Proceedings of 22th International Conference on Very Large Data Bases (VLDB), September 3-6, 1996, Mumbai (Bombay), India*, T. M. Vijayaraman, A. P. Buchmann, C. Mohan, and N. L. Sarda, Eds. Morgan Kaufmann, 1996, pp. 274–285.

[Jai91]   R. Jain, *The Art of Computer Systems Performance Analysis: Techniques for Experimental Design, Measurement, Simulation, and Modeling*, ser. Wiley professional computing, W. P. Computing, Ed. Wiley, 1991.

[Jam]   L. Jamen, "Oracle(c) Fusion Middleware - Performance and Tuning Guide," http://docs.oracle.com/cd/E17904_01/core. 1111/e10108/toc.htm, last visited June 2013.

[Jaz70]   A. H. Jazwinski, *Stochastic processes and filtering theory*. Academic press, 1970, vol. 63.

[JE06]   L. K. John and L. Eeckhout, *Performance Evaluation And Benchmarking*. CRC Press, 2006.

[JM11]   D. Jaffe and T. Muirhead, "Dell DVD Store," http://en.community.dell.com/techcenter/extras/w/wiki/dvd-store.aspx, 2011, last visited July 2013.

[JN12]   M. Jennings and D. Nolan, "Performance and Metrics on lonelyplanet.com," http://velocityconf.com/velocityeu2012/public/schedule/detail/26634, 2012, velocity 2012, last visited November 2012.

[JPS07]   G. Jung, C. Pu, and G. Swint, "Mulini: an automated staging framework for QoS of distributed multi-tier applications," in *Proceedings of the 2007 workshop on Automating service quality: Held at the International Conference on Automated Software Engineering (ASE)*, ser. WRASQ '07. New York, NY, USA: ACM, 2007, pp. 10–15.

[JTHL07]   Y. Jin, A. Tang, J. Han, and Y. Liu, "Performance Evaluation
             and Prediction for Legacy Information Systems," in *Proceed-*
             ings of the 29th international conference on Software Engi-
             neering, ser. ICSE '07.   Washington, DC, USA: IEEE Com-
             puter Society, 2007, pp. 540–549.

[KH11]   A. Kingsley-Hughes, "The BIG browser benchmark!
             Chrome 15 vs Opera 11 vs IE9 vs Firefox 8 vs Safari
             5," http://www.zdnet.com/blog/hardware/the-big-browser-
             benchmark-chrome-15-vs-opera-11-vs-ie9-vs-firefox-8-
             vs-safari-5/16041, 2011, last visited November 2012.

[KKR08]   M. Kuperberg, M. Krogmann, and R. Reussner, "ByCounter:
             Portable Runtime Counting of Bytecode Instructions and
             Method Invocations," in *Proceedings of the 3rd International*
             Workshop on Bytecode Semantics, Verification, Analysis and
             Transformation, Budapest, Hungary, 5th April 2008 (ETAPS
             2008, 11th European Joint Conferences on Theory and Prac-
             tice of Software), 2008.

[KKR10]   K. Krogmann, M. Kuperberg, and R. Reussner, "Using Ge-
             netic Search for Reverse Engineering of Parametric Be-
             haviour Models for Performance Prediction," *IEEE Transac-*
             tions on Software Engineering, vol. 36, no. 6, pp. 865–877,
             2010.

[KM97]   K. L. Karavanic and B. P. Miller, "Experiment management
             support for performance tuning," in *Proceedings of the 1997*
             ACM/IEEE conference on Supercomputing (CDROM), ser.
             Supercomputing '97.   New York, NY, USA: ACM, 1997,
             pp. 1–10.

[Koz93]   J. R. Koza, Ed., *Genetic Programming*, 3rd ed.   Cambridge,
             Mass.: MIT Press, 1993, vol. [1, book]:.

[Koz10]   H. Koziolek, "Performance evaluation of component-based software systems: A survey," *Performance Evaluation*, vol. 67, no. 8, pp. 634–658, 2010, special Issue on Software and Performance.

[KPSCD09]   S. Kraft, S. Pacheco-Sanchez, G. Casale, and S. Dawson, "Estimating service resource consumption from response time measurements," in *Proceedings of the Fourth International ICST Conference on Performance Evaluation Methodologies and Tools*, ser. VALUETOOLS '09, 2009, pp. 48:1—-48:10.

[Kri51]   D. G. Krige, "A Statistical Approach to Some Basic Mine Valuation Problems on the Witwatersrand," *Journal of the Chemical, Metallurgical and Mining Society of South Africa*, vol. 52, no. 6, pp. 119–139, 1951.

[Kro10]   K. Krogmann, "Reconstruction of Software Component Architectures and Behaviour Models using Static and Dynamic Analysis," Ph.D. dissertation, Karlsruhe Institute of Technology (KIT), Karlsruhe, Germany, 2010.

[KS00]   U. Krishnaswamy and I. D. Scherson, "A Framework for Computer Performance Evaluation Using Benchmark Sets," *IEEE Trans. Comput.*, vol. 49, no. 12, pp. 1325–1338, 2000.

[Laz84]   E. D. Lazowska, *Quantitative system performance: computer system analysis using queueing network models*. Prentice-Hall, 1984.

[LB05]   P. L'Ecuyer and E. Buist, "Simulation in Java with SSJ," in *Proc. of the 37th Conf. on Winter Simulation*. WSC 2005, 2005, pp. 611–620.

[LCZT07]   Y. Lu, I. Cohen, X. S. Zhou, and Q. Tian, "Feature selection using principal feature analysis," in *Proceedings of the 15th international conference on Multimedia.* ACM, 2007, pp. 301–304.

[Lep12] M. Leptien, "Media Markt - Doch Bloed? Or how Artists have gone over the edge," http://webforscher.wordpress.com/ tag/web-performance/, 2012, last visited June 2013.

[LH08] J. Li and A. D. Heap, *A review of spatial interpolation methods for environmental scientists.* Canberra: Geoscience Australia, 2008.

[Lil05] D. J. Lilja, *Measuring Computer Performance: A Practicioner's Guide.* Cambridge University Press, 2005.

[Liv08] J. Livingston, *Founders at Work: Stories of Startups' Early Days.* Berkely, CA, USA: Apress, 2008.

[MA01] D. A. Menasce and V. Almeida, *Capacity Planning for Web Services: metrics, models, and methods*, 1st ed. Prentice Hall PTR, Oct. 2001.

[Mar95] A. Marsan, *Modelling with generalized stochastic Petri nets*, ser. Wiley series in parallel computing. Wiley, 1995.

[MCC$^+$95] B. P. Miller, M. D. Callaghan, J. M. Cargille, J. K. Hollingsworth, R. B. Irvin, K. L. Karavanic, K. Kunchithapadam, and T. Newhall, "The paradyn parallel performance measurement tool," *Computer*, vol. 28, no. 11, pp. 37–46, Nov. 1995.

[Mee] P. Meenan, "WebPageTest," http://www.webpagetest.org/, last visited November 2012.

[Mic13] Microsoft, "MSHTML Reference," http://msdn.microsoft. com/en-us/library/aa741317.aspx, 2013, last visited July 2013.

[MM02]   A. Mos and J. Murphy, "A framework for performance monitoring, modelling and prediction of component oriented distributed systems," in *WOSP '02: Proc. of the 3rd international workshop on Software and performance*. New York, NY, USA: ACM, 2002, pp. 235–236.

[Moz13a]   Mozilla, "Gecko," https://developer.mozilla.org/en-US/docs/Mozilla/Gecko, 2013, last visited June 2013.

[Moz13b]   ——, "Spider Monkey," https://developer.mozilla.org/en/docs/SpiderMonkey, 2013, last visited June 2013.

[Nat12]   M. Natrella, *NIST/SEMATECH e-Handbook of Statistical Methods*, C. Croarkin and P. Tobias, Eds. NIST/SEMATECH, 2012.

[New13]   NewRelic, "New Relic," http://newrelic.com/, 2013, last visited June 2013.

[NYPF06]   F. Nadeem, M. M. Yousaf, R. Prodan, and T. Fahringer, "Soft benchmarks-based application performance prediction using a minimum training set," in *Proceedings of the Second IEEE International Conference on e-Science and Grid Computing*, ser. E-SCIENCE '06. Washington, DC, USA: IEEE Computer Society, 2006, pp. 71–.

[OAS13]   OASIS OData Technical Committee, "Open Data Protocol," http://www.odata.org, 2013, last visited June 2013.

[Ora12]   Oracle, "Tuning Garbage Collection with the 5.0 Java TM Virtual Machine," http://www.oracle.com/technetwork/java/gc-tuning-5-138395.html, 2012.

[Ora13]   ——, "Java EE at a Glance," http://www.oracle.com/technetwork/java/javaee/overview/index.html, 2013, last visited January 2013.

[Ost11]   I. Ostrovsky, "What really happens when you navigate to a URL," http://igoro.com/archive/what-really-happens-when-you-navigate-to-a-url/, 2011, last visited June 2013.

[OW209]   OW2 Consortium, "RUBiS: Rice University Bidding Systems," http://rubis.ow2.org/, 2009, last visited November 2012.

[Pea00]   J. Pearl, *Causality: models, reasoning, and inference.* New York, NY, USA: Cambridge University Press, 2000.

[Peb04]   E. J. Pebesma, "Multivariable geostatistics in S: the gstat package," *Computers and Geosciences*, vol. 30, pp. 683–691, 2004.

[PF04]   R. Prodan and T. Fahringer, "ZENTURIO: a grid middleware-based tool for experiment management of parallel and distributed applications," *Journal of Parallel and Distributed Computing*, vol. 64, no. 6, pp. 693–707, 2004.

[PF05]   ——, "ZEN: a directive based experiment specification language for performance and parameter studies of parallel scientific applications," *International Journal of High Performance Computing and Networking*, vol. 3, no. 2/3, pp. 103–121, 2005.

[PK05]   B. Page and W. Kreutzer, *The Java Simulation Handbook. Simulating Discrete Event Systems with UML and Java*, 2005.

[PM08]   T. Parsons and J. Murphy, "Detecting Performance Antipatterns in Component Based Enterprise Systems," *Journal of Object Technology*, vol. 7, no. 3, pp. 55–91, 2008.

[Pod05]   A. Podelko, "Workload Generation: Does One Approach Fit All?" in *Int. CMG Conference.* Computer Measurement Group, 2005, pp. 301–308.

[Poo00]   R. Pooley, "Software engineering and performance: a roadmap," in *Proceedings of the Conference on The Future of Software Engineering*, ser. ICSE '00.   New York, NY, USA: ACM, 2000, pp. 189–199.

[PSG01]   A. Podelko, A. Sokk, and L. Grinshpan, "Custom Load Generation," in *Int. CMG Conference*, 2001, pp. 179–184.

[PSST06]   G. Pacifici, W. Segmuller, M. Spreitzer, and A. Tantawi, "Dynamic estimation of CPU demand of web traffic," in *Proceedings of the 1st International Conference on Performance Evaluation Methodolgies and Tools, VALUETOOLS 2006, Pisa, Italy, October 11-13, 2006*, ser. ACM International Conference Proceeding Series, vol. 180.   New York, NY, USA: ACM, 2006.

[R D11]   R Development Core Team, "Classical (Metric) Multidimensional Scaling," http://stat.ethz.ch/R-manual/R-patched/library/stats/html/cmdscale.html, 2011, last visited November 2012.

[R F13]   R Foundation, "The R Project for Statistical Computing," http://www.r-project.org/, 2013, last visited June 2013.

[Rie11]   E. Ries, *The Lean Startup: How Today's Entrepreneurs Use Continuous Innovation to Create Radically Successful Businesses*, first edition ed.   Crown Business, 2011.

[RRMP08]   A. Rausch, R. Reussner, R. Mirandola, and F. Plasil, Eds., *The Common Component Modeling Example: Comparing Software Component Models*, ser. Lecture Notes in Computer Science, vol. 5153.   Springer, 2008.

[RSPM98]   R. H. Reussner, P. Sanders, L. Prechelt, and M. Müller, "SKaMPI: A Detailed, Accurate MPI Benchmark," in *Recent *advances in parallel virtual machine and message passing interface: 5th European PVM/MPI Users' Group Meeting, Liverpool, UK, September 7–9, 1998,* ser. Lecture Notes in Computer Science, V. Alexandrov and J. J. Dongarra, Eds., vol. 1497. Springer-Verlag Berlin Heidelberg, 1998, pp. 52–59.

[SAP12]   SAP, "SAP Sales and Distribution Benchmark," http://www.sap.com/campaigns/benchmark/appbmsd.epx, 2012, last visited November 2012.

[SAP13a]   ——, "SAP AG," http://www.sap.com/, 2013, last visited June 2013.

[SAP13b]   ——, "UI Development Toolkit for HTML5 Developer Center," http://scn.sap.com/community/developer-center/frontend, 2013, last visited July 2013.

[Sch06]   T. Schneider, *SAP Performance Optimisation Guide: Analyzing and Tuning SAP Systems.* Galileo Pr Inc, 2006.

[Shi03]   J. Shirazi, *Java performance tuning - efficient and effective tuning strategies.* O'Reilly, 2003.

[Sin09]   S. Sinek, *Start with Why: How Great Leaders Inspire Everyone to Take Action.* Penguin Group US, 2009.

[SM05]   M. Sopitkamol and D. A. Menascé, "A method for evaluating the impact of software configuration parameters on e-commerce sites," in *WOSP.* ACM, 2005, pp. 53–64.

[SMF⁺07]   J. Sankarasetty, K. Mobley, L. Foster, T. Hammer, and T. Calderone, "Software performance in the real world: personal lessons from the performance trauma team," in *Proceedings of the 6th international workshop on Software and performance,* ser. WOSP '07. New York, NY, USA: ACM, 2007, pp. 201–208.

[Smi81]   C. U. Smith, "Increasing Information Systems Productivity by Software Performance Engineering." in *Int. CMG Conference*, 1981, pp. 5–14.

[Smi82]   ——, "Software Performance Engineering." in *Int. CMG Conference*, 1982, pp. 331–332.

[Smi86]   ——, "The evolution of software performance engineering: a survey," in *Proceedings of 1986 ACM Fall joint computer conference*, ser. ACM '86.   Los Alamitos, CA, USA: IEEE Computer Society Press, 1986, pp. 778–783.

[Smi01]   ——, "Origins of Software Performance Engineering: Highlights and Outstanding Problems," in *Performance Engineering*, ser. Lecture Notes in Computer Science, R. Dumke, C. Rautenstrauch, A. Scholz, and A. Schmietendorf, Eds. Springer Berlin Heidelberg, 2001, vol. 2047, pp. 96–118.

[Smi07]   ——, "Introduction to software performance engineering: origins and outstanding problems," in *Proceedings of the 7th international conference on Formal methods for performance evaluation*, ser. SFM'07.   Berlin, Heidelberg: Springer-Verlag, 2007, pp. 395–428.

[Sou07]   S. Souders, *High Performance Web Sites: 14 Steps to Faster-Loading Web Sites*.   O'Reilly, 2007.

[Sou09]   ——, *Even Faster Web Sites: Performance Best Practices for Web Developers*.   O'Reilly, 2009.

[SPE05]   SPEC Standard Performance Evaluation Corporation, "SPECjbb2005 - Industry-standard server-side Java benchmark (J2SE 5.0)." http://www.spec.org/jbb2005/, 2005, last visited June 2013.

[SPE12]   ——, "SPEC's Benchmarks and Published Results," http:
                 //www.spec.org/benchmarks.html, 2012, last visited Novem-
                 ber 2012.

[SSN$^+$08]   S. R. Sandeep, M. Swapna, T. Niranjan, S. Susarla, and
                 S. Nandi, "CLUEBOX: a performance log analyser for auto-
                 mated troubleshooting," in *Proceedings of the First USENIX
                 conference on Analysis of system logs*, ser. WASL'08.
                 Berkeley, CA, USA: USENIX Association, 2008.

[Ste12]   S. Stefanov, "Book of Speed: The business, psychology
                 and technology of high-performance web apps," http://www.
                 bookofspeed.com, 2012, last visited November 2012.

[SW01]   C. U. Smith and L. G. Williams, *Performance Solutions: A
                 Practical Guide to Creating Responsive, Scalable Software*,
                 1st ed.   Addison-Wesley Professional, 2001.

[Swi06]   P. Switzer, *Kriging*.   John Wiley and Sons, Ltd, 2006.

[TAR11]   T. M. Therneau, B. Atkinson, and B. Ripley, "r-cran-rpart,"
                 http://mloss.org/software/view/115/, 2011, last visited June
                 2013.

[TDZN10]   E. Thereska, B. Doebel, A. X. Zheng, and P. Nobel, "Practi-
                 cal performance models for complex, popular applications,"
                 in *Proceedings of the 2010 ACM SIGMETRICS International
                 Conference on Measurement and Modeling of Computer Sys-
                 tems*.   ACM, 2010, pp. 1–12.

[THHF08]   D. Thakkar, A. E. Hassan, G. Hamann, and P. Flora, "A
                 framework for measurement based performance modeling,"
                 in *WOSP '08: Proceedings of the 7th international workshop
                 on Software and performance*.   New York, NY, USA: ACM,
                 2008, pp. 55–66.

[TPC13]   TPC, "Transaction Processing Performance Council," http:
             //www.tpc.org/, 2013.

[Tuk77]   J. W. Tukey, *Exploratory Data Analysis*.   Addison-Wesley,
             1977.

[TZV⁺08]   M. Tariq, A. Zeitoun, V. Valancius, N. Feamster, and
             M. Ammar, "Answering what-if deployment and configura-
             tion questions with wise," in *Proceedings of the ACM SIG-
             COMM 2008 conference on Data communication*, ser. SIG-
             COMM '08. New York, NY, USA: ACM, 2008, pp. 99–110.

[UH97]   P. Utton and B. Hill, "Performance prediction: An indus-
             try perspective," in *Computer Performance Evaluation Mod-
             elling Techniques and Tools*, ser. Lecture Notes in Computer
             Science, R. Marie, B. Plateau, M. Calzarossa, and G. Ru-
             bino, Eds. Springer Berlin Heidelberg, 1997, vol. 1245, pp.
             1–5.

[VW97]   V. Vetland and C. M. Woodside, "A Workbench for Automa-
             tion of Systematic Measurement of Resource Demands of
             Software Components," *Transactions of the Computer Mea-
             surement Group*, no. 92, pp. 42–48, 1997.

[W3C12a]   W3C, "HTML5 - A vocabulary and associated APIs
             for HTML and XHTML (W3C Candidate Recommenda-
             tion 17 December 2012)," http://www.w3.org/TR/html5/
             webappapis.html\#scripting, 2012, last visited June 2013.

[W3C12b]   ——, "Navigation Timing," http://www.w3.org/TR/
             navigation-timing/, 2012, last visited December 2012.

[W3C13]   ——, "Web Performance Working Group," http://www.w3.
             org/2010/webperf/, 2013, last visited June 2013.

[WAA⁺04]   M. Wang, K. Au, A. Ailamaki, A. Brockwell, C. Falout-
             sos, and G. R. Ganger, "Storage device performance pre-
             diction with CART models," in *Proceedings of the joint
             international conference on Measurement and modeling of
             computer systems*, ser. SIGMETRICS '04/Performance '04.
             New York, NY, USA: ACM, 2004, pp. 412–413.

[Wer13]   A. Wert, "Performance Problem Diagnostics by Systematic
             Experimentation," in *WCOP '13: Proceedings of the 18th
             international doctoral symposium on Components and Ar-
             chitecture*.   New York, NY, USA: ACM, 2013, pp. 1–6.

[Wes12]   D. Westermann, "A Generic Methodology to Derive
             Domain-Specific Performance Feedback for Developers," in
             *Proceedings of the 34th International Conference on Soft-
             ware Engineering (ICSE 2012), Doctoral Symposium*, ser.
             ICSE 2012.   Piscataway, NJ, USA: IEEE Press, 2012, pp.
             1527–1530.

[WFP07]   M. Woodside, G. Franks, and D. Petriu, "The Future of Soft-
             ware Performance Engineering," in *Future of Software Engi-
             neering (FOSE'07)*.   Los Alamitos, CA, USA: IEEE Com-
             puter Society, 2007, pp. 171–187.

[WH11]   D. Westermann and J. Happe, "Performance cockpit: sys-
             tematic measurements and analyses," in *Proceedings of the
             second joint WOSP/SIPEW international conference on Per-
             formance engineering*, ser. ICPE '11.   New York, NY, USA:
             ACM, 2011, pp. 421–422.

[WHF13]   D. Westermann, J. Happe, and R. Farahbod, "An experi-
             ment specification language for goal-driven, automated per-
             formance evaluations," in *Proceedings of the 28th Annual
             ACM Symposium on Applied Computing*, ser. SAC '13.   New
             York, NY, USA: ACM, 2013, pp. 1043–1048.

[WHH13] A. Wert, J. Happe, and L. Happe, "Supporting Swift Reaction: Automatically Uncovering Performance Problems by Systematic Experiments," in *Proceedings or the International Conference on Software Engineering 2013*. Piscataway, NJ, USA: IEEE Press, 2013, pp. 552–561.

[WHHH10] D. Westermann, J. Happe, M. Hauck, and C. Heupel, "The performance cockpit approach: A framework for systematic performance evaluations," in *Proceedings of the 2010 36th EUROMICRO Conference on Software Engineering and Advanced Applications*, ser. SEAA '10. Washington, DC, USA: IEEE Computer Society, 2010, pp. 31–38.

[WHKF12] D. Westermann, J. Happe, R. Krebs, and R. Farahbod, "Automated inference of goal-oriented performance prediction functions," in *Proceedings of the 27th IEEE/ACM International Conference on Automated Software Engineering*, ser. ASE 2012. New York, NY, USA: ACM, 2012, pp. 190–199.

[WHW12] A. Wert, J. Happe, and D. Westermann, "Integrating software performance curves with the palladio component model," in *Proceedings of the 3rd ACM/SPEC International Conference on Performance Engineering*, ser. ICPE '12. New York, NY, USA: ACM, 2012, pp. 283–286.

[WHW⁺13] D. Westermann, J. Happe, A. Wert, R. Farahbod, and C. Heger, "Software Performance Cockpit," http://www.sopeco.org/, 2013, last visited July 2013.

[WKH11] D. Westermann, R. Krebs, and J. Happe, "Efficient Experiment Selection in Automated Software Performance Evaluations," in *Computer Performance Engineering - 8th European Performance Engineering Workshop, EPEW 2011, Borrowdale, UK, October 12-13, 2011. Proceedings*. Springer, 2011, pp. 325–339.

[Wor05]   J. Worringen, "Experiment Management and Analysis with perfbase," in *IEEE International Conference on Cluster Computing (CLUSTER 2005)*.   IEEE, 2005, pp. 1–11.

[WS03]   L. G. Williams and C. U. Smith, "Making the Business Case for Software Performance Engineering," in *Proceedings of CMG*, 2003.

[WVCB01]   C. M. Woodside, V. Vetland, M. Courtois, and S. Bayarov, "Resource Function Capture for Performance Aspects of Software Components and Sub-Systems," in *Performance Engineering, State of the Art and Current Trends*.   London, UK: Springer-Verlag, 2001, pp. 239–256.

[WW08]   X. Wu and M. Woodside, "A Calibration Framework for Capturing and Calibrating Software Performance Models," in *EPEW '08: Proceedings of the 5th European Performance Engineering Workshop on Computer Performance Engineering*.   Berlin, Heidelberg: Springer-Verlag, 2008, pp. 32–47.

[WWHM13] C. Weiss, D. Westermann, C. Heger, and M. Moser, "Systematic performance evaluation based on tailored benchmark applications," in *Proceedings of the 4th ACM/SPEC International Conference on Performance Engineering*, ser. ICPE '13.   New York, NY, USA: ACM, 2013, pp. 411–420.

[Yah]   Yahoo, "YSlow," http://developer.yahoo.com/yslow/, last visited November 2012.

[YKM+05]   C. Yilmaz, A. S. Krishna, A. M. Memon, A. A. Porter, D. C. Schmidt, A. S. Gokhale, and B. Natarajan, "Main effects screening: a distributed continuous quality assurance process for monitoring performance degradation in evolving software systems," in *ICSE*, G.-C. Roman, W. G. Griswold, and B. Nuseibeh, Eds.   ACM, 2005, pp. 293–302.

The Karlsruhe Series on
Software Design and Quality

Edited by Prof. Dr. Ralf Reussner // ISSN 1867-0067

Band 1   Steffen Becker
          Coupled Model Transformations for QoS Enabled
          Component-Based Software Design. 2008
          ISBN 978-3-86644-271-9

Band 2   Heiko Koziolek
          Parameter Dependencies for Reusable Performance
          Specifications of Software Components. 2008
          ISBN 978-3-86644-272-6

Band 3   Jens Happe
          Predicting Software Performance in Symmetric
          Multi-core and Multiprocessor Environments. 2009
          ISBN 978-3-86644-381-5

Band 4   Klaus Krogmann
          Reconstruction of Software Component Architectures and
          Behaviour Models using Static and Dynamic Analysis. 2012
          ISBN 978-3-86644-804-9

Band 5   Michael Kuperberg
          Quantifying and Predicting the Influence of Execution
          Platform on Software Component Performance. 2010
          ISBN 978-3-86644-741-7

Band 6   Thomas Goldschmidt
          View-Based Textual Modelling. 2011
          ISBN 978-3-86644-642-7

The Karlsruhe Series on Software Design and Quality

Edited by Prof. Dr. Ralf Reussner // ISSN 1867-0067

Die Bände sind unter www.ksp.kit.edu als PDF frei verfügbar oder als Druckausgabe bestellbar.